The GREAT WALL of CHINA

By Robert Silverberg:

Treasures Beneath the Sea
Lost Cities and Vanished Civilizations
Sunken History: The Story of Underwater Archaeology
Great Adventures in Archaeology
Empires in the Dust
Akhnaten: The Rebel Pharaoh

THE GREAT WALL OF CHINA

By

ROBERT SILVERBERG

CHILTON BOOKS

A DIVISION OF CHILTON COMPANY/Publishers
Philadelphia and New York

ACKNOWLEDGMENTS

I am grateful to so many people for aid and comfort offered during the writing of this book that I am unable to list them all here. Only the greatest debts can be repaid: to my wife for her checking and rechecking of the manuscript; to those extraordinary booksellers, Max Faerber of the Paragon Book Gallery, New York, and J. F. Maggs of Maggs Brothers, London, for supplying vitally needed source materials. Librarians at the American Geographical Society, the New York Public Library, and Columbia University also helped to locate valuable material for me.

I gratefully acknowledge the services of Dr. Schuyler Van R. Cammann, of the University of Pennsylvania, who read the manuscript and offered suggestions and criticism. However, any errors that remain in the book are my responsibility alone.

Acknowledgment also is due to Arthur Waley and his publishers, George Allen & Unwin, Ltd., of London, for permission to quote extracts from Mr. Waley's translation of *The Book of Songs*.

CONTENTS

Introduction xiii

1 Before the Great Wall 1

2 The First Great Walls 17

3 The Rise of Ch'in 26

4 The Wall of Ch'in Shih
Huang Ti 41

5 "When Things Have Reached
Their Peak, They Decline" 56

6 The Sovereigns of Han 65

7 Westward Beyond the
Great Wall 76

8	The Downfall of Han	87
9	The Three Kingdoms and the Nomad Emperors	97
10	The Sui and the T'ang	111
11	Divided China	123
12	The Mongol Hordes	136
13	White Faces in the Yellow Realm	147
14	The Ming Dynasty	159
15	The Collapse of Ming	179
16	The Manchu Conquest	194
17	The Nineteenth Century and After	209
	The Chinese Dynasties	217
	Reference Notes	219
	Bibliography	222
	Index	225

*He [Dr. Johnson] expressed a
particular enthusiasm with respect
to visiting the wall of China.
I catched it for the moment, and said
I really believed I should go and
see the wall of China had I not
children, of whom it was my duty to
take care. "Sir," (said he) "by
doing so, you would do what would
be of importance in raising your
children to eminence. There would
be a lustre reflected on them from
your spirit and curiosity. They would
be at all times regarded as the
children of a man who had gone to
view the wall of China.
I am serious, sir."*

Boswell, *Life of Johnson*
(April 10, 1778)

: ix :

Author's Note

Two separate systems of notes have been used in this book. Where explanatory footnotes are necessary, they have been indicated by symbols and placed at the bottom of the page. Quotation sources are identified by superior figures. All these references are at the back of the book, and unless the reader is particularly interested in checking the source of a quotation, he need not interrupt his reading to refer to these numbered notes.

INTRODUCTION

Twenty-two centuries after the building of the Great Wall of China, the Chinese are still fond of telling stories about its construction. This is one of the most widely told:

"The Emperor Ch'in had a dream of two hares, one of which caught the sun in its arms. The other, jealous, struggled to get possession of the orb of day. A black hare arrived on the scene, separated the combatants, and took the sun away himself.

"Greatly troubled, Ch'in summoned the wise men of his court in the morning, and demanded from them, on pain of death, the proper reading of the dream. They conferred at length, and then told the Emperor, 'The first two hares are the two warring kingdoms of China. The black hare represents the Black Tartars of the north. The meaning of the dream is, if China remains weak and divided, the Tartars will triumph over us.'

" 'What steps do you suggest to prevent this?' asked the Emperor Ch'in.

"The wise men recommended building a great wall along the northern boundary of Ch'in's domain, to keep the barbarians out. Ch'in at once commanded that such a wall be built, and issued a decree that should have perpetual force, that in the present and all future time, any man found taking a nap on the wall should be buried alive in the construction."[1] *

We westerners are amused by such simple tales, but we prefer the sturdier joys of statistics. There is a marvelous superabundance of Great Wall statistics. Westerners have never ceased to delight in compiling them.

For example, it has been computed that the Great Wall—which traces a zig-zag course for nearly 2,500 miles across China—contains enough material to build a barrier eight feet high and three feet thick, completely encircling the globe at the Equator. In 1790, a member of the British Embassy to the Chinese Court estimated that the Great Wall contained more brick and stone than all the buildings of the United Kingdom. Superimposed on a map of the United States, the Great Wall would run from Philadelphia to Topeka, Kansas. Over-

---

* Superior figures refer to Reference Notes at end of text.

: xiii :

laid on a map of Europe, its terminal points would be near Lisbon and near Naples. The Wall covers one-twentieth of the circumference of the entire earth.

These arithmetical and geographical amusements are helpful in coming to terms with the stupendous bulk of the Wall. It is dizzyingly huge, a massive relic of the past, an architectural dinosaur—"the largest fossil on the planet," one traveler has called it. Supposedly it is the only work of man's hand that would be visible to the human eye from the moon. This hoary cliché of travel lecturers will soon enough be verified; meanwhile, astronauts and cosmonauts are able to contemplate the totality of the Wall from a height that old Emperor Ch'in would have envied.

Actually, as another Chinese Wall legend tells us, Ch'in *did* have an astronaut's-eye view of the site of his Wall. The story goes: "Ch'in was sleeping on a costly rug. It was when the darkness of the night was densest that he had a soul-stirring dream. His soul made a journey to the moon while his body remained on the earth. While on that lunar orb the bodiless Ch'in looked about him and then down on the far-off planet where he had left his body. From that distance his kingdom was as small as a dot. Then and there it was that Ch'in took on the idea of building the Great Wall, and in the midst of the moonshine he decided to construct a boundary line round his kingdom, that it might become as one family. The soul of Ch'in traveled from the moon to the earth, took on again its body, drafted men, put them to work, and intended to construct the big barrier so as to enclose an area vastly larger than the kingdom, that it might be encouraged to grow."[2]

Perhaps. This Emperor Ch'in—Ch'in Shih Huang Ti, to give him his full title—was an extraordinary man, a giant in his times, and it would be rash to deny him any of the supernatural powers with which he is credited. He built an empire that lasted two millennia, and a Wall that stretches for thousands of miles. Those are not an ordinary mortal's accomplishments.

The Wall is an overwhelming thing. It is one of the wonders of the world, though not one of the ancient Seven Wonders of the World. That canon was drawn up by a Greek who knew of China, if at all, only as a legendary land somewhere in the cloud-shrouded east. Moreover, the last of the classical Seven Wonders was built in 280 B.C., six decades before Ch'in Shih Huang Ti embarked on his wall-building project. Of the original Seven Wonders, only the Pyramid of Khufu survives today. The Wall endures; though, as we will see, little of Ch'in's own work remains.

Not only the size of the Wall, but the *idea* of it, exerts a fascination. China has always been a puzzle to Occidentals, and today it seems that the continued existence of civilization itself depends upon our ability to fathom the Chinese. The Wall has long been a symbol of the Chinese way of doing things. When the Romans were troubled by barbarians on their borders, they marched into the outlands and conquered their enemy. The Chinese built a Wall.* They withdrew behind a barrier which, for all its awesome breadth, is as much a monument to futility as to anything else. The Wall had psychological value

---

* The Romans built some long walls, too. But not nearly so long as China's Wall and not for the same reasons.

to the Chinese more than it had real military worth. It is the brick-and-stone realization of an idea, a summing up of China's concept of the relationship between itself and the hostile outer world.

All this deserves exploration: the Wall itself, the character of the man who built it, and the role it has played in Chinese history. But there was a China before Ch'in and walls in China before the Great Wall. We need perspective. To understand Ch'in Shih Huang Ti and his Wall, we must take the long view of China's four thousand years of recorded history.

The GREAT WALL of CHINA

One.
Before the
Great Wall

Being civilized is an old story for the Chinese. Of all the living civilizations of the world, theirs is by far the oldest; in many ways, China was shaped three or even four thousand years ago and has changed but little since. Chinese language, Chinese writing, modes of dress and manners of worship, ways of thought, literature—these have evolved with the years, of course, but there has been little fundamental change. Even the Chinese political system remained virtually unaltered from 221 B.C. to 1911, weathering dynastic changes and interregna without basic modification.

China is old, but she has by no means the oldest of cultures. According to modern historical and archaeological thought, civilization in China remained on a fairly primitive level until about 2000 B.C. Until that approximate date, there was no writing in China, no metal-working, and only the rudiments of agriculture and political organization.

By 2000 B.C., Egypt had at least a thousand years of highly complex civilization behind it. The cities of Sumer, in Mesopotamia, were hundreds of years past their primes, and entering a decadent period. In India, the remarkable cities we call Mohenjo-Daro and Harappa were already five hundred years old, and beginning their decline.

On that scale, China is a Johnny-come-lately among civilizations. We know more about the city of Ur, circa 2800 B.C., than we do about the China of 1500 B.C. The Pharaohs of the pyramid-building era (2700 B.C. and thereabouts) are better known to us than the shadowy men who ruled China a millennium and a half later.

The prehistoric phase of China's development, on the other hand, goes back an enormous way, and quite likely China was inhabited by human beings many thousands of years before Egypt or Mesopotamia. In 1929, the skull of one of these earliest Chinese was found at the village of Chou Kou Tien, near Peking. A Swedish paleontologist, J. G. Andersson, had noticed what seemed like a prehistoric human dwelling in limestone caves near Chou Kou Tien, in 1921. Six years later, teeth of a hitherto unknown type turned up at the site, and they were declared to be relics of a not-quite-human creature called *Pithecanthropus pekinensis,* or *Sinanthropus.* The discovery of a *Sinanthropus* skull followed shortly afterward. (The skull disappeared in 1941, when the Japanese occupied Peking, and was never seen again. But by that time other evidences of *Sinanthropus* had appeared—parts of the skeletons of 45 different individuals have been found to date.)

This cave-dwelling creature occupied China's central plains somewhere between 100,000 and 500,000 years ago. He stood upright, perhaps with a slight bend to his knees. He walked on two legs. The evidence of skull conformations leads paleontologists to conclude that he was capable of articulate speech.

It appears that even at that remote time, the familiar characteristics of the Chinese physiognomy had been formed. *Sinanthropus'* nose was broad, his cheekbones were high. Of the eyelid-fold that produces the so-called "slant," there is no surviving evidence, of course.

Sinanthropus occupied sites in what is now north and central China for some hundreds of thousands of years. Then there is a substantial gap in the record—and when skulls are found in the later strata, they are unmistakably *Homo sapiens* of the Asiatic sort.

The interruption was caused by a glacial period. A vast icecap thousands of feet thick rolled down from the north. The ice itself did not reach China. But the confrontation of cold northern air and the warmer air of the south stirred up winds of a velocity we find difficult to comprehend. These swirling winds skinned the plains of Mongolia bare, peeling away the soil as a knife does the skin of an onion, and depositing it far to the south.

It must have been impossible to live in China during the time when this was going on. The dry, cold winds, thick with yellow dirt, must have killed all vegetation, all animal life, and driven off the scattered bands of humans or proto-humans. Finally—some 10,000 to 12,000 years ago—the winds subsided, and men returned. The inhabitants of China began their journey toward civilization.

All the great civilizations of the past sprang up along the banks of rivers: Egypt along the Nile, Sumer along the Euphrates, the Harappa culture along the Indus. So it was, too, in China. The earliest human settlements in China developed in the valley of the Huang Ho—the Yellow River.

The geographical situation in the Huang Ho Valley is not really comparable to that along the Nile or the Euphrates. In the Near East, annual floods bring tons of fertile topsoil downstream, depositing it in the alluvial plain bordering the river beds. When the floods recede, farmers plant their crops in the newly deposited riverine mud. Thus Herodotus could accurately call Egypt "the gift of the Nile."

The Huang Ho is less benevolent. It flows through an area covered with yellow earth, a mixture of sand, clay, and limestone. The Chinese call it *huang-t'u,* but the German name of "loess" is the one we use.

Loess is the soil whipped from the Gobi Desert by the winds of the Ice Age. For thousands of years the wailing winds dropped their burden of loess on China's central plain, so that in some places the deposit of yellow earth is a thousand feet deep. In the loess regions of China, the wind easily raises the earth, plaguing the farmers with sandstorms known as "dry fogs," made up of tiny particles of yellow dust.

However irritating the dry fogs may be, there is no denying the wonderful fertility of the loess. When it is kept down by rain, the dry fogs disappear, and the soil takes on great fecundity. Although rain is infrequent in the loess regions of China, loess is remarkably porous, and is able to absorb much of the rainfall. This retained water gradually returns to the surface to provide nourishment for crops.

Through the plain of packed-down yellow dust cuts the Huang Ho. The loess affords no resistance, and the river has sliced nearly vertical banks. But the rushing flow carries along with it a great quantity of loess; hence the river's name. Choked with yellow mud, it winds a crooked course through much of northern China.

The mud that it carries tends to precipitate out and settle to the river bed. Accordingly, the bed keeps rising, and periodically the Yellow River overflows its banks—not a beneficial flow, as that of the Nile, but a disastrous, catastrophic flood. "China's Sorrow," the Huang Ho is called, and for good reason. It has long been proverbial in China that "Every eighty years the Yellow River is in flood, and every one hundred eighty years its course is changed." Each shift in course brings new woes to a different area.

If historian Arnold Toynbee is correct, civilization advances through a series of challenges and responses. The Huang Ho Valley provides a classic example. Fertility was there—when rainfall was scanty, the river and its tributaries provided water for irrigation—but the life-giving river held dangers as well. In order to reap the benefits of the area's fertility, it was necessary to hold the unruly river in check, and this technological challenge provided the impetus for China's progress.

That progress was not so rapid as in Egypt or Mesopotamia. The people of the Nile and Euphrates Valleys seem to have reached each successive landmark of civilization a thousand years or more ahead of the Chinese. But, by about 4000 B.C., a fairly complex culture had developed in the Huang Ho Valley. There were communities of moderate size, living in pits hollowed out of the loess (a poem of the eighth century B.C. tells us, "Of old Tan-fu the duke/Scraped shelters, scraped holes;/As yet they had no houses"[3]) and engaging in farming. Millet was the first important crop; later, wheat was introduced, and also rice in the warmer southern areas. The pig seems to have been domesticated at that time, and soon the dog. Crude pottery soon was succeeded by a more sophisticated kind.

"Then, suddenly," we read in J. G. Andersson's *Researches into the Prehistory of the Chinese*, "at the very end of the Neolithic, at a time only four thousand years distant from our own, the hitherto seemingly empty land becomes teeming with busy life. Hundreds, not to say thousands of villages occupy the valley bottoms. Many of these villages were surprisingly large and must have harboured a considerable population. Their inhabitants were hunters and stock-raisers but at the same time agriculturalists, as is evidenced by their implements and by the finding of husks of rice in a potsherd at Yang-shao-ts'un. The men were skilled carpenters and their womenfolk were clever at weaving and needlework. Their excellent ceramics, with few or no equals at that time, indicate that the then inhabitants of Honan and Kansu had developed a generally high standard of civilization. There must have been, by some means or other—new inventions or the introduction of new ideas from abroad—a rather sudden impetus that allowed the rapid spread of a fast growing population."

This took place about 2000 B.C. The Chinese prehistoric era now gives way to history.

II

Such history as we have of those times must be taken with caution. There are two important Chinese historical documents dealing with the origins of Chinese civilization—the *Shu ching*, or Book of History, and the *Shih ching*, or Book of Odes. They purport to deal with Chinese history from earliest times to about 800 B.C.

Even if they had come down to us without difficulties, these works, and the other early Chinese annals, would be open to some question. But all Chinese literature of early times has a dubious pedigree, thanks chiefly to the wall-building Emperor, Ch'in Shih Huang Ti, who, for reasons of his own, rooted out the scholars, burned the books, and did his best to obliterate any record of the China that had existed before his own reign.

From 213 B.C. to 207 B.C., any copies of the ancient books that were found were destroyed. Some survived the purge because they were hidden away until after Ch'in's reign; others were reconstituted from memory long after the time of the Burning of the Books. Thus, part of the *Shu ching* was recovered, the tradition holds, only because it was recited from memory by a 90-year-old man in the reign of the Emperor Wên (179–157 B.C.). Other chapters, hidden away carefully, were allegedly discovered when a house that had belonged to Confucius was demolished in the second century.

Granting the difficulties of preserving these documents through the years of purge, it is inevitable that distortions must have crept in. An entire section of the *Shu ching* is generally considered to be a forgery. And certainly there is an element of myth even in the genuine sections.

It seems to be a universal custom among the writers of annals to invent a few rulers of great longevity and lofty descent. Genesis gives us this:

"And Adam lived an hundred and thirty years, and begat a son in his own likeness, after his image; and called his name Seth:

"And the days of Adam after he had begotten Seth were eight hundred years: and he begat sons and daughters:

"And all the days that Adam lived were nine hundred and thirty years: and he died.

"And Seth lived an hundred and five years, and begat Enos:

"And Seth lived after he begat Enos eight hundred and seven years, and begat sons and daughters.

"And all the days of Seth were nine hundred twelve years: and he died." And so on.

The king lists of Sumer tell much the same story:

"When kingship first descended from heaven . . . A-lulim became king and ruled 28,800 years. Alalgar ruled 36,000 years. Two kings thus ruled it for 64,800 years. . . .

"En-men-lu-Anna ruled 43,200 years; En-men-gal-Anna ruled 28,800 years; the god Dumu-zi, a shepherd, ruled 36,000 years. Three kings thus ruled it for 108,000 years. . . ."

The traditional Chinese history begins with the Three August Ones (*San Huang*), Fu Hsi, Chu-jung, and Shên-nung. In the halcyon era of the August Ones, the earliest institutions of civilization developed—matrimony, agriculture, medicine, the calendar, cities. The consort of Shên-nung is said to have introduced the manufacture of silk.

The Three August Ones were succeeded by the Five Sovereigns (*Wu Ti*). First of these was Huang Ti, "Ruler of the Yellow," who—so the annals tell us—"established everywhere the order for the sun, the moon and the stars." Chuan-hu, Kao-Sin, Yao, and Shun complete the roster of the Five Sovereigns. A different, and slightly overlapping, arrangement is to be found in the *Shu ching*. Here, the Yellow Emperor, Huang Ti, is followed by three sovereigns, including two of the group of five from the other tradition. These alternate traditions stem from conflicts in theology, and their details need not detain us here, especially since they refer to rulers no more historical than Zeus, Cronos, and Uranus.

The tradition of the *Shu ching* is that the reign of the three sovereigns Yao, Shun, and Yü lasted 160 years—Yao reigning 102 years, Shun 50, Yü a mere 8. These mythical sovereigns were not hereditary monarchs, be it understood, nor were they despots. The venerable Yao declared, "I live for my people. The State exists for their benefit."

After he had ruled for many decades, the wise Yao heard of a young man named Shun, of great wisdom and forbearance, a model of filial piety. For twenty-eight years, Yao and Shun shared the throne, and then Shun ruled alone.

During Shun's rein, the Yellow River overflowed time and again. An energetic man named Yü performed miracles of engineering to stem the unruly tide, and Shun, hearing of Yü's accomplishments, declared, "My son has no such talents. The throne shall descend to the man who saved the people from the flood." Yü was named as Shun's successor.

Yü, the great engineer, became the first monarch to found a dynasty. According to the historian Ssǔ-ma Ch'ien, whose *Shih chi* (*Historical Records*) was set down about 100 B.C., Yü was "active, obliging, capable, diligent. . . . He restricted his clothing and his food, while he displayed an extreme piety towards the divine powers; he had only a humble dwelling, but he expended largely on ditches and canals." And Ssǔ-ma Ch'ien informs us that Yü "put into perfect order the six domains of Nature."

Yü named one Yi to be his successor. The princes of the land, however, refused to accept Yi's designation, and swore fealty instead to K'i, the son of the late Yü. And so the dynastic system came into being. The descendants of Yü ruled for some 400 years, and are known collectively as the Hsia Dynasty, China's earliest ruling dynasty.

There are traditional dates for all these rulers—in fact, there are several sets of dates, one dating the accession of Yao from 2357 B.C., the other from 2145 B.C. Chinese historians have been divided on the relative merits of these two chronologies for two thousand years, but the most widely accepted dates for the Hsia Dynasty are 1994–1523 B.C., and they will do for our purposes.

The Chinese annals list seventeen Hsia kings. There is no serious reason to doubt that the dynasty actually existed, but we have no definite archaeological proof of its existence. No artifacts have been positively identified as Hsia to this time. But while we can safely relegate Yao and Shun to the mythological or semi-mythical category, it would be risky to do the same with the Hsia. Archaeology is still a relatively new discipline, and many sites in China remain undug. Judgments on remote periods of antiquity must necessarily be tentative ones. After all, as recently as 1894 the great Egyptologist Flinders Petrie was able to write, "The first three dynasties [of Egypt] are a blank, so far as monuments are concerned. They are as purely on a literary basis as the kings of Rome or the primeval kings of Ireland. . . . We cannot regard the first three dynasties as anything but a series of statements made by a state chronographer, about three thousand years after date, concerning a period of which he had no contemporary material."⁴ Just eight years later, Flinders Petrie unearthed conclusive proof of the historicity of *eighteen* kings of the "blank" three dynasties!

Perhaps we will see the Hsia receive the official nod of history within the next decade or two. In any event, *some* series of kings ruled China in the first half of the second millennium before Christ.

Of course, the China that they ruled was not called "China," nor did it embrace anything like the territory we think of as China today. The kingdom of the Hsia probably was a relatively small group of city-states clustered along the Yellow River, perhaps in the region known today as Shansi, where the river takes a great bend to the north. The Chinese of the Hsia era probably knew the use of bronze, almost certainly had invented the wheel, and had begun to build carts and chariots and to manufacture silk. Furthermore, they had at least a rudimentary form of writing.

Tradition claims that the Hsia Dynasty was overthrown in 1523 B.C. The exact date is still in doubt within a matter of several centuries. But there is no doubt of the upheaval that took place along the Huang Ho at some time between 1800 and 1500 B.C. A warrior race exploded from we know not where and invaded the valleys of the Yellow River. The chariots of Shang swept down on the quiet villages of the Hsia kingdom, and the newcomers created what is the earliest undeniably historical unified state in China.

Until the late 1920's, the Shang were as dimly regarded by historians as their still unknown predecessors, the Hsia. But, beginning in 1927, archaeological explorations have left no doubt of the historical existence of the Shang Dynasty. We know now that theirs was a sophisticated and advanced culture—so advanced, in fact, that it poses one of the major puzzles of modern archaeology.

You need not look far to see examples of the craftsmanship of the Shang. Nearly every museum of art has at least one Shang bronze on display. The supply is an ample one; thousands of them are known. In fact, Chinese connoisseurs have been collecting them for a thousand years.

The Shang bronzes came into the art market in A.D. 1079. In that year, a

A Shang bronze vessel (from an old book of the Ming). *From the collection of the author*

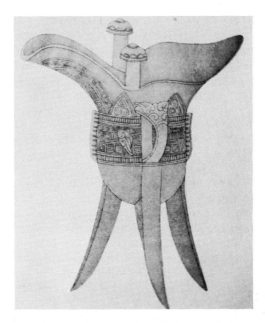

great storm struck the town of Anyang, in northern China. When calm returned, the people of Anyang were surprised to discover that a towering mound near the city had burst open, revealing what was obviously a tomb. Within were human bones, and the remains of horses and chariots, and also a multitude of splendid bronze vessels of strange shape and remarkable ornamentation. The good folk of Anyang promptly sold these bronzes to wealthy collectors. The demand grew, and over the centuries hundreds of bronzes were dug from the mounds at Anyang and sold to Chinese nobles. Particularly during the Ming period, these bronzes were so highly prized that modern imitations of them were produced. In time, a good many of the Anyang finds (and the imitations) made their way to the museums of America and Europe, where they are on view today.

These Shang bronzes are as wonderful in their way as the paintings of the Sung Dynasty and the porcelains of the Ch'ing. Richly patinaed with age, they display intricate ornamentation that bespeaks a highly developed esthetic sense. In his book on Chinese art, the British critic Finlay MacKenzie describes Shang decorations in this way:

"The wings [of an owl-shaped bronze vessel] are made up of a serpent within whose coils there are strange monsters crawling among the spirals of the 'Thunder Pattern.' This tendency to shift and alter before our eyes gives this decoration a dream-like, one might almost say nightmare, quality. For throughout the art of this period there runs an undercurrent of horror and darkness, a subtle blend of savagery and sophistication, and therein lies its peculiar fascination."[5]

The Shang employed these marvelous bronze vessels for sacrificial and ritual purposes, not for everyday uses. Some were goblets which must have held sacred wine; others were pans or ewers, still others were gigantic caldrons whose uses it is perhaps best not to try to guess. When a Shang chieftain died, these bronzes were placed in his tomb, as symbols of the puissance of the departed. In the tombs also went harness ornaments and musical instruments, pottery vessels, chariot fittings, bronze daggers and axes, and many other examples of Shang handiwork.

So extraordinary is this work, so qualitatively superior to anything that came before it, that the origins of the Shang tease the imagination. Where did they come from, with this full-blown culture? Did they spring from nowhere? Or were they emigrants from some other, more advanced part of the world?

We have no satisfactory answer. It is beyond belief that the Shang culture evolved overnight. But there is no archaeological evidence of the ancestry of the Shang. Nor do Shang artifacts resemble those of Egypt or Mesopotamia in any way. Examination of Shang skeletons shows that physically they were of the same stock as the earlier dwellers along the Huang Ho.

The traditional accounts say that the onrushing Shang hordes conquered 1,800 city-states. This is probably an exaggeration, like the 102 years of Yao's reign. It would seem that the Shang, highly organized and militarily superior, made themselves masters of a large area centering on the Huang Ho, and running from the shores of the Yellow Sea inland for perhaps eight hundred miles.

They had several capitals. Why they shifted from one to another, we do not know; perhaps the capitals were destroyed by resurgence of Hsia spirit, or possibly they were overwhelmed by floods. Little is known of the early Shang cities. But, about 1300 B.C., the Shang began building a new capital, the city of Shang, which in splendor and magnificence was the most imposing city in China at that time. It was part of this city of Shang, located near what is now modern Anyang, that was uncovered by the storm of 1079 A.D.

The Kings who ruled at Anyang were buried in huge pits—one of them was forty-three feet deep and sixty-five feet square—accompanied by articles of value and use for the afterlife. For many years the Anyang tombs were quarried on an amateur basis, chiefly for bronzes. Toward the end of the nineteenth century, however, another type of curio began to be found at the tombs: slivers of bone, covered with cracks and scratches. A good number of these bone slivers were powdered into medicine, thus sharing a fate that also befell some relics of *Sinanthropus*. Several scholars, though, got hold of these Anyang bones and studied them with care. They realized that the "scratches" were actually inscriptions—the earliest known examples of the written Chinese language.

Since 1927, systematic excavation at Anyang and other Shang sites has turned up thousands of these bones. Their inscriptions have been deciphered, yielding invaluable information not only about the Shang but about the evolution of writing in China.

From prehistoric times—as far back as 6000 B.C., perhaps—the Chinese had practiced a method of divination that we call "scapulimancy." Taking animal bones, usually shoulder blades, or scapulas, priests had applied hot points, and had read the future from the resulting cracks in the bone. Among the Shang,

: 8 :

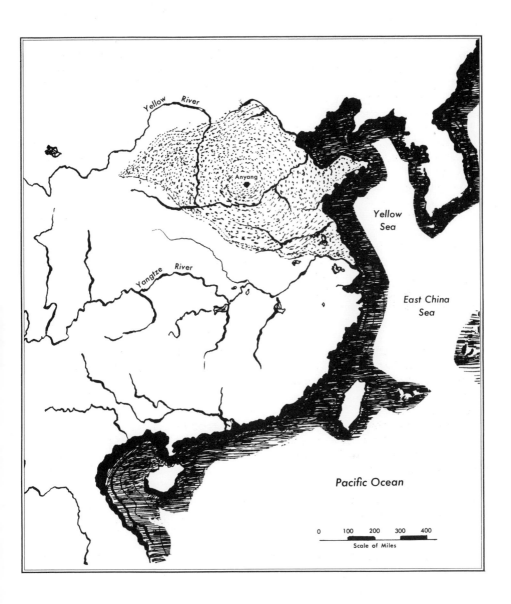

Shang China c. 1500 B.C.

A Shang jade knife. *Collection of Dr. A. N. Sockler, exhibited at the University Museum, University of Pennsylvania*

certain improvements in the technique of scapulimancy were introduced. For one thing, bronze points were used to produce the cracks. For another, the lower halves of tortoise shells were employed in place of deer bones. And, most important, the augurs of Shang developed a written script, and wrote on the bones themselves both the question and the oracular reply.

This Shang writing is the direct ancestor of the script in use in China today. The basic principle is the same: each character represents a single syllable, and the characters themselves have an ideographic origin, picturing in stylized form some real object. Sometimes the Shang ideographs can be correlated with modern Chinese characters. Out of 5,000 known Shang characters, 1,500 can be read at the present time.

Many of the "oracle bones" have thus been deciphered. Some contain simple sentences: "Rain or not?" "Is it permissible to go forth?" Others are more complex, as this one:

"Day *keng tzu,* oracle taken, Cheng [augur's name] asking, tomorrow, *hsin ch'ou,* will the weather be fine? asking, tomorrow, *hsin ch'ou,* will the weather not be fine?

"The king examined and said, this evening it will rain, tomorrow, *hsin ch'ou,* it will be fine.

"In that night rain was granted, on *hsin ch'ou* it was fine."[6]

Other oracle bones contain king lists that chronicle the names and doings of the Shang monarchs. The rich lode of these inscriptions is only now being tapped, and doubtless a decade hence we will know a great deal about this dynasty that so recently was classed as "legendary."

The Shang were doughty warriors. They carried their system of political organization over a wide-ranging area, and built up an elaborate structure of feudal domination. During the nearly five centuries of Shang rule, there were some thirty-one kings, according to the traditional annals, and the names of twenty-three of these have been confirmed by bone inscriptions. The Shang had a complex calendar, a good knowledge of astronomy, and a well-developed tradition of priestcraft. At their peak, they occupied a territory comprising about one-fifth of modern China.

It does not seem as though the Shang built boundary walls around their domain, though the major Shang cities themselves probably were walled. Walls are defensive instruments. They imply a certain cautiousness, a turtle-like tendency toward withdrawal. From what we know of the Shang, they were not turtles. Bold and aggressive, as fierce as the barbaric decorations on their bronze goblets would indicate, they expanded ever outward in a great imperialist surge, and had no interest in building walls to mark the bounds beyond which they would not venture.

A jade arrowhead, probably ceremonial. *Collection of Dr. A. N. Sockler, exhibited at the University Museum, University of Pennsylvania*

Imperialism is a transitory passion. The time comes when even the most aggressive of nations grows weak and lazy. Assyria lorded over Mesopotamia for half a millennium, but her fires grew feeble and the Persians put Nineveh and Assur to the torch. So, too, with the Shang. Having ruled for centuries, they lost their impetus, and gave themselves over to carousing and relaxation.

Possibly the Shang were approaching the stage when they would begin to think of consolidating their gains and building walls. They never had the chance, though. A new power arose in the west, and fell upon the Shang as mercilessly as the Shang had destroyed the Hsia.

These newcomers were the Chou, one-time vassals of the Shang. They came from the regions now known as Shensi and Kansu, sweeping eastward in a surge of conquest. For twenty years, the annals say, Chou and Shang contended, but it seems to have been a one-sided struggle, more of a lengthy mop-up than a real war. In 1027 B.C. (the date is traditional) the Chou made themselves unquestioned masters of China.

The story is told in many places, among them the *Shih ching*, the Book of Odes, which is often called the Confucian Odes. Confucius did not write them —they were set down between 800 B.C. and 600 B.C., and Confucius flourished around 500 B.C.—but he edited the text we now have, and used the poems for moral instruction. Some of the many poems are love lyrics, some are laments, others are philosophical in tone. A good many are dynastic chronicles, such as this one:

> *King Wên said, "Come!*
> *Come, you Yin and Shang!*
> *Why these violent men,*
> *Why these slaughterers—*
> *Why are they in office, why are they in power?*
> *Heaven has sent down to you an arrogant spirit;*
> *What you exalt is violence."*
>
> . . . .
>
> *King Wên said, "Come!*
> *Come, you Yin and Shang!*
> *Heaven did not flush you with wine.*
> *Not good are the ways you follow;*
> *Most disorderly are your manners.*
> *Not heeding whether it is dawn or dusk*
> *You shout and scream,*
> *Turning day into night."*
>
> . . . .
>
> *King Wên said, "Come!*
> *Come, you Yin and Shang!*
> *There is a saying among men:*
> *'When a towering tree crashes,*
> *The branches and leaves are still unharmed;*
> *It is the trunk that first decays.'*
> *A mirror for Yin is not far off;*
> *It is the times of the Lord of Hsia."*[7]

The last reference points up the fact that the Chou are now destroying the Shang (Yin was a Chou name for them) just as the Shang destroyed the Hsia.

The Chou pushed the last Shang king, Chou Hsin, from his throne, and established themselves in his place. Chou Hsin, according to the Chou-biased annals, was something of a Nero, a monster of depravity who had little popular support. With the Chou at the gates of his palace, Chou Hsin is supposed to have donned his most elegant regalia and to have ordered the palace set afire. He perished in the flames, The story is marvelously like the old fable of Sardanapalus, King of Assyria—who was really Assurbanipal, and whose death was in reality somewhat more prosaic.

The surviving members of the Shang royal family were pensioned off, with the privilege of continuing certain rituals of their line provided they undertook not to rebel against their Chou masters. Wu, the first Chou king, ascended the throne.

The age of the wall-builders was at hand.

III

The Shang had grown soft, as conquerors will over the course of centuries. The Chou, a tougher, culturally less advanced people, may have begun their eastward march in search of nothing more than booty, but they ended as masters of a realm.

It was not yet an empire. The Chou rulers extended and enlarged the Shang governmental system, which was essentially feudal—that is, local and hereditary chieftains ruled large tracts as fiefs granted by the dynastic overlord. The local chieftains had great power; the central overlord had no more than his vassals were willing to concede.

In many ways the change of dynasty represented simply a continuation of what had gone before, under a different group of rulers. The Chou were as Chinese as the Shang; not outsiders of different racial stock and language. They quickly learned those arts of civilization which the Shang had brought to a high level; Chou bronzes are nearly as good as Shang, for example, though they lack the strange power of the earlier works. The evolution of Chinese writing continued under the Chou.

The Chou rulers—who adopted the Shang title of *wang*, "king"—made their capital at Hao in the western part of their realm, near what is now the city of Sian in the province of Shensi. The Shang domain was sliced into fiefs, with a Chou noble at the head of each. Eventually the nobility was stratified into five grades: *kung, hou, po, tzŭ,* and *nan,* which are usually translated as "duke," "marquis," "count," "viscount," and "baron." Tribute and obeisance passed up the ranks of this hierarchy to the Chou *wang* at the pinnacle.

Tradition says that the Chou governmental system was devised by Tan, Duke of Chou, who died in 1105 B.C. The younger brother of Wu, first Chou king, he served as counselor and adviser, drawing up a legal code, "purifying the morals of the people," and organizing the state. The Duke of Chou acted as regent during the reign of his young nephew Ch'êng, crushing a Shang uprising and establishing the first four great feudal states of Wei, Yen, Lu, and Ch'i.

Early Chou history is cloudy and myth-shrouded, and we cannot rely on it too extensively. The chronicles tell us, for example, that the Duke of Chou had a wrist like a swivel, on which his hand could turn completely around; he is also credited with the invention of the compass. The unlikely anatomical detail tends to cast doubt on much else that is claimed for early Chou rule. It may be that the tale of Shang wantonness, and the whole Hsia dynasty, were Chou inventions designed to justify their own capture of the throne. In Chinese history, the last ruler of an outgoing dynasty is invariably described by the historians of the new rulers as a dissolute tyrant. We need not put too much faith in the tales of Shang atrocities. As for Hsia, supposedly overthrown by Shang when *it* grew decadent, that dynasty may have been invented simply to serve as precedent for the later, parallel, Chou conquest.

Chou nobility multiplied. So did the feudal states. The domain of Chou grew until it reached from Manchuria in the north to the Yangtze Valley in the south, and from the sea in the east to the eastern reaches of Kansu.* About half of modern China, in other words, was encompassed in the Chou expansion. To the south lay steaming jungles and impassable mountains, inhabited by barbarians of non-Chinese racial stock. To the north lay the grim, barren steppes of Mongolia, with the Gobi Desert beyond.

Some fifteen large states, loosely bound together by feudal obligations to the Chou king, emerged within the first two centuries of the Chou era. Hundreds of lesser states, most embracing only a single city, also came into being as the Chou rulers rewarded faithful followers with titles of nobility and land. The position of the Chou *wang* was something like that of Agamemnon in Homer's Greece; a horde of proud vassals looked to him for military and religious leadership, but did not necessarily follow him all the time.

The basic unit of Chou society was the walled city, with its surrounding countryside. In Shang days, too, cities had built walls of tamped earth, but now it became an obsession. Major cities surrounded themselves with towering walls whose gates were guarded well and locked at night. Lesser villages heaped up ramparts of mud. Beyond the city walls lay the zone of farms, for agriculture was the core of the Chinese economy. One city's farms shaded off, at the border, into the farms of another. Sweating peasants could look up at the walls behind which the proud aristocrats dwelled. Between the ruling class and the tillers of the soil came the artisans, the makers of bronze vessels and weapons, of chariots, of armor and musical instruments, of jewelry and mirrors.

Rivalry between state and state inevitably grew. Strong states expanded at the expense of weaker neighbors. The Chou monarch maintained order where he could, but often he found it wiser not to meddle. The Chou *wang* was himself a feudal lord, with territory of his own as well as an intangible claim over the rest of China. To the Chou capital came the tribute of the vassals; the Chou king offered arbitration of disputes, and performed the rituals of religion that he alone was entitled to perform.

About 800 B.C., the system began to crumble. The obeisance of the vassals became mere lip service. Each vassal was now absolute monarch in his own fief.

---

* The place names are the modern ones.

The Chou ruler was regarded as a kind of pope, his powers more spiritual than secular beyond the borders of his own small principality. The Chou "empire" was only a fiction.

A pretty story from Chinese annals mingles fact with fable to dramatize the final collapse of Chou authority. In 782 B.C., Yu Wang came to the throne, succeeding his father Hsuan. In Hsuan Wang's time there had been a prophecy that "Bows of mulberry wood and quivers of wicker will be the ruin of the Chou Dynasty." King Hsuan had learned that one old couple were famed for making mulberry bows and quivers of wicker, and had ordered them put to death. But they had escaped, fleeing westward.

On their flight, they found a baby girl wailing by the roadside. Like Moses, like Oedipus, like Romulus and Remus, she had been cast away by her parents to die. They carried her with them on their flight toward Pao, an obscure district in remote northwest China.

There they settled. The baby girl grew to womanhood, and her beauty was extraordinary. When Yu became king, it happened that the people of Pao inadvertently gave offense to the monarch, and to make amends they sent him the foundling girl to be his concubine. She was taken into the royal harem in 779, and was known as Ssŭ of Pao, or Pao Ssŭ.

Beautiful though she was, Pao Ssŭ was of a melancholy nature, and was never seen to smile. Yu Wang was fascinated as much by her somberness as by her beauty; he exiled his wife and her son, the heir apparent, and raised Pao Ssŭ to the throne beside him. When her first child was born, Yu named him heir to the throne. But still Pao Ssŭ did not smile. She said she loved the sound of tearing silk, and Yu Wang shredded many a bale of precious fabric to amuse her, but even that produced no flicker of mirth on her lovely face. Nor did dancers and jugglers, processions of dwarfs and clowns, boating trips, and other entertainments.

Now there was a chain of watchtowers ringing the Chou domain. A warning system was in use whereby, whenever the royal capital was besieged by barbarian invaders, fires were lit in these towers—a signal for the feudal vassals to send troops to the aid of the monarch. When Yu Wang offered a thousand ounces of gold to anyone who could suggest a way to make Pao Ssŭ smile, his chief minister put forth an idea: Why not light the signal fires on a night when no invasion was nigh, and have some fun at the expense of the vassals?

It was done. Beacons blazed in the watchtowers. In nearby towns, watchmen awakened their lords and told them to arm; new fires were lit, summoning troops from farther away. All across China the signals flared. The vassals prepared to go to the aid of the Chou king. Soldiers donned their armor and chariots were wheeled out.

Toward the capital the feudal legions streamed, banners flying gaily. When they arrived, they found no siege, no barbarians—only Yu Wang and his concubine. And Pao Ssŭ was smiling at the discomfiture of the vassals. "Go home," the king declared. "It was only a joke!" Peals of silvery laughter from Pao Ssŭ stirred the wrath of the feudal lords who had mobilized only to be mocked.

The rightful heir to the throne, at this time, had fled into exile in the west. He allied himself with the Jung, a barbarian tribe, and placed himself at the head of an army that marched toward the Chou capital. Once again the bonfires were lit, but the vassals, remembering the ruse and still smarting over it, refused to take up arms and be mocked a second time. They left Yu Wang to his own meager defenses. The barbarians swarmed through the royal city, slaughtering the king and his courtiers. Pao Ssŭ was carried off by a barbarian chief, and took her own life.

The true heir ascended his father's throne as P'ing Wang. But barbarians raged out of control in the capital, and P'ing, unable to quiet his unruly allies, was compelled to move his court far to the east, to Loyang in Honan. What once had been the Chou royal domain fell into the hands of Ch'in, western-most of the vassal states, and the soldiers of Ch'in drove the barbarians out.

Real historical truth underlies the tale of the unsmiling princess. No doubt the Chou capital was under pressure from the barbarian tribes of north and west for many years. The growing weakness of the central government left it unable to levy an army from the vassals, who by now were powerful enough to defy the king. The vassals, then, left the Chou king to his fate when a coalition of barbarians and western Chinese invaded the land in 771 B.C.

The death of Yu Wang effectively ended Chou rule except in name only. The Chou kings, in their flight eastward, gave up their ancestral lands in return for a token principality, a Chinese Vatican City. In the west, the state of Ch'in took possession of the fertile valley of the Wei River that once had been the heart of the Chou territory. A handful of powerful states now contended for supremacy over China and, to safeguard themselves, the contending states began to build long ramparts, barrier walls along their boundaries: the first great walls of China.

Two.
The First
Great Walls

When China shatters into several political units, as has happened many times in her long history, the cleavage tends to take place along fairly clear-cut geographical lines. In an agricultural society such as China's, unity is found where climate and growing conditions, as well as river transport, create natural bonds.

The breakup of the Chou realm after the disaster of 771 B.C. followed these lines. The one-time Shang domain, which had passed out of the hands of Chou into those of the princes of Ch'in, was the western highland region, where the Wei River meets the Huang Ho. Here, in the oldest inhabited section of China, the fertile yellow loess supported an economy based on wheat and nurtured by intensive irrigation.

To the east lay the great plains, sweeping on toward the province of Shantung, watered by the lower Huang Ho. One fundamental factor in the downfall of Chou was the gradual shift of China's political and economic center of gravity toward this eastern region, as the development of techniques of irrigation and flood control made the extension of agriculture possible.

The third power point lay to the south, in the valley of the Yangtze River. This area was quite beyond the original Shang-Chou zone of hegemony, and did not reach economic or political maturity until well after the splitup of the Chou regime. Here, the predominant crop was rice, not wheat; a warmer climate made for different basic attitudes toward the shaping factors of the economy.

Chou power, as we have seen, was extinguished in 771. For more than five hundred years, the Chou "kings" maintained a ceremonial importance at their court in Loyang. But real political power shifted from state to state as the feudal vassals, still nominally subservient to Chou, struggled for dominance.

The first to prevail was Ch'i, which attained the position of greatest power immediately after the Chou catastrophe, and held it until 636 B.C. Ch'i was a northeastern state, centering on the Shantung Peninsula, which is sometimes still called Ch'i today. Ch'i bordered on the tiny royal domain where the Chou king resided; on the north, though, Ch'i was adjacent to the barbarian

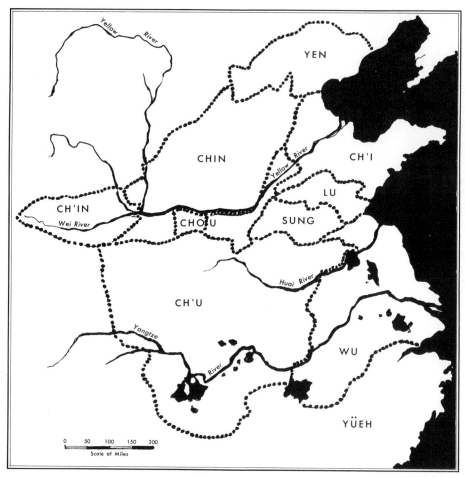

China c. 500 B.C.

districts of what is now Manchuria, and much of Ch'i's rapid growth in the seventh century B.C. was stimulated by its conflict with the Ti, a barbarian tribe.

Ch'i developed quickly into a tightly centralized state with a well-organized tax system and an army controlled by the government rather than by the whim of local potentates. For the first time in Chinese history, written law codes appeared, and an elaborate bureaucracy. Ch'i's nearness to the sea gave it the advantage of a monopoly over the lucrative salt trade, while its location at the mouth of the Huang Ho allowed it to control inland navigation.

At the same time, in the west, the state of Ch'in was beginning the explosive growth that would eventually give it total control of China. Between Ch'in and Ch'i there rose a third strong state, Chin,* in modern Shansi. Chin's

---

* The difference in pronunciation between Chin and Ch'in is slight. But the historical difference is a great one, and the two should not be confused.

time of maximum power was from 636 to 453, during which time it displaced Ch'i as the leader of the contending states. To the north of Chin lay the state of Yen; immediately south of Ch'i lay the small states of Lu and Sung. These seven states—Ch'in, Chin, Yen, Ch'i, Lu, Sung, and the royal domain of Chou —had swallowed up the hundreds of lesser states that had existed during the first three hundred years of the Chou era.

The rise of new states in the south posed a threat to the older ones. In the far southeast, in the modern Kiangsu and Chekiang, there grew the states of Wu and Yüeh. Far more dangerous to the northern states was Ch'u, centering on the Yangtze River, in what was then China's remote and almost uncivilized south.

As early as 704 B.C., the ruler of Ch'u had dared to call himself *wang*, "king," a title which until then had been reserved solely for the figurehead Chou ruler. Spreading outward from the point where the Han River meets the Yangtze, the Ch'u forces made themselves masters of a gigantic district nearly as great in area as that of all the northern states combined. While Ch'in and Chin and Ch'i bickered, Ch'u swelled and grew mighty. By about 450 B.C., it appeared likely that the Yangtze state would absorb the north and bring about a vast shift in Chinese political power.

It was a time of fierce stress. The northern states, never fully trusting one another, looked even more fearfully toward the expanding power of Ch'u in the south. But they were hard pressed on their northern frontiers, too, by the barbarians who lived beyond the boundaries of "civilization." It was a time to build walls. It was a time of fear.

II

The history of northern China, which is the history that concerns us here, is largely a record of the relationship between the Chinese and the invaders from the north. The outer barbarians bore many names during the twenty-five centuries of their threat to China: we will meet them as the Jung, the Ti, the Hsiung-nu, the Hsien-pi, the T'o-pa, the Khitan, the Jurchen, the Mongols, and the Manchus, among others. The essential fact linking them all is that they were not Chinese, though many of them eventually became more Chinese than the Chinese themselves.

The barbarians were of the same basic racial stock as the Chinese, though linguistically they were different, speaking languages unrelated to those of China. The real difference, however, lay in their way of life. The barbarians were pastoral nomads, depending on livestock for meat and milk, and moving from place to place in quest of new pastures for their herds. The Chinese were agricultural, raisers of wheat and millet in the north, rice in the south, and, of course, were rooted to their land.

The gulf between Chinese and barbarian was a natural geographic one. China, which is to say the land south of the Great Wall, is fertile and well-watered, ideal for cultivation once problems of flood control and irrigation are mastered. To the north of the Wall lie three differing but inhospitable zones where agriculture is impossible.

In the west is the Tibetan plateau, a high frozen desert suited only for a nomadic life, shepherds driving herds of yak and goats from one patch of alpine grass to the next. The plateau gives way to the huge steppe of Sinkiang and Mongolia, arid grassland along the Chinese border, bleak desert farther north. Here, too, the economy must be based on sheep, horses, camels, and cattle. The animals convert grass into meat and milk. Skins and furs yield food and clothing and shelter; animal dung provides fuel. Wells and oases are few. When rain is sparse, the pastures cease to support the grazing animals, and life is hard. Wheat must come from the south, from China, obtained through trade or, in hard times, through raiding.

The third frontier zone of the north is Manchuria, in the east. The geography here is less brutal; there are grassy steppes, watered plains, and, in the north, thick forests. But agriculture of the Chinese type could not flourish here until recently; it was a zone of shepherds in the steppes and hunters in the forest. Only in the present century has the Manchurian steppe been turned into farmland.

Thus there was a natural geographic barrier cutting off China from the barbarians. Just as naturally, the barbarians sought to plunder the rich, fertile south, carrying off the yield of the hard-working farmers of China. Hostility between Chinese and barbarian created a fluid situation along the border, an infinite series of shifts, alliances, and accommodations.

The traditional Chinese (and western) historical view is that the barbarians were "always" there, "always" nomads, "always" enemies to be feared. According to this interpretation, the Chinese from earliest times were subjected to periodic raids from the north, whenever economic conditions dictated a barbarian incursion.

This view has been called into question by modern scholars, most particularly by Owen Lattimore of Johns Hopkins University.[8] As Lattimore sees it, the Jung and Ti, those barbarian tribes who harassed the warring states of the middle and late Chou era, were not the vanguard of an invasion from the far north at all. Rather, he suggests, "these tribes . . . were in fact rearguard detachments lingering in territory into which the Chinese culture was expanding. They may not have been ethnically distinct from the Chinese. Possibly, and even probably, they were backward, less developed groups of the same stock as that from which the Chinese had evolved—a stock anciently holding the whole of North China, both the loess highlands in the west and the Great Plain in the east, and very likely also the southern parts of Mongolia and Manchuria."[9]

The Shang invasion no doubt forced the aboriginal peasantry of the loess highlands out into the marginal lands to the north. The outward pressure continued under Chou rule. Thus, the most backward inhabitants of the Chinese territory were inexorably squeezed into regions less desirable for agriculture. They turned to nomadism.

It is generally thought that nomads—wanderers—are the most primitive social groups, and that a nomad society gradually evolves toward agriculture. In his attack on the traditional beliefs of earlier historians, Lattimore has effectively demolished that notion, showing that "agriculture is earlier than pastoral nomadism and that farming peoples were the major contributors to the origin of nomadism."[10]

In this view, the spread of Chou civilization forced certain tribes into areas where agriculture was impracticable, if not altogether impossible. They struggled against drought and cold to raise crops in the Chinese manner. But the lack of rainfall—a million square miles of Mongolia gets less than fifteen inches of rain a year—defeated them. There were no rivers comparable to the Huang Ho to provide water for irrigation. Such rivers as there were either vanished in their valleys or discharged into marshy, salty, landlock lakes.

Eventually the struggle was abandoned. The border folk came to see that they could make better use of their parched fields for the grazing of livestock than for agriculture. The pressure of diminishing returns turned farmers into nomads; flocks were domesticated, and a pattern developed of continual migration from pasture to pasture. (At the same time, of course, the primitive reindeer-hunting people of the extreme north were also discovering domestication, and were descending *southward* into the steppe to become nomads. But the main stock of nomad "barbarians" came from the detached farmers thrust into the barren steppe by the pressure of Chinese expansion behind them.)

Thus the barbarian invasions that brought the Chou Dynasty down in the eighth century B.C. can be seen not as direct plunges out of the north, but as sidewise movements caused by local Chinese growth. The Jung, who swept into the Chou capital in 771 B.C., had formerly lived in the valleys of northeastern Shensi. The growth of the states of Ch'in in Shensi and Chin in Shansi forced the Jung barbarians to move in the direction of least resistance —which happened to be southward and eastward into the domain of Chou. As Lattimore puts it:

"The pressure of Ch'in and Chin on these Jung communities was greater than the resistance that Chou could offer to the Jung. Accordingly the Jung invaded Chou because they were retreating from Ch'in and Chin, not because they were 'invading nomads' pure and simple. Through this invasion-by-retreat, moreover, the land in which the Jung acquired a new foothold was not a terrain of open valleys and broad plains, favoring the rapid development of the Chinese economy, but the most hilly terrain in Honan and the most difficult to develop by irrigated agriculture on a large scale. The whole 'invasion' of these Jung, accordingly, comes down to the fact that they were forced to abandon better land to some Chinese but succeeded in taking poorer land from other Chinese."[11]

The process continued. The backward tribes were driven into ever less fertile land, until they gave up agriculture altogether and became stock-raising nomads. By the middle of the Chou era—the eighth to sixth centuries B.C.—the Mongolian steppe was rapidly filling with displaced tribes. Though the nomad population was always tiny in comparison to the teeming multitudes of China, the wanderers of Mongolia comprised a powerful threat to the settled lands.

The relationship between steppe and farm region was not easily subject to change by conquest. It was geographically impossible for the Chinese to extend their system of agriculture into Mongolia. Since the Chinese political system rested on a structure of fixed and walled towns surrounded by intensively cultivated countryside, obviously the steppe did not provide a lodging place for a Chinese method of administration. On the other hand, the nomads, though they could raid and harry the agricultural districts, lacked the techniques for governing them.

In the warfare that followed, the nomads had a considerable advantage. They were few in number, and highly mobile. Armed with bows and riding spirited horses, they could sweep down for a lightning strike at harvest time, carrying off grain and other plunder, then retreat deep into the steppe. They were striking at a fixed target: the Chinese city, with its bulging grain depots. Chinese punitive missions, however, were hard put to pursue and attack in the steppe, since the nomads could always remain on the move and beyond reach.

At a time when the Chinese central government was strong, border defenses could be maintained and the barbarians penned back into the steppe. When the government weakened, barbarian raids became more frequent, the frontier provinces were sapped of wealth, and the nomads grew bolder. On five major occasions, the barbarians were actually able to seize control of much or all of China itself, the nomad rulers putting the farmers of China to work for them while maintaining a power base in the steppe.

Some fifteen centuries after the breakup of Chou, the T'ang Dynasty poet Li Po described the barbarians of the steppe in these words:

> *The Huns have no trade but battle and carnage;*
> *They have no fields or ploughlands,*
> *But only wastes where white bones lie*
> *Among yellow sands. . . .*[12]

China had the barbarians under control in Li Po's time, early in the eighth century A.D. But when he wrote, China had only recently regained independence after hundreds of years of barbarian rule. He knew whereof he wrote. "They have no faces . . . only eyes," wrote another who had seen the barbarian armies at close range.

In Chou times the menace was new. The despised and outcast tribes of the northern hills became the warrior tribes of the steppe—the Jung, the Ti, the Hsien-yün, the Hsiung-nu. The divided states of China, quarreling among themselves, found new enemies on their northern border. The *Shih ching* sings of battle with the nomads as early as the reign of Hsuan Wang, the father of the luckless Yu:

> *We have no house, no home*
> *Because of the Hsien-yün.*
> *We cannot rest or bide*
> *Because of the Hsien-yün.*
>
> *We yoke the teams of four,*
> *Those steeds so strong,*
> *That our lord rides behind,*
> *The lesser men protect.*
> *The four steeds so grand,*
> *The ivory bow-ends, the fish-skin quiver.*
> *Yes, we must be always on our guard;*
> *The Hsien-yün are very swift.*[13]

The barbarians had ceased to retreat. By the seventh century B.C. they had begun to consolidate in the steppe and to attack those who had driven them out. And so the contending states of the later Chou era began to build walls.

They had gained engineering experience by building city walls. The wall of the capital of the northeastern state of Yen, built of rammed earth, was more than twenty feet thick in places, and parts of it still exist, rising to a height of over thirty feet. Archaeologists have studied other city walls of this era which are almost as sturdy.

Now came the first Long Ramparts—walls that enclosed not merely cities but entire states. The ruler of each state, feeling that his territory had reached the maximum area that could be conveniently ruled, chose to set bounds "forever" with long walls that marked, in Owen Lattimore's phrase, "the outer limit of desirable expansion."[14] To build these walls, which were hundreds of miles long, vast aggregations of laborers had to be assembled. The fact that they were built at all testifies to the strength of the feudal lord in each of the wall-building states. The Chou king, had he wanted to build walls, could never have summoned enough laborers to do the job. The Dukes of Ch'in, Chin, Ch'i, and the other individual states were able to command the necessary labor forces, though even they could not yet mobilize enough manpower to wall off every border. They had to be content with protecting those frontiers in greatest peril.

Some of the earliest walls were joint ventures by several states. In 658 B.C., a wall against the outer barbarians was erected in Hopei, in eastern China, by men of Ch'i, Sung, and the short-lived state of Ch'ao. Ten years later, several states, again led by Ch'i, put up a wall in northern Honan.

Usually the walls were enterprises of a single state, however, and this became more often the case as the rivalries between the contending states grew more bitter. Wall-building was intensified after 453 B.C., the year in which the state of Chin broke into three new states, Chao, Han, and Wei.

These three states were active wall-builders. In 353 B.C., Wei built a wall running north–south in Shensi, along the banks of the Lo to the northeast corner of the great bend of the Huang Ho. The northern half of this north–south wall was intended to keep out the barbarians of the area northwest of Wei. But for much of the distance, Wei was walling itself off from its "civilized" neighbor to the west, the State of Ch'in. (Ch'in broke through the wall and appropriated a slice of Wei, whereupon Wei built a new wall to defend its reduced territory.) Ch'in had a wall of its own, built in the fourth century B.C., that ran along its northern border to separate it from the Jung barbarians on the other side. Han, the southernmost of the three states that had emerged from the collapse of Chin, built a wall along its southern border to keep back the soldiers of the burgeoning Ch'u state. Ch'u built a wall on its northwest boundary to guard against trouble from Ch'in. Ch'i, in the east, ran a wall three hundred miles long on its southern border in the fifth century B.C. as a defense against Ch'u. Ch'i's wall, which ran from east to west

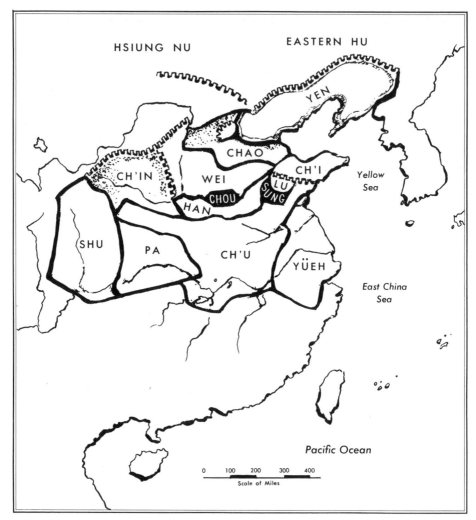

China c. 300 B.C.
This map shows the earliest Great Walls.

across Shantung, also functioned as an embankment to contain the floods of the lower Huang Ho.

It can be seen from all this that the walls in this era of contending states were designed as protection against other Chinese states as much as to ward off the barbarians. Three states in particular, however, bordered barbarian territory: Ch'in in the west, Chao (the northernmost segment of old Chin) in the center, and Yen in the east. All three built northern walls.

Chao's wall was the work of King Wu Ling, who ruled from 325 to 298 B.C. But Wu Ling was not content to abide behind his static fortification. The *Shih chi,* the great historical work written about 100 B.C., tells us that Wu Ling "changed the customs [of Chao], wore the costume of the Hu [a tribe of nomad barbarians], and trained cavalry and archers." On one campaign he "set out, dressed as a Hu, at the head of his war councilors, to the northwest, and won possession of the Hu territory in that region, with the intention of making an attack southward . . . to invade Ch'in."[15] Li Mu, a general of Chao, also trained his troops to fight in the nomad manner, using mounted archers who drew unsuspecting barbarians into a prepared ambush and slaughtered them. These adaptations of nomad fighting methods were significant changes in the Chinese way of waging war. In Shang and early Chou days, the feudal nobility had traditionally fought from chariots; the introduction of cavalry undermined the old and already collapsing power structure. The new armies of mounted archers could wheel and strike with a flexibility unknown to the warriors of Shang. This means of warfare, borrowed from the nomads, had far-reaching social consequences in China during the troubled decades that lay ahead.

The wall of Chao ran from a point northeast of Ninghsia, in what is now Inner Mongolia, to a point midway between the modern cities of Kalgan and Peiping in the east. About 290 B.C., the state of Yen extended this wall eastward through its own territory, into the lower valley of the Liao River, in modern Manchuria. This wall ran deep into the steppe, providing a considerable buffer zone between the outer fortifications and the cultivated fields.

West of Chao was Ch'in, with its Long Rampart running from the valley of the T'ao River, in Kansu, north to the Huang Ho, then eastward along the Huang Ho to the vicinity of Ninghsia, and southeastward from there along the steppe region known as the Ordos, to the Huang Ho again. Thus, by 300 B.C., the general outlines of what would eventually be the Great Wall of China were beginning to take shape.

In this troubled time there were many attempts to reach political stability, with various states combining against the one currently making itself dominant. Thus there were "vertical" alliances led by Ch'u, encompassing the southern and eastern states, directed against the rising power of Ch'in. There were "horizontal alliances" of the northern states from Ch'in to Ch'i, directed against Ch'u. In the sixth century, a balance of power was struck between Chin in the north and Ch'u in the south, but the breakup of Chin in 453 ended that.

State absorbed state. In the southeast, Wu rose to power in the sixth century, threatening Ch'u's eastern border, but in 473 was conquered and annexed by the neighboring state of Yüeh. Yüeh in turn was devoured by Ch'u in 334. Ch'i, the strong eastern state, engulfed Sung in 286. Ch'u gobbled up the central state of Lu in 249.

These conquests soon would be unimportant. The state of Ch'in was growing stronger. Within a span of little more than thirty years it took possession of all the other states, and welded them for the first time into a unified Chinese Empire. The Great Wall of China is the outstanding symbol of that stunning achievement.

Three. The Rise of Ch'in

Ch'in began modestly, but, as the Han Dynasty historian Ssŭ-ma Ch'ien wrote, it "ate up its neighbors as a silkworm devours a leaf." In the ninth century B.C., Ch'in was a minor principality in central Shensi, along the borders of the Wei River. The flight of the Chou monarch to an eastern capital left Ch'in free to seize the land that once had been the heart of the Chou royal domain. But at the northeast and southwest Ch'in was threatened by the expansion of neighboring Chin.

Ch'in strengthened its position by defeating and driving out the Jung barbarians in two battles, in 714 and 697 B.C. In 687, it annexed the small state of Kuo. Further conquests and alliances permitted Ch'in to expand northwestward along the Huang Ho, until it was powerful enough to withstand the menace of Chin.

Its growth continued, spurred by the downfall and partition of Chin in 453. Ch'in now occupied a large area in the northwest and was poised for striking in any direction. As Ssŭ-ma Ch'ien wrote:

"The country of Ch'in was a state whose position alone predestined its victory. Rendered difficult of access by the girdle formed around it by the Yellow River and the mountains, it was suspended a thousand *li* [there are three *li* to a mile] above the rest of the empire. With twenty thousand men it could hold back a million spearmen. The position of its territory was so advantageous that, when it poured out its soldiers on the seigniories, it was like a man emptying a jug of water from the top of a high house."[16]

Ch'in was regarded with suspicion by the other states, not only for its warlike ways, but because its northwesterly position made it seem more barbarian than Chinese. For a rough parallel in European history, we have the rise of Macedonia in the fourth century B.C. Macedonia, too, was a vigorous, expansionist northern state. Uncouth in its manners, it was willing to learn from its betters as it conquered them, and ultimately it brought unity to a horde of warring states of a more refined cultural status. Without pressing the parallel too far, we can see a Macedonia in Ch'in, and even an Alexander the Great in Ch'in Shih Huang Ti, the Ch'in emperor who built the Great Wall.

The barbaric cast of Ch'in culture set it apart from the other states. As late as 361 B.C., Ch'in still was not invited to the conferences held by the other feudal rulers. A chronicler of the era observed that "Ch'in has the same customs as the Jung and the Ti. It has the heart of a tiger or a wolf. It is avaricious, perverse, eager for profit, and without sincerity. It knows nothing about etiquette, proper relationships, and virtuous conduct, and, if there be any opportunity for material gain, it will disregard its relatives as if they were animals."[17]

The Ch'in rulers were not averse to acquiring barbarian customs. At Ye, in the district of Wei, the peasants held an annual ceremony in which a beautiful girl was cast into the river as a bride for "the Count of the River." When Ch'in annexed the region in 417 B.C. the ceremony was continued under Ch'in auspices, and each year thereafter a Ch'in princess went into the whirlpool where the river god dwelled.

Other aspects of Ch'in culture were equally barbaric by Chinese standards. In 237 B.C., a Ch'in statesman, Li Ssŭ, observed in a letter to the Ch'in king that the state had made great progress musically. Only a short while before, he wrote, "The beating on earthen jugs, knocking on jars, plucking of the *cheng,* and striking on thigh bones, the while singing and crying 'Wu! Wu!' as a means of delighting the ear and eye, such indeed was the music of Ch'in. . . . Today [the people of Ch'in] have done away with this beating on earthen jugs and knocking on jars. . . ."[18]

In warfare the Ch'in armies were ruthless in their ferocity and unique among the Chinese states in their method. In the seventh and sixth centuries B.C., the warfare between the states did not involve the annexation or destruction of the defeated state. A conquered noble acknowledged his defeat, and paid a tribute—while retaining control of his own territory. This gentlemanly system gave way, largely as a result of the Ch'in conquests, to a more bitter strife in which the ruling family of a defeated state was exterminated and the state itself absorbed into the victorious state.

Ch'in made this tactic a state policy. Prisoners no longer were ransomed, but were put to death in mass executions. Corpses were decapitated; Ch'in soldiers were paid bounties for the heads of enemies. Cities that were particularly stubborn in their resistance to Ch'in often were wholly depopulated. Conquered rulers sometimes were thrown into boiling caldrons, with Ch'in generals proudly drinking the human soup that resulted.

The Ch'in military machine was invincible. The opposing states were washed away in streams of blood. Appeasers offered Ch'in slices of territory to buy favor; Ch'in accepted the gifts, then asked for more. One factor in the Ch'in success may have been its use of iron swords. The earliest use of iron weapons in China dates only from 600 B.C., several centuries after the Iron Age had reached Europe, and nearly eight hundred years after the Hittites of Asia Minor had terrified the Near East with their awesome iron weapons. Iron swords were not generally used in China until about 250 B.C., and quite probably their spread was the direct result of their adoption by Ch'in. In 318 B.C. Ch'in had annexed the barbarian "states" of Shu and Pa in modern Szechuan, thereby gaining possession of important deposits of iron ore.

The unification of China was well under way by that time. In 364, the three states that had made up Chin—Chao, Wei, and Han—had leagued themselves against Ch'in, only to meet disastrous defeat. The battered states retrenched, and in 318 B.C. challenged Ch'in again, this time in alliance with the eastern states of Yen and Ch'i, and even with some support from a barbarian tribe, the Hsiung-nu. Ch'in threw back this assault and added new territory. Six years later, it was the turn of the southern state of Ch'u to try to halt the Ch'in advance—without success.

The six major states—Chao, Wei, Han, Ch'i, Yen, and Ch'u—still maintained their independence after their defeats by Ch'in. The time was not long in coming, though, when they would be absorbed. An indication of what was in store came in 256 B.C., when Ch'in turned against the small state of Chou, where the descendants of the ancient Chou kings still performed their ceremonial functions. Ch'in seized the royal domain, dethroning the Chou figurehead and ending a dynasty more than eight centuries old.

The myth of a Chou monarchy had been obliterated. Ch'in paused in its path of conquest shortly afterward, undergoing a change of rulers. In 246 B.C., thirteen-year-old Prince Chêng came to the throne of Ch'in. Soon the juggernaut rolled again—and this time it did not halt.

II

"High-pointed nose, slit eyes, pigeon breast, wolf voice, tiger heart, stingy, cringing, graceless"—so did Ssŭ-ma Ch'ien describe Emperor Ch'in Shih Huang Ti a little more than a century after the building of the Great Wall. But Ssŭ-ma Ch'ien, the Grand Historian of China, was writing in the days of the successor dynasty, the Han. Like Shakespeare, who painted the overthrown Richard III as a monstrous villain to please his Tudor monarch, Ssŭ-ma Ch'ien must have found it difficult to praise a Ch'in Emperor in the days of Han rule. Ch'in Shih Huang Ti has had a bad press through the centuries, in any event. His short reign was determinedly anti-intellectual, and Chinese historians have repaid his persecution with everlasting hatred. *"Fen Shu K'en Ju"* is the epitaph they coined for him—"He burned the books and buried the scholars."

Yet he also built the *Wan-li Ch'ang Ch'eng*, or Wall of Ten Thousand Miles,* and he built a system of government that endured for twenty centuries. "Stingy, cringing, and graceless" he may have been, and certainly there was little lovable about him. Even when we filter out the deliberate distortions of his record introduced by historians of later dynasties, what remains looks megalomaniac and unpleasantly paranoid. The Chinese view of the First Emperor may be balanced somewhat by the opinion of a twentieth-century French historian, René Grousset, who called him "a personality without equal . . . not only a conqueror, but an administrator of genius . . . an achievement equal to that of Caesar or Alexander the Great, but . . .

---

* A literary exaggeration—it means "ten thousand *li*," or about 3,300 miles, but the Wall was not quite that long.

was to endure much longer than theirs. . . . He was one of the mightiest geniuses to whose lot the reshaping of humanity has fallen."[19]

Ch'in Shih Huang Ti was born in 259 B.C., a few years before Ch'in's conquest of the Chou domain. The circumstances of his paternity have been placed under a cloud by the Han historians, who evidently invented an elaborate story to prove that Shih Huang Ti was not of royal blood.

The story goes that the old King of Ch'in, Chao (306–251 B.C.) had named his second son, the Prince of An-kuo, as heir apparent. The Prince of An-kuo himself had more than twenty sons. One of them, Tzŭ-ch'u—a secondary son by a concubine—had been sent to the state of Chao as a hostage, in accordance with an established custom whereby the royal families of the different states exchanged lesser sons as guarantees against treachery.

There came to the state of Chao a clever merchant, who "bought cheap and sold dear" and had grown wealthy thereby. He encountered the Ch'in princeling Tzŭ-ch'u at the court of Chao, and saw in him a means toward political advancement.

This merchant, Lü Pu-wei by name, drew Tzŭ-ch'u into conversation, and pointed out, "At present you have more than twenty elder and younger brothers, and moreover hold but a middle position among them. You have not received much favor, and for a long time have been a hostage among the feudal lords. When the great King dies, the Prince of An-kuo will become King, and then you will have no chance to compete with your elder and other brothers, who are ever before him, for the position of Crown Prince."[20]

"What, then, is to be done about this?" the prince asked.

Lü Pu-wei offered to return to Ch'in and place some judicious bribes, at his own expense, to insure Tzŭ-ch'u's succession to the throne. In return, of course, he expected a position of high favor when the young prince came to rule.

So did it occur. The Prince of An-kuo, influenced by the bribed sister of one of his wives, named Tzŭ-ch'u as his successor. Lü Pu-wei further consolidated his position in another way, according to Ssŭ-ma Ch'ien. He presented one of his concubines to the young prince, who took such a fancy to her that he made her his wife. The concubine, however, was already pregnant by Lü Pu-wei. In time, a child was born, and named Chêng. It was this Chêng who one day would rule all China as Ch'in Shih Huang Ti—the child of a tricky merchant and his concubine, not of a royal prince, so Ssŭ-ma Ch'ien would have posterity believe.

King Chao died in 251 B.C., the fifty-sixth year of his reign. The Prince of An-kuo became King of Ch'in, but died within a year. Tzŭ-ch'u took his place, becoming King Chuang-hsiang. As he had promised, he named the merchant Lü Pu-wei his chief minister, and the young Prince Chêng became heir apparent. When King Chuang-hsiang died in the fourth year of his reign, 246 B.C., thirteen-year-old Chêng ascended the throne of Ch'in.

That is the account given in the *Shih chi* of Ssŭ-ma Ch'ien. Derk Bodde, who has translated and analyzed this part of the Grand Historian's vast work, finds it hard to believe that Ssŭ-ma Ch'ien himself was responsible for the legend. He thinks that the text at this point was tampered with in later times,

The only known picture of Ch'in Shih Huang Ti, detail from a Han tomb engraving. Chavannes, *Mission Archaeologique*

or perhaps was not Ssŭ-ma Ch'ien's work at all. "In all likelihood," Bodde concludes, "the story that Lü Pu-wei was the father of the First Emperor is a pure invention, probably created by some Confucian of the Han dynasty in order to cast slander on the First Emperor. If this has been its purpose, the attempt has certainly been successful, for even now, two thousand years later, the story is commonly believed by most Chinese."[21]

During the boyhood of King Chêng, Ch'in was governed by Lü Pu-wei. The annals on which we have to depend show him as vain, untrustworthy, depraved, and scheming. How much of this is factual, and how much is gross propaganda aimed at the merchant class to which Lü Pu-wei belonged, we can never know. But in 238, Lü's intrigues touched off a rebellion in Ch'in which King Chêng subdued, and the following year, learning of some of the chief minister's activities, Chêng sent him into exile. Lü Pu-wei drank poison after leaving the capital, and a new minister, Li Ssŭ, rose to prominence.

The cautious, self-serving Lü Pu-wei had been content to consolidate the gains made by Ch'in in previous decades, and young King Chêng had not had enough power to act on his own. From 235 onward, when his rise to power began, Li Ssŭ advised the king to complete the conquest of China that his ancestors had begun. "Ours," he said, "is such a chance as does not come once in ten thousand years."

In 234, King Chêng's armies took the field. A year later, the King of Han asked to become his subject, but Chêng rejected such feudal overtures. Vassalage alone would not content him. He conquered and annexed Han in 230,

Chao in 228, and Wei in 225. Thus Ch'in engulfed all three sections of the ancient and once-mighty state of Chin.

Having disposed of his immediate rivals in the north, King Chêng turned next toward Ch'u, the large southern state. Ch'u fell in 223. A year later, it was the turn of Yen, in the extreme northeast, and in 221 the last of the old states, Ch'i, succumbed to the armies of Ch'in.

All China now lay under a single authority. Not for five and a half centuries, since the collapse of Chou prestige in 771, had the contending states owed a common allegiance. But Ch'in rule was totally different from the decentralized feudalism of Chou. King Chêng refused to accept the homage of the defeated kings. "The six kings were subjected to all the penalties befitting their crimes," and the entire feudal structure of the Chinese states was dismantled. The dukes, marquises, counts, and barons lost their titles and their local authority. Chêng divided China into thirty-six prefectures, and appointed men of his own to rule over each. The local administrators were not given the right to hand on their powers to their sons. All power flowed from the center, from the king, and there would be no more minor potentates to threaten the authority of the central government.

With China pacified, King Chêng demanded of his ministers that they find him a title "which was in proportion to his merits." The ministers considered the problem, observing that now "the laws and ordinances emanated from a single chief, and that from remote antiquity there had never been anything of the sort." In place of the obsolete title of *wang*, now too puny a designation, they offered *T'ai Huang*, "The Great Sovereign."

Chêng improved on their suggestion. He hearkened back to the legendary golden age of the remote past, and to those two groups of early monarchs, the *San Huang*, or Three August Ones, and the *Wu Ti*, or Five Sovereigns. He combined the titles of these deities into the appellation *Huang Ti*, "August Sovereign," and dubbed himself *Shih Huang Ti*, "First August Sovereign." His intention was that his successors would be known as "Second August Sovereign," "Third August Sovereign," and so on even unto the ten-thousandth generation of his dynasty.

China now had an emperor where once it had had many kings. The First Emperor—the Only First, as he was sometimes called—flourished his new style grandly. The Chinese usage is to prefix the name of the dynasty to the royal title, and so it is that the founder of the Ch'in Dynasty is formally known, after the year 221 B.C., as Ch'in Shih Huang Ti.

III

Behind the Only First was a cunning adviser, Li Ssŭ. And Li Ssŭ represented a school of philosophy, known as the Legalists, which provided the framework on which the new and unified China was ruled.

The Legalists arose partly in reaction to an earlier philosophy better known in the West: Confucianism. K'ung-fu-tzŭ, whose name we Latinize as Confucius, was a man of the unimportant state of Lu. The dates traditionally given for him, 551–479 B.C., are probably reasonably correct.

Confucius, an educated man who held petty bureaucratic posts and aspired unsuccessfully to higher ones, was an itinerant philosopher who wandered from state to state in search of a prince who would accept his advice. Eventually he returned to Lu at the end of his life, having accomplished little. Like Socrates, he left behind no books of his own, but his disciples gathered together his sayings, and his posthumous influence has been great.

What Confucius taught was a conservative philosophy. He accepted the rule of hereditary feudal lords, and directed his teaching at the aristocracy, believing that if the rulers maintained high ethical standards of conduct all society would remain orderly. He addressed the *chün-tzu*, or "Superior Man," setting forth codes of behavior.

The *chün-tzu* had to have certain inner virtues—righteousness, loyalty, love for others. He also had to have *wen*, meaning "culture" or "polish," and above all he had to have *li*.

Li can be defined as "proper deportment" or "attitude," but it meant much more than that to Confucius. As one commentator puts it, "This is a word with an extraordinarily wide range of meanings. In its narrowest (and probably original) sense, it denotes the correct performance of all kinds of religious ritual: sacrificing to the ancestors at the right time and place and with the proper deportment and attitude is *li*; so is the proper performance of divination. In this sense *li* is often translated as ritual or rites. In a broader sense, however, *li* covers the entire gamut of ceremonial or polite behavior, secular as well as religious. There are numerous rules of *li* for all customary situations involving social relationships, such as receiving a guest, acquiring a wife, going into battle, and the many other varied duties and activities of polite society. In this sense, *li* is often translated as ceremonial, politeness, etiquette, or rules of proper conduct. Finally, *li* in its broadest sense is a designation for all the institutions and relationships, both political and social, which make for harmonius living in a Confucian society. The *li*, in short, constitute both the concrete institutions and the accepted modes of behavior in a civilized state."[22]

In the Confucian philosophy of *noblesse oblige,* there was no need for any formal codification of the attitudes and virtues that comprised *li*. The fundamentals of *li* were broad moral principles, received *a priori*. Law alone was not sufficient to insure order in society. "To have good laws (*fa*) and yet experience order—examples of this have existed," wrote one Confucian philosopher. "But to have a Superior Man (*chün-tzu*) and yet experience disorder —this is something which from antiquity until today has never been heard of."[23] Let there arise a class of men with an innate appreciation of *li*, Confucius felt, and law and order would stem from them. *Fa*, laws, were suited only for regulating the common people. "The rules of polite behavior (*li*) do not reach down to the common people; the punishments (*hsing*) do not reach up to the great dignitaries."[24]

The Confucian tradition, with its emphasis on moderation and balance, had great appeal for the Chinese in the strife-ridden era of the warring states. Confucius' tenets of respect for age and wealth and position suited the conservative needs of a society trying desperately to hold itself together. But an opposing school of thought, developing in the third century B.C., challenged many of the Confucian assumptions.

Hsün-tzu, who lived from about 300 to 237 B.C., was the first philosopher of this school, which became known as *Fa Chia,* the Legalists. Confucius had said that man was by nature good, a rational being, capable of bettering himself. Hsün-tzu felt that most men acted out of self-interest, not out of innate virtue and altruism. Confucian philosophers declared, "Lead the people by regulations, keep them in order by punishments (*hsing*), and they will flee from you and lose all respect. But lead them by virtue and keep them in order by established morality (*li*), and they will keep their self-respect and come to you."[25] To this the Legalist reply was, "For governing the people there is no permanent principle save that it is the laws (*fa*) and nothing else that determine the government,"[26] and, "When punishments are heavy, the people dare not transgress, and therefore there will be no punishments."[27]

Li Ssŭ, the chief minister of Ch'in Shih Huang Ti, was a disciple of Hsüntzu. A fellow disciple was Han Fei Tzŭ, who died in 233 B.C. Han Fei Tzŭ was one of the chief exponents of Legalist thought, devoting particular attention to the problems of the ruler and the ruled. He argued for an all-powerful ruler; the monarch alone, he said, took the long view, whereas his subjects, hating toil and danger, craving only immediate ease and peace, are shortsighted and stupid. "A wise ruler when he makes his laws is bound to find himself in conflict with the world," Han Fei Tzŭ declared. For the subjects would not be willing to bestir themselves to take the precautions that the ruler knew to be necessary for public safety. Harsh, repressive laws thus would be needed for the good of society.

"If we had to depend upon an arrow being perfectly straight of itself," he wrote, "there would be no arrows in a hundred generations. If we had to depend on a piece of wood being perfectly round of itself, there would be no wheels in a thousand generations. . . . How is it, then, that everyone in the world rides carriages and shoots birds? It is the result of applying the art of stretching and bending. . . . Therefore, the ruler who possesses methods of government does not follow the good that happens by chance, but practices according to necessary principles."[28]

Philosophies that prefer ends to means are rarely popular, either in the societies in which they are applied, or in the judgment of later commentators. Thus the Legalists have been denounced, with some justice, as forerunners of modern totalitarianism. Certainly a man who could declare, as did Han Fei Tzŭ, that "benevolence, righteousness, love and favor are not worth adopting, while severe punishment and heavy penalties can maintain the State in order," is not likely to be regarded in a friendly light.

The actions of which Han Fei Tzŭ approved strike us as bizarrely unjust in their pursuit of justice. Thus he tells of Prince Chao of the Han state, who got drunk and fell asleep outdoors. To protect him from the cold, the keeper of the royal crown threw a coat over him. When he awoke, the prince asked who had covered him; upon being told, he punished the coat-keeper for negligence, but put the crown-keeper to death for transgressing on the legally appointed duties of another official.

The book of Han Fei Tzǔ is one of the two basic documents of Legalism. The other is the *Book of Lord Shang*, written in the third century B.C., and falsely attributed to Shang Yang, a Ch'in statesman who died in 338 B.C.

Shang Yang, who came to power in 361, practiced Legalist government before the philosophy as such had been formally set forth. Born Kung-sun Yang in the state of Wei, he served Wei's ruler for a while, until learning that he was about to be put to death as a potential rival for the throne. Kung-sun Yang fled across the border into Ch'in, and offered his services to Duke Hsiao, the ruler. He received the title of Shang Yang, or Lord Shang, and became the chief minister of Ch'in.

Shang Yang reorganized Ch'in completely, instituting a strict system of rewards and punishments, compelling all persons to take up "productive" occupations, and establishing an informer system to prevent shirking. As Ch'in Shih Huang Ti would do on a larger scale fifteen decades later, Shang Yang broke up the feudal aristocracy of Ch'in, taking power from the old hereditary nobles and bestowing it on men of talent and achievement, many of whom, like himself, were immigrants from other states. He divided Ch'in into thirty-one prefectures, each under a government-appointed officer, and built a powerful central government. It is said that under Shang Yang the people of Ch'in became so law-abiding that a jewel dropped in the street would lie there forever; no one dared pick it up.

Reformers such as Shang Yang rarely met natural deaths in China. In 338 B.C. Duke Hsiao died, and his successor, who had as a young prince chafed under Shang Yang's tutelage, looked menacingly toward the chief minister. Shang Yang once again found it expedient to flee from his employer. He crossed back into his native state of Wei, where, however, he was regarded as a renegade and an enemy. He returned to Ch'in, and tried to take shelter at an inn, but was refused, the innkeeper pointing out that Shang Yang was violating his own laws because he was not carrying a passport. The minister made his way to his own estate and put up armed resistance to the soldiers of his ruler, but he was overpowered and executed, his whole family being exterminated .

He had, at any rate, established the governmental principles by which the state of Ch'in, and afterward all of China, would be ruled. Nearly a century after his death, a group of anonymous Legalists compiled the collection of Machiavellian maxims now known as the *Book of Lord Shang*—as chilling a platform for rule as anyone has ever written, with the possible exception of *Mein Kampf*.

This coldly cynical book provided the principles by which Ch'in Shih Huang Ti and his minister, Li Ssǔ, governed. The aim of the state, it declared, was to maintain and if possible to expand its strength. This could be accomplished by establishing a powerful army and a productive agriculture:

"If there is no hope of gain except from the soil, the people will work hard in their fields; if there is no hope of fame except through services in warfare, the people will be ready to lay down their lives. If at home they work to their uttermost, then land will not be left uncultivated; if abroad they are ready to lay down their lives, then the enemy will be defeated. If the enemy is defeated and land is not left uncultivated, then without more ado a country becomes rich and strong."[29]

War was the stick the ruler used to beat his people into compliance. So long as an external threat existed, the subjects would obey, for their lives were in jeopardy. Peace merely bred "the Six Maggots, to wit, Rites and Music, the Songs and the Book [the Confucian works], the cultivation of goodness, filial piety and respect for elders, sincerity and truth, purity and integrity, kindness and morality, detraction of warfare and shame at taking part in it. In a country which has these twelve things, the ruler will not promote agriculture and warfare, with the result that he will become impoverished and his territory diminished."[30]

This was the philosophy of Legalism. Its triumph was brief; within five years after the death of Ch'in Shih Huang Ti a new dynasty was forming, and Legalism was expressly repudiated in favor of Confucianism. Yet the Confucianism of the Han Dynasty and later times was not that of Confucius; it had absorbed much of the Legalist thinking, so that the rule of law, abhorred by Confucius, now became the means toward the achievement of *li*. Legalism disappeared as a separate school, but its ideas and practices subtly infiltrated Confucianism, leading to the elaborate and most un-Confucian penal codes that were promulgated by dynasty after dynasty, with lip service given to Confucius and the concept of *li* all the while.

Li Ssŭ, Ch'in Shih Huang Ti's Legalist minister, was a native of the state of Ch'u. Born about 280 B.C., he served as a petty bureaucrat for a while, then enrolled as a pupil of the philosopher Hsün-tzu. Upon completing his studies, Li Ssŭ looked for a king worthy of receiving his services, and selected the newly-crowned King Chêng of Ch'in.

It was the year 246, and Chêng was only thirteen. Ssŭ-ma Ch'ien, in his biography of Li Ssŭ, would have us believe that Li Ssŭ foresaw Chêng's future greatness. He causes Li Ssŭ to make this declaration to his mentor Hsün-tzu:

"I have heard that when one attains the opportune moment one should not be tardy. Now is the time, when ten thousand chariots are at war. . . . At present, the king of Ch'in desires to swallow up the world and rule with the title of Emperor. This is the time for the commoners to be busy. It is the golden age of the traveling politicians. One who [at such a time], abiding in a mean position, decides to remain passive, is like a bird or deer that will merely look at meat [but not touch it]. But one who possesses a human countenance can act vigorously. . . . Therefore, I intend to go westward to give counsel to the king of Ch'in."[31]

Li Ssŭ took employment with Lü Pu-wei, then the chief minister of Ch'in. The young scholar met the future Shih Huang Ti and impressed him favorably with his suggestion that Ch'in sweep away the other feudal lords and conquer all of China. Li Ssŭ was given the post of Senior Scribe, and quietly feathered his own nest while Lu Pü-wei was nearing his downfall. When the wily old merchant finally was forced from power, Li Ssŭ moved into a position of authority.

He had enemies at court. There were those who, in the hope of ridding themselves of Li Ssŭ, recommended to King Chêng that he expel all foreigners

An attempt on Ch'in Shih Huang Ti's life (from the same Han tomb engraving).
Chavannes, *Mission Archaeologique*

from Ch'in. Li Ssŭ reminded his sovereign of the advantages Ch'in had long
enjoyed through making use of imported advisers as well as imported luxuries,
and he brought about cancellation of the expulsion order. That was in 237
B.C., soon after the fall of Lü Pu-wei.

Li Ssŭ's fellow student, the celebrated Legalist philosopher Han Fei Tzŭ,
was at this time serving as adviser to the king of the neighboring state of Han.
It happened that King Chêng saw the writings of Han Fei Tzŭ and was pleased
by the ideas that the Legalist advocated. "If I could once catch sight of this
man and move with him, I should die without regret," King Chêng declared.

The opportunity soon presented itself. Ch'in had begun to make warlike
gestures toward Han, and the ruler of Han sent Han Fei Tzŭ to Chêng's court
as an emissary. Li Ssŭ recognized a possible rival in his old classmate, and
warned Chêng against him, saying that any advice he might give would be
aimed at the eventual destruction of Ch'in and the enhancement of Han.
The slander was effective; at Li Ssŭ's suggestion, Chêng did not return Han
Fei Tzŭ to the Han prince, but ordered him tried as an enemy. Han Fei Tzŭ
was ordered to commit suicide. He attempted to state his case to Chêng, "but
was unable to secure an interview." Thus he died, the apostle of expediency
undone by one who played the game even more briskly and effectively.

Han Fei Tzŭ died in 233. Li Ssŭ next turned his plotting against the state
of Han itself. Part of his plan to destroy that state required him to make a
journey to the Han capital, and this he did, despite the possibility that there
might be retribution for the fate of his counterpart, the emissary Han Fei Tzŭ.
Li Ssŭ was unable to accomplish his mission in Han, but he succeeded, at
least, in returning intact to Ch'in. Soon after, Ch'in forces conquered Han,
and the great drive toward unification began—a campaign that met with complete success within ten years.

IV

Ch'in Shih Huang Ti, guided by the suave and durable Li Ssŭ, now commenced his rule of all China. He met with immediate difficulties of a ceremonial kind, according to the later chroniclers. Attempting to carry out a

ritual pilgrimage to the holy places of China, he ascended the sacred mountain T'ai-shan only to be met with "a storm of wind and rain," and when he tried to reach the mountain Siang, where the divine daughters of the legendary sovereign Yao dwelled, the divinities of the place greeted him with so furious a wind that he could scarcely get across the Yangtze. In return, Ch'in Shih Huang Ti ordered three thousand condemned criminals to level every tree on the mountain and paint it red, the brand of a criminal.

There was also trouble over the Nine Tripods of Yü. Yü, the legendary sovereign whose descendants supposedly founded the Hsia Dynasty, was said to have cast the nine talismans in 2202 B.C. from copper sent as tribute by the nine provinces of his day. Every ruler since Yü had maintained possession of these tripods as a sign that he held a mandate from heaven. When King Chao of Ch'in, great-grandfather of the First Emperor, overthrew the last Chou king in 256 B.C., he presumably took the tripods. Yet they were nowhere to be found when Ch'in Shih Huang Ti made himself Emperor, nor have they ever come to light. A Han Dynasty bas-relief at Shantung shows Ch'in Shih Huang Ti trying to draw them from the River Ssŭ, but being prevented by a guardian dragon.

Tripods or no, the Only First enforced his sway. He broke up the feudal domains and set up a nonhereditary bureaucracy to rule the many new prefectures. The laws of the various states were nullified and replaced by those of Ch'in. He unified weights and measures, standardized the coinage, and ordered the use of a revised system of writing that could be read in every part of the empire. The axles of wagons were now to be of a standard length, so that one network of roads could serve equally well for all vehicles. The armies of the old states were demobilized, the soldiers becoming farmers. Those weapons not needed by the army of the central government were melted down. The highest nobles of each conquered state were put to death; the rest were transported in wholesale lots to live at the Emperor's capital, where he could keep watch over them.

Heeding the advice of the *Book of Lord Shang,* Ch'in Shih Huang Ti took steps to foster agrarianism in the new empire, thus implicitly recognizing that agriculture was the practice that chiefly set the Chinese off from the non-Chinese nomads beyond the northern borders. He redistributed landed estates, making the peasants themselves landowners, subject to a tax proportional to the area of their fields. In an inscription of 215 B.C., he declared that his "favors are extended to cattle and to horses" and that his "benefits have enriched the soil of the land." Merchants, on the other hand, were regarded as nonproductive, and the Emperor distrusted them. In 219 B.C. he praised himself "on having honored agriculture and proscribing the lowest of the professions, commerce." Five years later, he deported many shopkeepers whom he regarded as troublemakers. Yet the very measures which the First Emperor took to standardize and unify the country benefited the merchants whom he disliked and feared; in Han Dynasty times Ssŭ-ma Ch'ien observed that "the country within the seas was unified; passes and bridges were opened; prohibitions which closed the mountains and lakes were removed. That is why rich merchants ran to and fro about the empire; there was no object of exchange which did not go everywhere."[32]

Ch'in Shih Huang Ti required a capital and a palace in keeping with his new magnificence. For his capital he chose Hsien-yang, in Shansi, then a petty provincial town.* Here he caused to be erected twelve huge metal statues, said to have weighed sixty tons apiece, fashioned from the melted weapons of the defeated states. Here, also, he built replicas of the palaces of the conquered kings, as reminders of his triumph. He settled the city with the richest of China's noble families: thousands of once-powerful aristocrats, compelled to take up residence as satellites of their conqueror.

The opulence of the Only First's palace became a Chinese legend. We are told that it extended for seventy miles, and included two hundred and seventy separate royal residences, each equipped with its full complement of furnishings and servants. The main palace was said to have taken the labor of seven hundred thousand prisoners to build; its entrance hall alone reputedly was five hundred paces by fifty, and so high that a sixty-foot banner could be unfurled in it, while the upper story was capacious enough to hold ten thousand people—doubtless a convenient way of saying "a great many."

As his reign progressed, Ch'in Shih Huang Ti less and less often left the sprawling confines of the royal residence. He declared that he ruled without being seen and without making his voice heard. At the suggestion of a court magician, Lu, he withdrew from nearly all contact with his subjects so that nothing impure might soil him. Within a radius of 200 *li* (about seventy miles) around his palace, the roadways were flanked by walls, and the Emperor remained behind that barrier. When he emerged to inspect his capital, it was at night, and when he traveled about the empire he did so incognito, within a closed carriage.

Like most autocrats, Ch'in Shih Huang Ti was fond of erecting inscriptions in praise of himself. "For the first time he has united the world," read an inscription at T'ai-shan. An inscription at Chieh-shih declared, "The inner ramparts have been cast down and destroyed. He has regulated and made equal the laws, measures, and standards for all men; . . . he has quelled the battles. . . . The black-haired people [the Chinese] enjoy calm and repose; arms are no longer necessary and each is tranquil in his dwelling. The Sovereign Emperor has pacified in turn the four ends of the earth."[33]

The Sovereign Emperor developed a powerful streak of mysticism. He surrounded himself with sorcerers and necromancers; he sought in vain for elixirs of immortality; he envied the miracle-workers who "enter water without becoming wet, fire without being burnt, and raise themselves on clouds and vapors." Near the holy mountain of T'ai-shan he set up a plain granite shaft, fifteen feet high, which he called "the letterless mountain" and regarded as an offering to the spirits that dwelled there. He sent an expedition eastward across the sea to a mysterious land of islands where spirits were said to drink from "the sweet wine-fountain of jade," thus becoming immortal. The expedition returned with word that a larger party should be sent, including "youths and maidens of good family." This was done, and nothing further was heard. In legend the members of this expedition are said to have reached Japan and become the first settlers of that country.

---

* A thousand years earlier it had been the site of the first Chou capital.

The Emperor relied heavily on the judgment of his chief minister, Li Ssŭ, but not all the members of the court agreed with Li Ssŭ's policies. The refusal to establish a new feudal system caused particular discontent. In 213, eight years after the conquest, there came to the Emperor one Shun-yü Yüeh, a native of the old state of Ch'i and "a mandarin of vast knowledge." He remonstrated with the Emperor in these words, according to the historian Ssŭ-ma Ch'ien:

"Your subject has heard it said that the reigns of the Yin [Shang] and the Chou lasted more than a thousand years. The sovereigns of these dynasties gave fiefs to their sons, to their younger brothers, to their distinguished subjects, in order to gain support. Now your Majesty possesses all that is within the seas, whilst his sons and his younger brothers are private individuals. . . . For a person, in any matter, not to model himself on antiquity, and yet to achieve duration—that to my knowledge has never happened."[34]

The minister Li Ssŭ rejected this reactionary argument. He pointed out, "The Five Sovereigns did not repeat each other's actions, the Three Royal Dynasties did not imitate each other . . . for the times had changed. Now, your Majesty has for the first time accomplished a great work and has founded a glory which will last for ten thousand generations. The stupid mandarins are incapable of understanding this. . . . In ancient days China was divided up and troubled; there was no one who could unify her. That is why all the nobles flourished. In their discourses the mandarins all talk of the ancient days, in order to blacken the present. . . . They encourage the people to forge calumnies."[35]

Li Ssŭ offered a proposal in the drastic Legalist manner that would forever rid the empire of this chatter about obsolete methods of governing. Though himself a member of the scholar class, he suggested that nearly all the classical literature of China be destroyed to eradicate "dangerous thoughts" and prevent the use of "the past to discredit the present." He recommended this course of action:

"Your servant suggests that all books in the Bureau of History, save the records of Ch'in, be burned; that all persons in the empire, save those who hold a function under the control of the bureau of the scholars of wide learning, daring to store the *Shih,* the *Shu,* and the discussions of the various philosophers, should destroy them with the remission of all penalty.

"Those who have not burned them within thirty days after the issuing of the order are to be branded and sent to do forced labor. Books not to be destroyed are those on medicine and pharmacy, divination by the tortoise and milfoil, and agriculture and arboriculture. As for persons who wish to study the laws and ordinances, let them take the officials as their teachers."[36]

Ch'in Shih Huang Ti gave his assent. The books would be destroyed; Chinese history would begin anew with the annals of the Ch'in Dynasty.

Printing was still a thousand years in China's future. The books that existed were carved by hand on bamboo tablets, a process extremely slow. Books were hard to produce, harder to conceal, and easily burned. Most of the classics existed in editions of only a few copies.

The books were collected. The fires burned for days. The classics of China, set down in the great days of the Chou era, were consigned to the flames—the

Book of Rites, the Book of Odes, the Book of History, the annals of the earlier princely houses of the many states. Many works were destroyed altogether, except for the copies preserved in the imperial library—and those, too, went up in flames not many years later, when invading armies sacked the First Emperor's capital. Thus many of the literary treasures of the Chou era, a time of miraculous fertility in literature, were lost forever. Some were hidden by defiant scholars, and were thus preserved, the hidden books sometimes not coming to light again for centuries. Other books were reconstituted after the First Emperor's death by aged mandarins, whose sometimes faulty memories yielded corrupt texts. Tradition holds that four hundred and sixty of the scholars were put to death for opposing the burning of the books.

That unhappy event took place in 213. Li Ssŭ was at the zenith of his power in Ch'in. His sons and daughters married the daughters and sons of the Emperor; he was laden with wealth; when he gave a great banquet the chariots and horsemen at his door numbered into the thousands. He had not forgotten, however, a maxim of his old teacher Hsün-tzu: "Things should not be allowed to become too flourishing."

Aware of this, Li Ssŭ remarked, "When things have reached their peak, they decline." His career and the career of Ch'in Shih Huang Ti, which were so closely entwined, attained their peak simultaneously in the year of the burning of the books. The decline would be sharp and remarkably swift.

Those of lesser wisdom than Li Ssŭ made no such gloomy predictions. The First Emperor's line, they declared, would endure for ten thousand generations. Had he not overcome the warring states? Had he not triumphed over the scholars? Had he not unified the land?

Above all else, had he not built a Wall?

Four.
The Wall of
Ch'in Shih Huang Ti

The First Emperor was nothing if not a shrewd administrator. For all his megalomania, for all his autocracy, he understood the dynamics of power. Through a decade and a half, from his first independent decisions in 235 to his total victory in 221, Ch'in Shih Huang Ti had maintained the momentum of his mighty enterprise by finding ever new enemies to attack. Now there were no enemies left; all China acknowledged his rule.

There was need of an external focus, a foe against which the energies of the Ch'in empire could be directed. There were barbarian tribes in the mountainous south who could be attacked, but their terrain was unsuited for the Ch'in methods of warfare, and it must have seemed that there was less to gain than to lose by choosing them as the new enemy. Other barbarians lurked in the grassy steppe north of China proper, but the First Emperor was equally cool to the idea of leading his forces into what is now called Mongolia. The nomads of the steppe were too hard to catch, and they had nothing to offer, anyway.

No, there was no suitable enemy to serve as the badly-needed focus for the imperial energies. Ch'in Shih Huang Ti chose a different technique for holding his empire together. He organized an incredibly vast public works project, thereby mobilizing millions of men not needed for agriculture and otherwise likely to become a source of trouble.

Public works had long been a means by which the Ch'in kings had maintained order. Long before the time of the First Emperor, the states of Wei and Han had sent a hydraulic engineer, Chêng Kuo, to Ch'in to encourage the building of a canal linking the Ching and Lo Rivers. The rulers of Wei and Han believed that the enterprise would sap the strength of Ch'in and reduce its military strength. But the canal was successfully built, and served to irrigate a vast region of Ch'in, creating additional wealth in grain that permitted the Ch'in king to enlarge his armed forces. After that, canal-building became a fixed policy of Ch'in. In 246, the year of Chêng's accession, a canal almost a hundred miles long was cut across Shensi; this, it is said by the chronicler, increased grain production in the region by twenty-eight pecks

The Great Wall of China, from a 19th century sketch. *Picture collection, New York Public Library*

per square mile. It became possible, as a result, to quarter troops in the area when Ch'in began its final onslaught against the other states.

Ch'in Shih Huang Ti's program of agrarian reform had set free from the land large numbers of men who were not landowners or heads of families. This floating population of unemployed men could not be used for a standing army, for there were no feudal kingdoms left to conquer. It was vital to the survival of the new empire that this great force be harnessed. Ch'in Shih Huang Ti chose to do it by linking the existing border walls of the old states of Yen, Chao, and Ch'in into one new Great Wall running from the sea westward for fifteen hundred miles.

The standard explanation of this decision is that the First Emperor felt "threatened" by the barbarians to the north. The evidence does not support this. The nomads seem to have been weak and divided at the time, posing no real threat to the stability of the empire. The reasons for building the Wall were more complex than the simple wish to exclude the warlike tribes of the steppe. The "hordes" of nomad barbarians had not yet begun their campaign of terror and looting.

The old nomad tribes, the Jung and the Ti, who had menaced the Chinese states in Chou times, apparently had broken up. In their place were the Hu and the Hsiung-nu, quite probably new tribes of the old stock. They spoke languages of the group called Turkic, and lived by herding livestock. (The Hsiung-nu are probably the Huns who invaded Europe many centuries later.) The Hu, or Tung-hu, occupied what is now Manchuria; the Hsiung-nu territory was the central steppe land, the present-day Inner Mongolia. Further to the west was a third nomad confederation, the Yüeh-chih, occupying the region embracing modern Kansu, Chinese Turkestan, and the borders of Tibet.

There were sharp differences of language separating these various nomad groups, but their way of life was similar.

Only the Hsiung-nu then encroached on Chinese land. The nomads had moved across the great loop of the Huang Ho into the district known as the Ordos. They were still north of the old state wall of Ch'in, but they were occupying land that the Emperor now felt should be included in Chinese dominions. Accordingly, he proposed to drive them out and build a new wall north of the Ordos, following the line of the Yellow River.

Building walls was not the best of all possible ways of thrusting back the nomads. Wu Ling of the state of Chao had shown that a century before; although he built a wall, he also carried military action into the steppe, adopting the fighting methods of the nomads and savagely defeating them. But Ch'in Shih Huang Ti had no interest in sending small detachments of mounted raiders into nomad country. A Great Wall best suited his purpose, which was not to eradicate a nomad menace but to achieve certain goals within China.

The Wall would be a cultural barrier, a line drawn across the geographical divide between grassy steppe and fertile farmland. It was not a line that could be drawn sharply, of course; there was no hard and fast area of cleavage separating geographical China from geographical Mongolia, as there is separating desert from fertile land in the valley of the Nile, for example. The line would have to be arbitrary and approximate. On one side, China, with its walled cities and tilled fields; on the other, the steppe land, fit only for grazing—that was the ideal. In practice, the Wall would have to run through marginal land, not quite steppe, not quite cultivable. Beyond the Wall, there would stretch zone after zone of ever less useful land, shading off imperceptibly from the steppe to the utter desolation of the Gobi Desert.

Nothing could be gained by trying to extend the highly centralized Chinese system of government into that desolation. Instead, Ch'in Shih Huang Ti preferred to use the border wall as a device that would keep his own people in, as well as keep the nomads out. All along the frontier, the steppe country exerted a powerful pull on the farmers of the marginal lands of China. They were forever tempted to break free of China and drift off into nomadism. Ch'in Shih Huang Ti intended to put a stop to this process of loss. Regarding the Wall as the boundary of what Owen Lattimore has called the "outer limit of desirable expansion," the Emperor chose to limit the risks of border trouble, to make the empire inward-looking rather than have it outward-looking, with all the chance of population loss that an unguarded frontier entailed.

The Great Wall was an instrument of economic policy. It consolidated the conquest; it fixed a terminal point for the Chinese style of government; it absorbed the energy of a restless army of landless men.

The Emperor could not, however, altogether resist the temptation to reach beyond his own Wall into the steppe. When the Great Wall was built, he attempted to develop a buffer zone of friendly barbarians just beyond it. The "barbarian auxiliary" idea, involving the maintenance of a tributary relationship with the tribes just beyond the barrier, provided a second line of demarcation and defense for the empire. North of the Wall dwelled the "friendly" barbarians, with the true outer barbarians roaming far to the north. Nearly every Chinese government since the days of the Only First attempted to maintain such a reservoir of allies beyond the Great Wall, and the distinction still can be seen on the maps: Inner Mongolia has long been regarded as part of China, while Outer Mongolia, the present-day Mongolian People's Republic, is an independent political entity.

But the concept of reservoir zones proved to be a double-edged one. The "friendly" nomads gave up their nomad ways when they took up residence just beyond the Great Wall; as they grew more settled, they developed a keener interest in possessing the luxuries of the Chinese on the other side of the Wall. It became a regular occurrence for the people of the reservoir zones to penetrate the Wall and make themselves masters of northern China, and on several occasions masters of all China. The "friendly" barbarians, not the wilder nomads of the distant north, became the greatest threats to Chinese security.

All that was far in the future when Ch'in Shih Huang Ti ordered that a Great Wall be built. It was to be a wall impressive enough to keep back the barbarians, a wall that in many places would be twenty-four feet high and wide enough for eight men to march in formation along its top. Watchtowers every few hundred yards would serve as warning stations from which signals of flame could rise, precisely as in the days of Yu Wang and his glum concubine Pao Ssŭ. At greater intervals, garrison towers would hold hundreds of soldiers, provisioned by China's agricultural fertility.

Across plain and mountain the Wall would go, a serpent of stone snaking an unbelievable distance, cutting through soft loess and rising to the rims of mountains thousands of feet high. At one point, the Wall would be eighty feet below sea level; at another, ten thousand feet above. It would pass through twenty-two meridians—from 120° E. to 98° E.—and it would curve back and forth across the region from the 35th parallel North to the 41st. Which is to say that Ch'in Shih Huang Ti asked for a Wall that would arc across one-twentieth of the world's circumference.

II

The actual task of construction was entrusted to an energetic, successful military officer, Mêng T'ien. Like so many of the great men of Ch'in, Mêng T'ien came of outlander stock; his ancestors were men of Ch'i. In the reign of King Chao of Ch'in, great-grandfather of the First Emperor, the grandfather of Mêng T'ien had left Ch'i to take service in Ch'in. His name was Mêng Ao; he advanced rapidly to the post of High Dignitary. In the reign of King Chuang-hsiang, immediately preceding that of the First Emperor, Mêng Ao distinguished himself in service against the states of Han, Chao, and Wei. His son, Mêng Wu, who became Adjutant-General of Ch'in, led the army that conquered the state of Ch'u in 223.

The third generation of this family of generals included two sons, Mêng T'ien and his younger brother, Mêng I. It was Mêng T'ien who conquered Ch'i, his family's ancestral homeland, in the year 221. For this, General Mêng was named Prefect of the Capital. His younger brother, Mêng I, was an intimate of Ch'in Shih Huang Ti, with the title of High Dignitary; he was one of the few courtiers with the privilege of direct access to the Emperor.

Ssŭ-ma Ch'ien's biography of Mêng T'ien tells us quite simply what his task was:

"After Ch'in had unified the world [in 221], Mêng T'ien was sent to command a host of three hundred thousand to drive out the Jung and Ti along the north.* He took from them the territory to the south of the [Yellow] river, and built a Great Wall, constructing its defiles and passes in accordance with the configurations of the terrain. It started at Lin-t'ao [in modern Kansu] and extended to Liao-tung [just west of Korea], reaching a distance of more than ten thousand *li*.† After crossing the [Yellow] river, it wound northward, touching Mount Yang."[37]

The Grand Historian's casual phrase "He . . . built a Great Wall" cloaks perhaps the greatest and most strenuous single engineering achievement of the ancient world. Khufu, when he built his Great Pyramid at Gizeh, kept thousands of men busy for twenty years, and raised a great pile of stone; but there is something simple-minded and brutal about heaping one block of granite atop another for twenty years. Mêng T'ien spent no more than seven years building the Great Wall, completing it about 214 B.C., and he had the advantage of being able to incorporate long sections of earlier walls into it. Nevertheless his accomplishment is more remarkable than that of the pyramid builder, for Mêng T'ien worked in extremes of climate, under uncertain conditions in a newly pacified empire, with unruly barbarians roaming not far to the north. The Chinese general flung up his mighty rampart in broiling heat and in winter snow; he ascended mountains and pressed on through endless plains. Freezing gales, sizzling sandstorms, raging storms assailed the builders. On and on went the making of bricks, the digging of trenches, the pounding of clay. Though Ssŭ-ma Ch'ien credits Mêng T'ien with a mere three hundred thousand laborers, other sources indicate that more than a million men may have worked on the Wall during its years of construction. Indeed, one writer says that four hundred thousand men perished in building what has been called "the longest cemetery in the world."

We know tantalizingly little about Mêng T'ien. Ssŭ-ma Ch'ien tells us that he was a great general, and of a family of great generals, and we know from Mêng's later actions that he was an honorable and patriotic man, who, like many honorable and patriotic men in China's history, went to an unjust death. As though troubled by the lack of detail in Mêng T'ien's life, the mythmakers of China have supplied a second great accomplishment for him, as delicate as the building of the Wall was grand. "*Tien pi Lun chih*," the proverb goes: "Mêng T'ien invented the writing brush and Ts'ai Lun invented paper."

This has become accepted history; Mêng T'ien is the semi-deified patron of Chinese brush sellers to this day. The tradition has been traced back no farther than to a work by Chang Hua (232–300 A.D.) which states explicitly that "Mêng T'ien created the writing brush." A later source, Hsü Chien (659–729), denies this: "Before Ch'in, the writing brush already existed; yet

---

* Actually, he drove out the Hsiung-nu.

† As before, a figurative exaggeration—the actual distance being about 1,500 miles.

Ch'in alone has gained the reputation of [first having it], and of Mêng T'ien, moreover, as having invented it. This [later belief] is a still greater error."[38]

The evidence of archaeology tends to support Hsü Chien's debunking of the legend. Bronzes of the Shang era clearly show the hair writing brush, sometimes loaded with ink, sometimes with its hairs outspread. As far back as 1500 B.C., it seems, the stylized representation of a writing brush was used as the written character for *yü*, "writing instrument." Two possible bases for the legend exist: perhaps Mêng T'ien was responsible for some improvement in the design of writing brushes, or possibly his sole connection with them was to introduce them into the rather backward state of Ch'in. Certainly an improved type of writing brush did make its appearance in China several centuries before the Christian era, and with the invention of paper (traditionally in 105 A.D.) the typical flowing Chinese calligraphy became possible.

It is pleasant, at any rate, to think of General Mêng taking time off from building walls and defeating nomads to ponder improvements in the writing brush. It makes a cheerful image: the general, at the close of a hard day of construction, inditing poems in tranquility, covering tablets of bamboo with lovely Chinese characters.

We have little real information about the methods by which the first Great Wall was built. Not much, if any, of Mêng T'ien's Great Wall has survived. In the east, repeated repairs in later dynasties have all but swept away the original Wall. In the west, time has done its work.

There is good reason to think that Mêng T'ien began by erecting supply bases along the line of the Wall—thirty-four in all, says one account. Since the Great Wall was to run through land of steppelike barrenness in the main, the workers' food had to come from the southern farms, by slow convoy. Lines of communication were still uncertain in the new empire, and the roving bandits—survivors of the old feudal armies—were not yet under control, so there was immense waste and pillage as these supplies moved northward. One chronicler remarks that of 182 loads of grain sent from Shantung, only one reached the Wall, the rest vanishing en route.

The supply bases served as command headquarters for the engineers. Next came the watchtowers and the garrison towers. The towers, which may have numbered 25,000 in all during the height of the Wall's usefulness, were of various sizes, but most of them were forty feet high and forty feet square at the base, sloping inward to thirty feet square at the top. They were built as close together as was practicable; the ideal was to place them two bow-shot-lengths apart, so that the tower archers could cover every square foot below. For the same reason, the watchtowers were designed to stand out a few feet from the body of the Wall itself on the outer side, thus enabling the defenders to lean over and pick off attackers at the base.

Besides these towers, which were planned as integral parts of the Wall, there were others, maybe 15,000 in all, placed north of the Wall as free-standing outposts. These were located at sites chosen for maximum command of the nomad country: on hilltops, at the mouths of valleys, and flanking passes through which invaders were likely to come. Each of these outlying towers was designed to be self-sufficient, and was provisioned to withstand a siege of four months. They served as a kind of Early Warning Line, flashing information back to the guardians of the Wall.

Once he had erected his line of towers, Mêng T'ien drew a curtain of wall between them. The construction of the Wall varied widely in technique from district to district. In the rocky, mountainous country north of what is now Peking, for instance, the Wall was made of brick and stone. We can reconstruct Mêng T'ien's methods, as they probably were, by studying the tactics used in Ming Dynasty days, seventeen centuries later, to repair this section.

The workmen dug a pair of parallel furrows in the solid rock, about twenty-five feet apart. Along these two lines they piled up a foundation of squared granite blocks, six to twelve feet high and about four feet wide. This served as the base for a brick face that tapered to a thickness of about eighteen inches, twenty or more feet high. Between these two granite-based brick walls the builders used clay or earth, rammed down by foot-power or perhaps by timber pile drivers. Lastly, a brick platform was constructed over the clay, linking the inner and outer faces of the wall and providing a roadway along which the defenders could march or ride. The builders tried to follow the strongest lines of defense; for example, the eastern section of the Wall, which today is the best preserved and the most familiar to travelers, leaps agilely along the crests of mountains and across the mouths of narrow gorges. Thus the Great Wall served as an added line of defense in a region that was well-nigh impassable anyway.

Further to the west, differing geography produced another kind of Wall. This was the loess country, the original heartland of China, where the Huang Ho makes a huge northward loop through the yellow plains. Here there was no stone for foundations, no clay for bricks. Mêng T'ien's workmen built a wall of loess. Loess is a curious substance. One geographer describes the loess country of China this way:

"Sprinkled over the countryside as though by a gigantic flour-sifter, a veneer of fine wind-blown silt blankets over a hundred thousand square miles of the north-western provinces. Although this formation is described by the German word *löss,* derived from deposits along the Rhine, it would not be inappropriate for these far more extensive accumulations to be known by their Chinese name of *huang t'u,* or 'yellow earth.' The material consists of very fine silt, yellowish brown in color, so fine that when rubbed between the fingers it disappears into the pores of the skin without noticeable gritty material. The porosity exceeds 45 per cent, enabling loess to hold considerable moisture, while the fineness of the openings facilitates capillary action."[39]

In some places the loess is hundreds of feet deep, with bedrock below. The fine yellow earth, unmixed with stones or pebbles, is easily excavated, and the people of the loess district build cave homes for themselves by burrowing into the loess cliffs. The soil is naturally fertile, and holds rainfall well, so that it yields good harvests even in dry years. However excellent loess is in agriculture, though, it makes poor material out of which to build a wall. Mêng T'ien's men strung their Wall through the loess lands by chopping the soil away to leave a projecting rampart of loess itself. Where materials were available, they veneered this loess wall over with a face of brick or stone. In other places, they erected a wooden framework and filled it with rammed earth. Nowhere did the Wall take on the solid, fortresslike appearance that it had east of the Huang Ho.

Unsurprisingly, the Great Wall in the loess region was subject to destruction at the hands of the elements. What *is* surprising is the extent to which this section of the Wall survived at all. At the beginning of the present century, an American traveler, William Edgar Geil, toured the length of the Great Wall and found sections of the loess wall still in fairly impressive condition.

"It has been sneeringly said," Geil wrote, "that the Wall in Shensi and Kansu is only a heap of hard mud; but if mud will do to keep people out, why not use it? . . . Even now, after long neglect, when our men measured the ruins, the remains were found in many places over 15 ft. high, nearly 15 ft. thick, with towers 35 ft. square at the base, and rising 30 ft. This would be awkward to climb over at any time, but when men are waiting on them with something humorous like boiling oil for a welcome, they would seem to furnish a good defence."[40]

It was necessary to drive the Hsiung-nu out of the Ordos before the Wall could be built there. The Ordos consists of nothing but hills and sandy valleys, and it is hard to see why Ch'in Shih Huang Ti chose to envelop it in his domain, unless perhaps, as seems quite probable, its climate was more gracious twenty-two centuries ago. Since walled cities and ancient highways have been found buried in the shifting sand dunes, it may well have been that the Ordos region was a valuable prize in the First Emperor's day. Today it is so much a desert that it is not even used for pasture except in sparse grazing zones south of the river. Nonetheless, Mêng T'ien not only walled it in but, at the orders of Ch'in Shih Huang Ti, transported thousands of Chinese into the Ordos as colonists with instructions to begin farming it in the Chinese manner. The colony was a failure; before many years had passed, the Ordos was abandoned to the Hsiung-nu once again.

Having completed the loess section of the Great Wall, Mêng T'ien moved westward into even less promising territory, the edge of the desert of Chinese Turkestan. (Or perhaps he built the western section of the Wall first, and worked his way eastward; the record is unclear.) Even the exact location of this desert loop of the Wall is uncertain; there are several lines of walls here, one within another. Probably the original Wall of Ch'in is the one from Ninghsia to Liangchow, in Kansu Province. Much of it today is fronted by the Gobi Desert,* and the sand has swept up over the earthworks that comprise the Great Wall. Beyond is the final stretch of the Ch'in Great Wall, dividing Kansu from Mongolia and enclosing the cities of Kanchow and Suchow. Twenty-three miles west of Suchow the Great Wall came to an end.

The Great Wall of Ch'in Shih Huang Ti thus falls into three main sections. It begins at Shanhaikuan (40° N., 119°44′ E.) on the Yellow Sea, and its first

---

* The name is redundant, really. "Gobi" is a Mongol word which means simply "a desert."

The solitary dedication stone, west of Kia-yü-kuan. Geil, *The Great Wall of China*

section, running to the Huang Ho, passes through mountainous terrain where the Wall is built of brick and stone, and is still in good condition today, thanks to the work of later dynasties. The second section is the earthen rampart, in large measure destroyed, running first from the Huang Ho's eastern arm to the western end of the great river's loop—this is the Ordos, or loess section—and then from the second intersection with the Huang Ho to Liangchow, the desert loop. Finally, there is the section that runs through the mountainous Ala country from Liangchow to the western terminal point, Kia-yü-kuan (98° 14′ E.).

This is a distance of 1,850 miles, including the bends and twists: 800 miles from Shanhaikuan to the Huang Ho, 600 miles through the loess and desert country, and 450 miles from Liangchow to Kia-yü-kuan. Of course, there is much more than this to the Great Wall of China, for later emperors extended it in various directions to meet changing needs. As we will see, there is a 300-mile extension west of Kia-yü-kuan; there is a 400-mile loop through Manchuria; there are more than a thousand miles of inner walls; and there are perhaps a hundred miles of false starts and useless limbs of wall. All told, the Great Wall of China has been reckoned at 3,930 miles in length, according to the measurements of Frederick G. Clapp, an American geographer who explored the Wall during the First World War. But the first Great Wall, of Ch'in Shih Huang Ti and Mêng T'ien, was somewhat less than half this length—a mere 1,850 miles.

The terminal points of the original Great Wall, Shanhaikuan and Kia-yü-kuan, have special interest as the alpha and omega of this mighty enterprise. Shanhaikuan, the eastern terminus, is a city three miles from the waters of the Gulf of Liao-tung. Its name means "Mountain-Sea Barrier," or "Between Mountain and Sea." There was no need to extend the Wall along the sea-coast itself, since China feared no invaders from that direction, and so at Shanhaikuan the Wall rose, and still rises, from the water's edge. Adam Warwick, a traveler who visited the Shanhaikuan terminus about 1920, wrote that "the terminal sea end of the wall is immensely impressive, where the blocks of granite, beaten upon by the waves and their ally, the wind, have broken loose and extend all awry into the water, toys for the rising tide."[41] The Wall here is a high earthen core coated with bricks. It runs from the sea to the city, which it enters at the gate known as Hsia-t'ien-ti-i-mên, "Under Heaven, Number One Gate," or "The First Gate in the World." Thence the Wall rises toward the mountains, on which it rests for the first three hundred miles of its western course. A dedication tablet at Shanhaikuan's Wall declares, "Heaven made the Sea and the Mountains."

At the other end of the Wall, at Kia-yü-kuan, stands another dedication tablet, this one inscribed, "The Martial Barrier of All under Heaven." Kia-yü-kuan, often called "The Jade Gate,"* is a city located between rising hills. The city's name means "Barrier of the Pleasant Valley," and here some of the most poignant scenes in Chinese literature took place, for all travelers going westward out of China passed through the gate at Kia-yü-kuan, bidding a tearful farewell to their homeland as they entered the unknown and probably hostile non-Chinese world outside. An inscription on a stone tablet at Kia-yü-kuan, fairly recent in date, seems intended to reassure those who were leaving the known world for the strange lands beyond:

> "Looking West we see the vast road leading to
>   the New Dominion
> But only brave ones go through the Martial Barrier.
> Who fears not the desert of a thousand square li,
> Why should he fear the scorching heat of Heaven?"[42]

The Great Wall ends some five miles southwest of the city of Kia-yü-kuan proper. One traveler who visited the true terminus was William Edgar Geil, who rode out of Kia-yü-kuan's gate on muleback. "During the journey thither no human being crossed our path," he wrote, "and there was not a house in sight the whole way. Five antelopes were the principal sign of life, as they hurried out of our track, and lizards, magpies, and crows, of which there were

---

* The Chinese imported jade (yü) from the west, and so the westernmost fortification of China was known as the Jade Gate. For some centuries the boundary lay far west of Kia-yü-kuan, and at that time the Jade Gate (Yü-men) was near the town of Tun-huang. That is the famous Jade Gate of Han Dynasty times, but after the loss of the western provinces the name was loosely applied to Kia-yü-kuan once more.

The ruins of the westernmost tower of the Wall with the mountains of Tibet in the distance. Geil, *The Great Wall of China*

some to be seen at the start, soon disappeared. There was nothing to attract the eye beyond whirling spirals of sand and tufts of brown sage-brush, while the whole landscape was earth-color, save that on the lofty Southern Mountains there lay, as ever, the snow."[43] The mountains of Tibet were in sight, but the Great Wall, Geil found, did not run to them. Instead the Wall ended suddenly, dramatically, at the brink of a precipice, "as perpendicular as if cut by engineers to a plumb-line." It was a 200-foot drop to the waters of the Tapai Ho, or Big White River, which flowed by below, milky with dissolved limestone.

Beyond Kia-yü-kuan lies the haunted land known to the Chinese as K'ou Wai, "Outside the Passes." On one hand the sky-piercing fangs of Tibet's mountains, on the other the lifeless wastes of the Gobi; between the two is a narrow panhandle dotted with oases, along which caravans have moved for twenty centuries. This forbidding zone played an important role in the history of the succeeding dynasty, but in Ch'in Shih Huang Ti's time no one ventured into the howling, demon-ridden wilderness that lay beyond the Barrier of the Pleasant Valley.

IV

So monumental a project as the construction of the Great Wall of China stirs even the dullest imagination. The Chinese are far from dull; poetry springs naturally to the Chinese mind, and just as naturally the story of the

Great Wall has become encrusted by legend. Twenty-two centuries of fantasy shroud the story of the building of the Wall.

And so we read that the First Emperor rode horseback across the empire, and the horse stamped three times in every *li,* and where it stamped a watchtower sprang up. We read that eighteen suns lit the sky while the Wall was building, and that the men labored so long on it that grass grew in the dust which accumulated in their hair. A legend tells of Ch'in Shih Huang Ti's magic whip, with which he could slice off mountains or make the Huang Ho change its course. The Only First was equipped, too, with a magic staff, seven feet long, studded with knobs of iron or gold; the Wall was built of any material that was handy, and when Ch'in Shih Huang Ti struck it with his staff, the material was changed to stone.

Then, too, the Emperor had a wonderful white horse, the one that stamped the earth to produce towers. The horse was allowed to wander freely over mountains and plains, and the imperial architects followed it, plotting the line of the Wall by the path of the horse. At one point a dust storm arose, and the track of the horse was obscured; the surveyors continued along the original line for ten miles, until they realized they had gone astray and the horse was elsewhere. The surveyors, architects, and workmen hastily returned to the horse's route, but forty *li* of abandoned wall going in the wrong direction remain to prove the tale.

There is a city along the Wall where the great rampart curves capriciously. The explanation is that while the workmen were resting, a dragon appeared and curled up along the just-completed stretch of Wall for a nap. So great was his bulk that the Wall was pushed out of shape; the workmen took this as an omen and completed the section by continuing the curve.

Other tales tell of the medicinal value of the mortar with which the Wall is held together—a belief that was current in China until very recently, though perhaps it has been suppressed by the prosaic Marxists who rule the land today. William Edgar Geil quotes an old recipe for skin cuts: "Take of the Magic Mortar quantum suff. and pulverize, take an unborn mouse and mash it into the powdered lime; apply the ointment. . . . Should the mouse not be available, substitute oil."[44] Geil goes on to note, "The same mixture is good for burns. If applied internally it will cure stomach-ache; for an average stomach and an average ache take a pill the size and shape of a lotus seed, for a baby, less."

Many of the legends of the Great Wall are love stories. One relates how the Emperor lost his magic whip. He fell in love with a mason's daughter, who refused to marry him because of his cruelty toward the hard-driven workmen on the Wall. When he insisted, she took her life. Arriving in heaven, she told her story to the Dragon King, who was deeply moved by the account of the suffering men.

The Dragon King sent his own wife to earth, in the guise of an irresistibly beautiful woman; she easily caught the Emperor's fancy, and wangled his whip away from him. The moment she had it, she flew off to heaven, and thereafter Ch'in Shih Huang Ti had to make do without it.

Probably the most familiar of the Great Wall legends is the story of Mêng

Chiang Nu, which has been told and retold for centuries. One version of the Ballad of Mêng Chiang Nu begins with an account of her father, Yüen Wai, "who often fasted and did good deeds." The lovely and gifted Mêng Chiang Nu married Fan San-lang, "who was himself a golden child come down from heaven," a scholar of such brilliance that at sixteen he had taken the highest degree in the Chinese academic system. The newlyweds settled in Chiang-li. Then, the ballad relates:

> Half a month had hardly gone: before the tyrant Emperor
> Ch'in Shih Huang Ti: began to build the Great Wall.
> Her husband's name was pricked: so he took in his hands
> The carrying-pole: and the ropes and baskets
> Thus husband and wife: were torn apart and scattered. . . .[45]

Fan San-lang told his bride sadly, "I am now departing to work at the Great Wall; you in the family must wait upon the old ones. . . . We must wait till the Wall is successfully completed." Leaving his wife behind, the frail scholar joined the labor force at the Wall. Winter came, and there was no news from him. Mêng Chiang Nu began to make winter clothes for him. One midnight, the spirit of her husband visited her while she slept.

> Weeping, weeping: he entered the chamber
> Stooped over the bed: with tears falling
> "I am freezing to death": he seemed to say
> "Quickly make for me: a padded gown."

> "Separated am I: so far from the family
> The wicked king has sent me: to build the Great Wall
> Since boyhood by my books I bided: I have little brute strength
> How can I be expected: to do this cruel work?"

He told Mêng Chiang Nu how he had weakened and fallen to the ground, and was buried in the Wall. She did not know whether her dream had been truthful or not, and she resolved to take his warm winter clothes to him at the Wall, hoping to find him alive.

Sadly she set out, not knowing the distance. Kuan Yin, the Buddhist goddess of mercy, took pity on her, and instantaneously transported her the three thousand li to the Wall—an anachronistic favor, since Buddhism did not enter China until several centuries after the Wall was built.

> The width of the wall: was several times ten feet
> To east and west: you could never see the end of it.

Mêng Chiang Nu looked for her husband, asking the workmen if they had seen the scholar Fan San-lang. They told her that they had heard of his death. Mêng Chiang Nu began to weep; and in heaven, the Jade Emperor looked down and pitied the young widow. He directed spirits to find the bones of Fan San-lang and give them to Mêng Chiang Nu so that she could bury them properly.

There was a sound as of thunder, and a gaping rent, several *li* long, appeared in the newly built Great Wall. The bones of thousands of dead workmen were exposed. Which ones were those of Fan San-lang?

Mêng Chiang Nu had her own way of telling. She bit her finger, and the blood ran through the boneyard. Most of the bones were unstained by the droplets, but her husband's bones soaked up the blood and stood out, red against the whiteness of the charnel heap. Hastily, Mêng Chiang Nu gathered up her husband's remains and prepared to return to her home with them.

> *Now hardly was she started: on her long journey*
> *Than the wicked Ch'in Shih Huang Ti: came by that way*
> *With officials and soldiers: noble and numberless*
> *With spears, pikes and swords: like a forest of hemp*
>
> *With ladies of honor: and maidens in pairs*
> *With canopies and fans: bright like the sun and moon*
> *In the middle there stood: an imperial baldaquin*
> *Under which sat stately: the wicked Emperor.*

Struck by the beauty of the passing Mêng Chiang Nu, the Emperor ordered her to stop, and asked her where she was going. She related her entire story, and showed him the bones of her husband. Ch'in Shih Huang Ti promptly invited her to become a lady of his court. The alternative, he remarked, would be a sentence of death, since she had committed a capital crime by causing a section of the Great Wall to be destroyed.

Of course, Mêng Chiang Nu abhorred the tyrant who was the instrument of her husband's death. But she wished to live long enough to bury her husband. Accordingly, she asked the Emperor for a hundred days to consider his proposition.

Laughing, the Emperor agreed to the delay, but directed that she remain in his retinue for the hundred days. He asked her to spend the time embroidering a gown for him; when the task was done, he told her, he would allow her to go home with the bones. Mêng Chiang Nu wove an elaborate purple-and-gold gown, and presented it to the Emperor. Struck by her skill and cleverness, he withdrew his promise to let her go, and insisted that she join his harem at once.

Mêng Chiang Nu, seeing that there was no alternative and no possibility of burying Fan San-lang on ancestral soil, agreed—with one condition. She would join the harem provided that her husband received a formal state funeral by the shores of the Eastern Sea.

The Emperor granted the wish. The nobles of the court were present, and Ch'in Shih Huang Ti himself took part in the elaborate ceremony. At the end of the funeral, the Emperor turned to Mêng Chiang Nu, but she thwarted his design by leaping into the sea, so that her soul would be reunited with that of her husband.

The surprised Emperor gasped in anger, "and his face turned yellow." But then he declared:

> *"To live alone for love: is rare in the world*
> *There are very few girls like this: now to be found."*

And he decreed:

> "Let a monument of stone: be erected on this coast
> In memory of Mêng Chiang Nu: who jumped into the sea
> And now make ready: my chariot royal
> For I will soon return: into my Court."

Another version of this legend goes on to state that the breach in the Wall never was closed, and that through all the succeeding centuries the gap remained, until our own day, when the Peking–Kalgan railway line was built through the Wall at that point.

The idea that hundreds of thousands of men were buried in and under the Wall is a persistent one. Story after story tells how the workmen, as they dropped, were immured under the growing rampart. One more such story, and then we will have done with fables of the Great Wall:

One of the First Emperor's many sorcerers told him that the Wall could never be completed unless ten thousand men were buried alive in it. Not even Ch'in Shih Huang Ti would lightly undertake such a deed, and he hesitated, while the Wall remained incomplete.

At last he found a characteristically Chinese way of sidestepping the terrible necessity. Heralds went out through the land in search of a man whose name contained the character *wan* (10,000). The man was found, and buried in the foundations of the Wall, and thereafter the work proceeded rapidly.

Five.
"When Things Have Reached Their Peak, They Decline"

And so the Great Wall was built. It was flung across the land from Shanhaikuan to Kia-yü-kuan, a great collar shackling China, holding back the barbarian tide and keeping the Chinese within their proper territory.

Not even the building of the Wall and the expulsion of the Hsiung-nu served to exhaust the energies of the empire. Ch'in Shih Huang Ti turned to military adventures in the south, pushing his troops beyond the traditional borders of Ch'u in a remarkable campaign. Chinese forces invaded the coastal province of Fukien, forested and mountainous; they marched into Kuangsi and Kuangtung; they reached as far as Tongking in what was later called Indochina, and is now North Vietnam.

He built roads. In 212 B.C. Mêng T'ien was ordered to build a grand highway across the empire. The tireless general "made cuts through the mountains and filled in the valleys, over a distance of one thousand eight hundred *li,*" notes Ssŭ-ma Ch'ien.

Less than a decade had passed since the unification of China. Vast changes had been worked. The Great Wall vividly blazoned the distinction between "we" and "they," and brought alive the concept of China "within the Wall" that remained alive thenceforward. Indeed, the Ch'in ruler invented the concept of China as a nation, as opposed to a group of states. Most scholars think that China's very name is derived from Ch'in—though the Chinese themselves, loathing the First Emperor's memory, have never called their own land by that name.

It was a majestic accomplishment. But, as the pessimistic Li Ssŭ observed at the time, "When things have reached their peak, they decline." Ssŭ-ma Ch'ien, the historian of the succeeding dynasty, summed up Ch'in Shih Huang Ti's rule in these dry, unfriendly words:

"Having united the empire, Ch'in Shih Huang Ti made public works within, and expelled the I and Ti tribes without. He received a tax amounting to the greater half, and sent forth as soldiers [all] to the left of the village gate. The men's exertions in cultivation were insufficient for the grain taxes, and the spinning of the women was insufficient for clothing. The resources

: 56 :

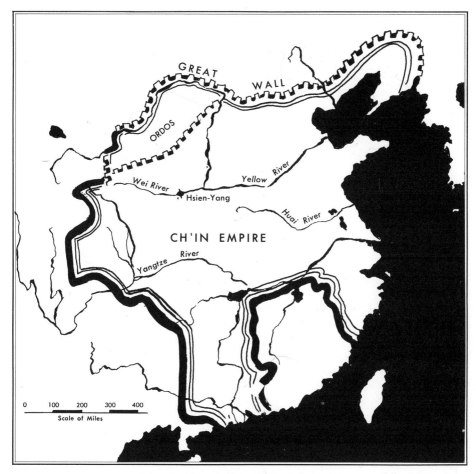

The Empire of Ch'in Shih Huang Ti

of the empire were exhausted in supplying [Shih Huang Ti's] government, and yet were insufficient to satisfy his desires. Within the seas there was sadness and dissatisfaction, and this developed into disorder and rebellion."[46]

Ch'in Shih Huang Ti's own official pronouncements were considerably more grandiose. Moving from palace to palace in the imperial compound at Hsien-yang, using underground passageways so he could not be seen, the Emperor issued decrees listing the benefits of his rule and boasting of the ten thousand generations that his dynasty would endure. He consulted his sorcerers and waited none too patiently for one of them to bring him the elixir of immortality.

The sorcerers were too slow. Time ran out for the Only First in the winter of his thirty-seventh year of rule and fiftieth year of life. He had left Hsien-yang early in 210 B.C. for an inspection tour of his domain. Accompanied by Mêng I, the brother of the wall-builder, the lonely, aging Emperor traveled, as always, in his closed carriage. He was proceeding north along the sea to Lang-ya in modern Shantung, more than a thousand miles from his capital, when he fell ill. Ch'in Shih Huang Ti sent Mêng I hurriedly back "to pray for the mountains and streams." Death overtook the Emperor at a place called Sha-ch'iu, in Hopei.

His death created an awesome rift in the political structure he had built. The empire had been undergoing strain during the last years of his life; the war juggernaut of Ch'in was less capable of dealing with the problems of peace, and in outlying districts of the huge land there was talk of rebellion and restoration of the feudal families. The Great Wall had drawn off much of the energy that might otherwise have gone into rebellion, but a fundamental instability plagued the empire all the same. It threatened now to fly to pieces.

Mêng T'ien, perhaps the most trustworthy man in the realm, was in no position to take action when the Emperor died. He was in the north, building a road parallel to the Great Wall. With him was the Emperor's eldest son and heir apparent, Fu Su, who had fallen into the royal disfavor by objecting to the burning of the books, and who had been sent to the remote provinces as a mark of his disgrace.

Clustered around the body of the dead Emperor were three figures who now played principal roles in the many-sided struggle for control of the tottering empire. One was Li Ssŭ, the architect of Ch'in's greatness, past sixty and a man of unquestioned power. Another was the imperial prince Hu Hai, weak and rapacious, younger brother of the exiled Fu Su. The third was the eunuch Chao Kao, who emerged into sudden prominence at the time of Shih Huang Ti's death.

Chao Kao is the archetype of the many sinister eunuchs who occupied so powerful a position in China's later history. His title at the Emperor's court was Keeper of the Chariots; he was descended from the royal house of the former state of Chao, but, according to Ssŭ-ma Ch'ien, "for generation after generation the family had been mean and lowly." The Emperor, impressed with Chao Kao's knowledge of the penal code, had raised him to high rank. Privately, the eunuch affixed himself to Prince Hu Hai, seeing that the young man was pliable and open to the eunuch's influence.

While the Emperor still lived, Chao Kao "committed a great crime"—not otherwise identified by Ssŭ-ma Ch'ien. The Emperor ordered Mêng I to judge the eunuch, and the wall-builder's brother sentenced Chao Kao to death. In view of Chao Kao's career of diligent service, however, Ch'in Shih Huang Ti reversed the verdict and restored him to his former rank. The incident left Chao Kao with a fierce hatred toward the family of Mêng.

Now the Emperor was dead, and he had never formally named a successor. Ch'in Shih Huang Ti's last order had instructed Chao Kao to write a letter to the eldest prince, Fu Su, telling him to accompany the funeral cortege to the capital and officiate at the burial. The letter was never sent. Chao Kao quietly retained it, along with the imperial seal.

Evidently it had been the old Emperor's decision that Fu Su was to succeed him, despite the estrangement. Chao Kao planned otherwise. He summoned Hu Hai and told him of the letter to Fu Su. "When this eldest son arrives, he will become established as Sovereign Emperor while you will remain without a foot or inch of territory," the eunuch said. It was an easy matter to lead Hu Hai into a *coup d'état* that would place the prince on the imperial throne.

The cunning Chao Kao next sought out the chief minister of the empire, Grand Councilor Li Ssŭ. Here was a match for the eunuch's shrewdness—a wily, durable man who had managed to survive thirty-five years of public life unscathed. Cleverly Chao Kao pointed out the risks Li Ssŭ faced if Fu Su came to the throne. The Emperor's eldest son, as was well known, respected no one more profoundly than Mêng T'ien. Chao Kao noted that "the eldest son is firm, resolute, warlike, and courageous. He is a sincere man and a spirited gentleman, and, when he succeeds to the throne, it is inevitable that he will use Mêng T'ien as his Grand Councilor. Hence it is inevitable that your lordship will not possess for an entire lifetime your seal as Marquis of the Highest Rank, but will someday be returning to your village."[47]

Li Ssŭ allowed himself to be drawn into the conspiracy to place Hu Hai on the throne. He saw no alternative; Fu Su was likely, as Chao Kao had observed, to dismiss him from office and replace him with Mêng T'ien. With the weakling Hu Hai in power, Li Ssŭ felt he would be free to continue his own policies and perhaps even attain greater influence than under Ch'in Shih Huang Ti.

Thus a letter was forged, using the imperial seal, and sent to Prince Fu Su at his frontier post near the Great Wall. It was supposedly a command from the dying Emperor that Fu Su and Mêng T'ien commit suicide:

"As to Fu Su, who, never having done anything worthy of merit himself, yet dares to complain and speak ill of all I do; and as to Mêng T'ien, who has not been able to correct my son's fault during this past year: I permit them both to take their own lives."

Mêng T'ien was suspicious of the letter. He urged that they send a message back, asking for confirmation, before they obeyed the imperial command. Fu Su pointed to the royal seal, and declared that it was his filial duty to obey. He killed himself on the spot. Mêng T'ien nevertheless sent a messenger to the capital, but received no reply, for Li Ssŭ had the man taken prisoner. Troubled by all this, the loyal general set out for the capital himself, accompanied only by a small bodyguard.

Events elsewhere were moving rapidly. With Fu Su out of the way, Hu Hai was preparing to seize the throne. No one knew of the Emperor's death but Chao Kao, Li Ssŭ, and Hu Hai. They feared that if the news spread before they were in full command of the empire, rebellion might break out. So, as the closed carriage of Ch'in Shih Huang Ti began the slow journey back to the capital, no hint was given that the monarch was dead.

Warm weather had come, however, and the imperial remains began to decay. To smother the odor, Chao Kao caused a hundred pounds of dried fish—a favorite delicacy of the court—to be loaded on each of the chariots in the procession. The stinking reek of elderly fish masked the smell of mortal corruption as the grand cortege entered the capital city.

Hu Hai mounted the throne as Erh Shih Huang Ti, the Second August Sovereign. Spoiled and self-indulgent, the new Emperor was content to leave the running of the empire to his ministers. Unlike Ch'in Shih Huang Ti, who took so personal an interest in government that he "handled one hundred twenty pounds of documents a day," Erh Shih Huang Ti spent his time in drinking and wenching.

Somewhat to his dismay, Grand Councilor Li Ssŭ now found that his own power had been usurped by Chao Kao, the Second Emperor's favorite. One of Chao Kao's first acts was to arrest his old enemy, Mêng I. Soon after, Mêng T'ien was taken into custody. Chao Kao asked the new Emperor to put the Mêng brothers to death.

Li Ssŭ vainly defended them, citing Mêng T'ien's great military achievements and his feat of building the Wall, and praising Mêng I's services as a minister to the First Emperor. It was to no avail, nor did the entreaties of Tzŭ-ying, grandson of Ch'in Shih Huang Ti and son of the late Fu Su, sway the eunuch. Prodded by Chao Kao, Erh Shih Huang Ti ordered the execution of Mêng I.

The Second Emperor next sent an emissary to Mêng T'ien in prison, bearing the imperial command that he take poison. The captive general replied by declaring, "My family has served in Ch'in during three generations. With three hundred thousand men under my command, nothing could have been easier than for me to rebel. Yet I would rather die than take up arms against the imperial house." And he asked: "What crime have I before heaven? I die without fault!"

But after reflection, Mêng T'ien remarked, "Indeed I have a crime for which to die. Beginning at Lin-t'ao, and extending to Liao-tung, I have made ramparts and ditches over more than ten thousand *li*, and in this distance it is impossible that I have not cut through the veins of the earth. This is my crime."[48] So saying, he took the poison.

Ssŭ-ma Ch'ien, in reporting the wall-builder's farewell speech, scoffs at the fanciful confession. "What did his crime have to do with the veins of the earth?" the Grand Historian asks sarcastically. "Mêng T'ien was a noted general, but [he did not] alleviate the distress of the common people, support the aged, care for the orphaned, or busy himself with restoring harmony among the masses. On the contrary he gave in to the ideas of the Emperor and conscripted forced labor. Is it not fitting that he and his younger brother should meet death for this?"

The Grand Historian to the contrary, it appears that Mêng T'ien's remorse for having "cut through the veins of the earth" was genuine. The ancient Chinese belief of *fêng shui,* the "science of winds and waters," held that the earth had veins through which cleansing winds and waters passed, affecting the course of events for good and ill. Until recent times in China, no large construction could be undertaken without first consulting the principles of *fêng shui* to determine whether the local spirits of winds and waters would be injured. This was one reason for the slowness with which railroad construction proceeded in nineteenth-century China. Perhaps some superstitious Chinese of the Han Dynasty put the pious allusion to *fêng shui* into Mêng T'ien's mouth, by way of showing that he had belatedly come to recognize the heinous crime of building the Great Wall. Ssŭ-ma Ch'ien, more rational, mocked the whole idea.

III

The new regime, having disposed of its chief enemies, Fu Su and the brothers Mêng, turned its attention now to the task of providing a tomb for the First Emperor. If we can credit the accounts we have, it was a tomb on a fitting scale for such a monarch.

The Emperor had chosen the site himself, some twenty miles from his capital, and construction had begun during his lifetime. A great hill of sand had been heaped up south of the River Wei, at the foot of Mount Li. Within this mound was a palace, and the palace contained a relief map of China, modeled in bronze and depicting the rivers, mountains, valleys, and plains. The two chief rivers, the Yangtze and the Huang Ho, were represented as channels two fathoms deep, filled with quicksilver. The banks of these rivers were bordered by models of cities and palaces, and high overhead there rose a great burnished copper dome on which were outlined the moon and the constellations of the night sky.

The First Emperor's sarcophagus, shaped like a boat, floated on one of the quicksilver rivers. A powerful bow was mounted at the coffin's side, so artfully crafted that it would fire an arrow at anyone who dared to approach the Emperor's sarcophagus. There were tales, too, of elaborate trapdoors and hidden knives and thunder-making machines to bedevil those who would rob the tomb. And it was said that hundreds of slaves and artisans were buried in the tomb when it was sealed for the last time.

No doubt most of this is fantasy. Yet a mound called the Mound of Ch'in still exists near the Wei, and when Geil saw it about 1908 it was 120 feet high, and measured 350 yards on each side. No wall or monument was to be seen, though there was evidence that the mound once had been surrounded by a protective barrier. Though the site was still reputed to be the burying-place of Ch'in Shih Huang Ti, no later monarch had cared to erect a temple to the First Emperor's memory—a clear indication of the hatred with which posterity regarded him, in a land where even the most minor of emperors had his funerary monuments somewhere.

Unloved but not unremembered, Ch'in Shih Huang Ti disappeared within his great mound. The scholars never forgave him for the burning of the books; the common people never forgave him for the heartless conscription of laborers to build the Great Wall; the great families never forgave him for destroying feudalism. Yet he had taken scattered states and welded them into an empire, and he had built a Wall that served to give that empire identity as a nation. The verdict on Ch'in Shih Huang Ti must be a mixed one, for he was tyrant and statesman, blinded by belief in magic and far-sighted enough to create the world's most enduring state. Ssŭ-ma Ch'ien, who had no reason to be fond of the Only First, offered this summary:

"Ch'in Shih Huang Ti, brandishing his great horse-whip, governed the world. . . . He destroyed the nobles . . . and imposed his law on the six directions of space. He handled the whip and the rod to beat the Empire. His prestige made the Four Seas tremble. In the south . . . the princes, with bowed heads, handed over their destiny to subaltern officers. . . . In the north, the Hu dared no longer come down to the south to pasture their horses. . . . But Ch'in neglected to follow the example of conduct set by the ancient kings; he burnt the teachings of the Hundred Schools in order to make the people stupid. . . . He killed the eminent men. . . . He cherished greedy and base sentiments. . . . He made the foundations of the Empire rest on tyranny. . . . If he had administered the realm according to the principles of ancient generations . . . calamity would not have resulted."[49]

But calamity could not be forestalled. Chao Kao, the Keeper of the Chariots, was in the driver's seat and wielding a furious whip. "Exterminate the great ministers," he urged his puppet Erh Shih Huang Ti. "Exile your own flesh and blood. Enrich the poor; give honor to the humble, and completely do away with the old ministers of the former Emperor. Appoint, furthermore, those with whom your Majesty is intimate, and bring near those whom you trust. When this is done, your Majesty will then recline peacefully on a lofty pillow, giving free vent to his desires and favoring what he takes pleasure in."

A reign of terror followed. In keeping with a standard Oriental practice, the royal family was the first to be purged; twelve of the Second Emperor's brothers were executed, and ten of his sisters. Several others took their own lives. Old Li Ssŭ watched in horror as the empire trembled. Rebellions were beginning in outlying provinces, but the Second Emperor was taking no action against them. Rumor reached Li Ssŭ that Chao Kao himself was conspiring with the rebels, planning a partition of the empire.

The breakdown of central authority was the undoing of Li Ssŭ. His son, Li Yu, was administrator of the province of San Ch'uan. The province was overrun by bandits, and Li Yu could not control them. When an investigator from the capital came to San Ch'uan to look into the situation, Li Yu stopped his ears with a heavy bribe. The story leaked out and came to Chao Kao, who whispered it to Erh Shih Huang Ti. "Li Ssŭ is dangerous," the eunuch argued, hinting that the old man and his son were plotting with brigands to wreck the empire.

Li Ssŭ himself was unable to see the Emperor. Even more than his father, Erh Shih Huang Ti had withdrawn to the security of the inner palaces. "When I wish to see him," the Grand Councilor complained, "he has no leisure." Cut off from direct contact, Li Ssŭ resorted to his pen, writing ever more agitated letters to the Emperor, attacking Chao Kao, warning the young monarch, citing historical precedent of ambitious ministers who had overthrown their masters. The Emperor replied with testimonials to Chao Kao's "incorruptible spirit and strong vitality," and bluntly told Li Ssŭ that he was "old . . . and out of contact with the empire." Chao Kao, seeing the correspondence, urged that Li Ssŭ be liquidated.

The Second Emperor placed Li Ssŭ's fate in Chao Kao's hands. He was seized, bound, and imprisoned. Groaning, he exclaimed, "Alas for an unprincipled ruler. How can one make any plans?"

The trial was brief. Li Ssŭ and his son were accused of subversion. Sentenced to a certainly fatal thousand-stroke flogging, Li Ssŭ made a "voluntary" confession, whose self-accusing tone reminds one of the endless protestations of iniquity recited by hopeless defendants in Communist trials. A last appeal to the Emperor was intercepted by Chao Kao. Father and son were led out to execution in the marketplace of Hsien-yang in August of 208 B.C.

Chao Kao now was supreme—at least in the capital city. Rebellions were rising elsewhere; in what is now southern Honan, a group of supporters of the late rightful heir Fu Su had briefly set up a rival kingdom, though a Ch'in general suppressed it, and defeated the so-called "Avenging Army" of Ch'u, which had hoped to restore feudalism. In eastern China, whole provinces broke away from the government, slaughtering the Ch'in officials. One by one, the old states were reasserting their existence, only thirteen years after the unification of the empire.

Safe in well-defended Hsien-yang, Chao Kao contented himself with the exercise of local power. To root out possible opposition at the court, he caused a deer to be presented to the Second Emperor, while announcing that it was a horse.

"Surely this is a deer!" the befuddled Emperor declared. He turned to his courtiers for confirmation. Those who dared to say that the "horse" was a deer were ticketed for destruction by Chao Kao. The Emperor, having been assured by most of his court that the beast was a horse, summoned the Great Diviner of the court, who informed him that "your Majesty has not been pure in his fasting, and that is why he is come to this. . . ."

The total demoralization of the puppet monarch was swift. Chao Kao took the Emperor on a hunting trip, shot an onlooker, and insisted that the fatal arrow had sped from Erh Shih Huang Ti's bow. Baffled, the Emperor retreated to an inner palace to make amends for the accident. Chao Kao, wearying of his satellite, now staged a strange charade, dressing members of the palace guard as "rebels" and ordering them to pretend to storm the palace. While angry shouts echoed in the courtyards, Chao Kao came to Erh Shih Huang Ti and informed him that an armed mob had invaded the palace to take his life. The Second Emperor committed suicide.

Chao Kao took the imperial seal from the dead Erh Shih Huang Ti and fastened it round his waist. He hoped to make himself Emperor in this way, although how a eunuch intended to found a dynasty is not made clear in the records. None of the officials of the court, however, would make obeisance to him:

"When he ascended the audience hall, three persons there wished to do him harm. Chao Kao himself realized that Heaven refused to grant him the empire and that the body of officials would not consent."[50] So the eunuch brought forth Tzŭ-ying, son of Fu Su and grandson of the First Emperor, and proclaimed him Third August Sovereign.

It was not long before the Third Emperor discovered that Chao Kao was in league with one of the rebels. The eunuch's plan was to split the empire, taking the northwestern region for himself, handing the rest over to the rebels, and putting the Third Emperor to death. The new Emperor acted swiftly. In 207 B.C., the first and only year of his rule, he ordered that Chao Kao be assassinated. This was carried out, but it was too late to save the dynasty. The rebel forces were marching toward the capital.

A day came, in 206, when the Third Emperor exchanged his imperial robes for the clothes of a commoner, wrapped a cord around his neck in token of submission, and carefully packed the imperial seals and insignia. He rode out of Hsien-yang in a chariot drawn by white horses—a Chinese sign of mourning. The rebel general Liu Pang received him courteously, removing the cord of submission from the Third Emperor's neck, and accepted the seals of office from him. Soon after, the Third Emperor was slain, not by Liu Pang but by an opposing general, and thus did the dynasty that was to have lasted ten thousand generations come to its end, within fifteen years.

Early in his reign, a sorcerer had warned Ch'in Shih Huang Ti that "the destruction of China will be accomplished through 'Hu.'" The Only First took this to mean the northern barbarians, the story goes, and so he built the Great Wall. The oracle had been insufficiently precise, as oracles often are. Destruction came through "Hu," but the agent of doom was Hu Hai, the Second Emperor, the puppet weakling who let the great achievements of his father and of his father's minister, Li Ssŭ, come to naught.

Six.
The Sovereigns
of Han

It was inevitable, of course, that the First Emperor's domain would break apart. The mismanagement of Erh Shih Huang Ti contributed to the cataclysm, but the fundamental weaknesses of the empire were so great that even a wiser ruler could not have held it together.

The empire was an amalgamation of proud states with a long tradition of independence. Shrewdly, the First Emperor and Li Ssŭ had done as much as they could to shatter the old statist power structure and to replace it with a central authority. Ch'in was a northwestern state, and it was not easy to extend the imperial tentacles into the remote reaches of the east and south. The great effort of building the Wall had helped to give coherence to the northern part of the empire, but did little to secure the restless rice-growing country of Ch'u. Ch'in's fierce momentum of conquest could not be converted rapidly enough into an administrative force. Hordes of uprooted peasants, set free from feudalism but not yet integrated into a new system, provided a reservoir of discontent that could easily be tapped by powerful war lords in the outlying regions.

A sharp, violent internal reaction thus followed the unification of the empire. The huge land cracked apart in the valley of the Huai River, midway between the valleys of the Huang Ho and the Yangtze. Southern China, which had never been fully assimilated into the Ch'in empire, rose in revolt once the heel of the First Emperor was lifted.

Liu Pang, the founder of China's second and most enduring dynasty, came of peasant stock. He was born in 247 B.C. in P'ei in modern Kiangsu, a coastal province through which the Yangtze finds its way to the sea. His birthplace was "a house where the window was made of the neck of a broken pitcher and where a cord served as a hinge on the door," Ssŭ-ma Ch'ien informs us.

He is a sympathetic character, though we must remember that the historians who praised his modesty and generosity wrote during the reign of his immediate descendants. He was "good and kind; he loved to show liberality," writes Ssŭ-ma Ch'ien. He had wise and just advisers, and "he knew how to make use of them, and that is why he got possession of the empire." The benevolent Liu Pang was no remote autocrat; he is said to have been fond of wine and women, relaxed by nature, but prudent and artful.

Though he came from a humble level of society, his "integrity and winning manners" helped him in his steady rise through the ranks. He was first placed in charge of a party of laborers working on some project of the First Emperor's —not the Great Wall. So many of the men died that Liu Pang released the rest from their duties, and fled with ten of them into the mountains. They formed the nucleus of his eventual army.

In 210, upon the death of the First Emperor, the little rebel band left the hills. Liu Pang and his men joined the army of Ch'ên Shêng, who was leading an uprising in Ch'u. When that was crushed, Liu Pang became part of the rebel forces of Hsiang Liang and Hsiang Yü, two descendants of the royal house of Ch'u. In 209, the people of Liu Pang's native city of P'ei put to death their magistrate and named Liu Pang to rule over them; he took the title of Duke of P'ei. The following year, he aided Hsiang Liang in reviving the old Ch'u kingdom. They placed the grandson of the former king on the throne.

Soon after, Hsiang Liang was slain by a Ch'in general, and the leadership of the rebel forces passed to his nephew, Hsiang Yü, who maintained the Ch'u king as a puppet. Friction developed between Hsiang Yü, a man of aristocratic lineage, and the peasant Liu Pang. In the period of anarchy that followed the death of the Second Emperor, Hsiang Yü and Liu Pang fought each other as energetically as they did the collapsing armies of Ch'in. Each man commanded an army; each had aspirations to gain complete authority. It was agreed between them that the first to enter the Ch'in capital, Hsien-yang, would be rewarded with the fief of the old Ch'in state in the new feudal regime that was to be established. Liu Pang reached the capital first, and received the submission of the Third Emperor. Immediately, he issued a proclamation repealing the harsh Ch'in legal code, substituting only three simple laws dealing with murder, bodily injury, and theft.

A few days later the army of Hsiang Yü arrived. The rival generals confronted one another; Hsiang Yü asserted his higher rank, and Liu Pang withdrew. At once, the soldiers of Hsiang Yü put the city to the torch and the sword. The captive Third Emperor was slain; the many palaces of Ch'in Shih Huang Ti were gutted; the imperial library, containing the only copies in existence of many literary classics, was destroyed. Liu Pang had to be content for the moment with ruling the region around the valley of the Han River, and received the title, Prince of Han.

Hsiang Yü now put aside his Ch'u puppet and attempted to establish his own rule. Civil war broke out, Liu Pang leading the opposing faction. A terrible battle in 205 is said to have cost the lives of a hundred thousand of Liu Pang's men, but gradually the tide turned, and after a defeat in 202 Hsiang Yü took his own life, crying out blasphemously, "It is Heaven which has caused my ruin!" Liu Pang became the first Emperor of the Han Dynasty. In Chinese history he is known thereafter by his posthumously awarded title of Kao Tsu ("High Ancestor.")*

---

* The practice of awarding posthumous titles to Emperors confuses the historical record. Generally, in what follows, we will use the posthumous title even while relating the events of an Emperor's life.

Kao Tsu inherited an empire in chaos. His first decree after accepting the throne (supposedly he refused the crown three times) was an amnesty: "The troops have not had rest for eight years. All the people have suffered severely. Now my efforts in settling the control of the world have been brought to completion. Let an amnesty [be proclaimed] throughout the world [for all crimes] below [those deserving] capital punishment."

The historian Pan Ku, who died in 92 A.D. and in whose history of the Han Dynasty that decree is quoted, also relates that before settling at his capital, the new Emperor returned to his native village and "invited all those, young and old, whom he had known in former times and passed around the wine. He drank and danced with them. Old men, married women, and all the former friends of Liu Pang passed days in drinking and rejoicing."[51]

Kao Tsu chose as his capital Ch'ang-an, not far from the ruins of the Ch'in Dynasty's capital of Hsien-yang.* He dated his dynasty's reign from 206 B.C., when he received the title of Prince of Han, but it was actually 202 before he attained control of the empire.

Although the revolution that overthrew Ch'in had been designed in part to restore feudalism, Kao Tsu did not entirely return to the former system. He recognized the need for a strong central government. However, the uncertain state of the land at his accession forced him to make certain concessions to the feudal interests. Many cities had been looted or destroyed; the capital had burned for three months after its sacking; dikes and dams and granaries had been ruined; great sections of the country withheld their allegiance from the new ruler. For the sake of averting total disaster, Kao Tsu parcelled out much of the country to relatives and favorites, giving them feudal powers but hoping to bring them under central control once the situation was stabilized. China teemed with kings again. There were thirteen large provinces in the newly reconstituted empire, subdivided into vassal kingdoms and marquisates. Only in this way could Kao Tsu hope to maintain order in the farthest districts, though he knew the dangers of letting a system of hereditary feudalism return.

Kao Tsu devoted much of his short reign of seven years to whittling away at the powers of the new feudal potentates. He had found it necessary to name seven kings not of his own family, but he succeeded in eliminating them all before his death in 195 B.C., ruling that only members of the imperial clan of Liu should hold this rank henceforth. The task of removing the entrenched nobles of the royal family was one that he left to later emperors.

That task was made easier by the Han Dynasty's attitude toward the scholars of the kingdom. Ch'in Shih Huang Ti had shown the scholars short shrift, and by so doing had fatally injured his own chances of maintaining control over his empire. Control could safely be asserted only through a bureaucracy of appointed officials, a scholar gentry. It has never been an easy matter to read and write the Chinese language, with its thousands of characters, and literacy has always been a key to power in China. With a cadre of scholars to govern the provinces, it would not be necessary to rely on feudal lords.

---

* Which itself had been built near the site of an earlier capital, that of the first Chou kings.

Kao Tsu did not grasp this at first, evidently. A member of his court was fond of quoting the classics to him, particularly the *Odes* and the *Annals,* two books which the Ch'in Emperor had burned. Irritated, Kao Tsu cried, "I conquered the empire on horseback; what is the good of these *Annals* and *Odes?"*

The minister replied, "You conquered it on horseback, but can you govern it on horseback?"

The point went home. Kao Tsu, realizing that scholars could not conquer an empire but could help to preserve it, began to recruit a bureaucracy of Confucianist civil servants, to be chosen by competitive examination, whose powers would not be hereditary. With that decision, Chinese feudalism received its deathblow, though it was a while in dying. In 154 B.C., seven of the feudal kings rebelled against the fifth Han Emperor, and the revolt was put down with a finality that broke the feudal system. Wu Ti, the succeeding Emperor, adopted a policy of depriving a feudal prince of territory every time he offended the throne, and in 127 decreed that the property of a feudal lord should be subdivided among all his sons upon his death—a process that swiftly minced the remaining fiefs to impotence.

Kao Tsu's abilities as a leader prevented the dissolution of the empire, and in the few years that were granted him to rule he rendered China safe against the internal forces that threatened it. But hardly was the internal problem under control than the Han Emperor was faced with an external difficulty. The Hsiung-nu, beyond the Great Wall, were stirring. The barbarians had acquired an emperor of their own, and were looking with interest at the wealthy but troubled land south of Ch'in Shih Huang Ti's Long Rampart.

II

The First Emperor had had no difficulties dealing with the barbarians. They were fierce warriors, but they had no unity, and it had been a relatively simple matter for Mêng T'ien to thrust them into the outer darkness of the steppe. During the latter days of Ch'in Shih Huang Ti's rule, though, a powerful nomad chieftain had united the Hsiung-nu, taking a title which the Chinese wrote as *shan-yü.*

The first *shan-yü* was named T'u-man, according to Chinese annals. T'u-man was a contemporary of the First Emperor. When Mêng T'ien's army entered the Ordos, Ssǔ-ma Ch'ien records, T'u-man was "unable to prevail against Ch'in" and led his people away. After the fall of the Ch'in Dynasty, the Hsiung-nu, still led by T'u-man, "again gradually crossed the Yellow River southward into China, and set the boundary of their nation at its old limit." In the chaos of the interregnal period, no one prevented the Hsiung-nu from reclaiming their ancestral land, which, in any event, was useless to the Chinese except for strategic purposes, since it could not be farmed.

T'u-man died about 210 B.C. Ssǔ-ma Ch'ien relates that he fell victim to the ambitions of his own son, Mao Tun. Since the Hsiung-nu themselves had no historians, we must rely on Ssǔ-ma Ch'ien, who probably used as his source a mythologizing nomad epic. The story goes that T'u-man feared his son and sent him as a hostage to a westerly nomad tribe, the Yüeh-chih. Then he attacked the Yüeh-chih, expecting to cause the execution of Mao Tun. However, the nomad prince escaped and returned to his father. For this exploit, T'u-man reluctantly gave Mao Tun command of ten thousand horsemen.

Mao Tun trained his men to obey the sound of a "whistling" arrow—aiming the arrow at a target of his choice, and putting to death any man who did not himself fire at the same target. The first target of the whistling arrow was Mao Tun's favorite horse, and he winnowed from his ranks those who failed to aim at the animal. Next, Mao Tun directed the arrow at one of his favorite wives, and then at a fine horse of his father's. (The ascending scale of values here is an interesting one!) In a pre-Pavlovian manner he conditioned his men to aim and shoot at whatever target he selected, without pausing to ponder.

At length Mao Tun went riding with his father. He drew his bow; the target was T'u-man. No man dared hesitate, and so all shared the guilt of the shan-yü's assassination. Mao Tun took command of the tribe.

Immediately the new leader was challenged by the Tung-hu nomads to the east. Mao Tun followed a policy of appeasement, yielding to Tung-hu demands while he consolidated his own tribal power. When the Tung-hu grew bold and demanded a stretch of borderland Mao Tun turned on them in a surprise campaign and defeated them. Without hesitating, he swung his army around and drove away the Yüeh-chih in the west, giving the Hsiung-nu supremacy along the entire Great Wall frontier.

Suddenly China faced an enemy such as it had never known before: unified, purposeful barbarians under a single chieftain. The Great Wall, that mighty whim of Ch'in Shih Huang Ti, assumed magnified importance now. Mao Tun ranged the border, the first of the great nomad heroes, a superb horseman and a ruthless leader who coveted the rich lands of China.

Emperor Kao Tsu found it necessary to turn from the task of pacifying the interior of China to safeguard his northern frontier. The operation was complicated by the tendency of Chinese generals to come to terms with the Hsiung-nu rather than to attack them. Thus, in 201 B.C., Chinese annals record a Hsiung-nu invasion of what is now Shansi. The general in charge of the Chinese battalions, though he had been a loyal comrade of Liu Pang in the time of civil war, promptly surrendered to the Hsiung-nu, and defected outright to them when the Emperor personally took the field in the area. The result was the brief existence of a puppet state along the border, ruled by the general under the "protection" of the Hsiung-nu. Kao Tsu was discovering that holding an empire together was like carrying water on both shoulders.

A year later, the Hsiung-nu attacked in earnest, raiding their puppet kingdoms in northern Shansi. The defecting general fled, throwing himself on Kao Tsu's mercy—and was forgiven and made a marquis. Kao Tsu was buying loyalty; he had to overlook the defection of the past for the sake of regaining border strength in the present.

Mao Tun evidently realized that though he might be able to conquer China, he could never hope to administer it. He made no serious attempt at penetration deep into China, confining his raids to the border area. Several times he found himself in a position to seize the empire, and declined the opportunity.

On one occasion, Mao Tun bottled Emperor Kao Tsu up in a fortified town, something none of the Emperor's Chinese foes had ever succeeded in doing. The trapped monarch had to buy his freedom through a treaty giving Mao Tun a Chinese princess as a bride, as well as sizable quantities of grain, wine, silks, and other forms of tribute. It became a familiar pattern in Han times to buy off the Hsiung-nu. In 174 B.C., the tribute included "thirty pieces of many-colored woven silk, ten lengths of embroidered silk, several embroidered silk gowns woven with many-colored patterns"; in 51 B.C., "seventy-seven sets of bedcovers"; in 49 B.C., "one hundred ten suits of clothes"; and so on for almost two centuries. The Hsiung-nu proved sharp bargainers once they found that the Chinese were willing to bribe for peace. The northward flow of silk and treasure was immense; and princess after royal princess made the melancholy journey through the gates of the Great Wall, so many that the Hsiung-nu rulers could claim with justice that they were of Han descent as well as of the line of Mao Tun.

III

The Hsiung-nu pressure rarely relaxed. Raid was followed by tribute, again and again. The people of the northern provinces became resigned to sharing their produce with the horsemen of the steppe. The Great Wall proved to be a futile barrier; the Han rulers, preoccupied with internal difficulties, were able neither to provide proper garrisons for the Wall nor to keep it in good repair for all its vast length.

China's problems were complicated by the early death of Kao Tsu, in 195 B.C. Liu Ying, the Emperor's eldest son, was a boy of ten. Power was seized by his mother, the Empress Lü, a grim and awesome regent. She began her reign by mutilating her late husband's favorite concubine, with results so horrifying that they affected the sanity of the boy ruler when he saw what had been done. She endowed her own family with feudal fiefs, poisoned enemies in the manner of a Borgia, and shook the empire with her reign of terror. When Liu Ying died in 188, the dowager Empress put a second son of Kao Tsu on the throne, but retained her own grasp of power. On the death of the second young puppet emperor, Empress Lü entertained some thoughts of effecting a shift of dynasty by placing one of her own male relatives on the throne, but her death in 180 B.C. touched off an uprising that resulted in the massacre of her entire clan. Liu Hêng, another son of Kao Tsu by a different wife, ascended the throne and ruled successfully for more than twenty years, winning the posthumous title of Wên Ti, "Cultured Emperor."*

Wên Ti's "sole preoccupation," remarks Ssŭ-ma Ch'ien, was "to reform the people by his virtue: that is why the whole country in the Interior of the Seas was prosperous and flourishing through the execution of rites and justice."[52] His was another reign of consolidation; he shored up the damaged empire, undoing the harm that had come about during the fifteen years of Empress

---

* Since *Ti* in the imperial titles means "emperor," it is redundant, though common, to speak of Emperor Wên Ti. Wên Ti will do, or Emperor Wên, but not both.

Lü's ascendancy, and through his frugality brought about an economic revival. For the first time in anyone's memory, there was peace throughout the land. A rising middle class came to power, helping to counterbalance the not-yet-checked feudal lords. On the northern border an uneasy quiet prevailed; Mao Tun was growing old and the nomad raids were less frequent, although the pressure never entirely ceased.

Mao Tun died in 174 B.C. A few years later, Wên Ti despatched an ambassador to the Hsiung-nu court, who returned with these observations:

"The Hsiung-nu are not more numerous than the population of a single Chinese province. What renders them intractable is that their habits and their diet are entirely different from those of the Han; they have no desire for our things. If only they acquired the taste, if they had only two-tenths of our needs, they would become our tributaries. But so far they have not. We have sent them silk costumes; they have worn them to shreds hunting in thickets and then declared that silk was not as good as their hides. We have sent them delicacies to eat; they have found them infinitely inferior to their milk and their koumiss [fermented mare's milk]."[53]

As the Hsiung-nu raids grew frequent once again, Wên Ti consulted his ministers on the possibility of launching all-out war against them and carrying the campaign beyond the Great Wall into the steppe. The Minister of War warned against such an attempt, pointing out that the nomad methods of waging war were very different from those the Chinese employed:

"Scaling and descending the most precipitous mountains with astonishing rapidity; swimming the deepest rivers and torrents; suffering wind, rain, hunger, and thirst; making forced marches; not being halted even by precipices; accustoming their horses to pass along the narrowest tracks; expert with bow and arrow, and in surprise attacks discharging their arrows even at full gallop; such are the Hsiung-nu. They attack, retreat, and rally again . . . if they suffer a setback they simply disappear without trace, like a cloud."[54]

Wên Ti attempted instead to meet the nomad threat by setting up a buffer zone of friendly barbarians just outside the Great Wall. Through subsidies and the gift of arms, he hoped to win their assistance, and protect the border against the wilder nomads beyond. He did not succeed, and perhaps that was fortunate for him, for, as Owen Lattimore pointed out in his discussion of such nomad "reservoirs," the system "was a method that haunted the imperial state responsible for it, because it created a sword of two edges capable of striking outward when held in a strong hand but of cutting inward when the hand weakened."[55]

In 166 B.C., a nomad horde drove so deep into China that it came within sight of the capital. Four years later, the attack was repeated, leading Wên Ti to declare humbly, "It is because I am not perfect that I am incapable of spreading my virtue afar. That is why, sometimes, the countries outside my territory have not had repose, and those who live outside the Four Desert Zones have not lived a tranquil life."[56] The Hsiung-nu were at the gates of Ch'ang-an again in 158 B.C., and Wên Ti's death the following year was ascribed to grief and chagrin at his inability to pacify the horsemen of the north.

Nonetheless, the Cultured Emperor had achieved much. Building on the foundation set up by his father Liu Pang, Wên Ti had created a stable and secure nation. He was succeeded by his son, Liu Ch'i, a man of no particular stature, who ruled for sixteen years and whose chief accomplishment was the successful conveyance of the empire to his successor. During Liu Ch'i's reign, the Hsiung-nu afforded constant threats, making and breaking treaties as it pleased them. The customary gift of a royal princess was tendered in 152 B.C. It was in this reign, too, that the feudal lords made their last stand, in the revolt of 154 B.C. The rebellion was quelled within a matter of months, and there was never any further question of the supremacy of the central government.

In 140 B.C. the government was delivered into the hands of Liu Ch'i's son, sixteen-year-old Liu Ch'ê, the sixth Han Emperor. History knows him as Wu Ti, "the Martial Emperor," and his long and extraordinary reign was one of the most memorable of China's times of glory.

IV

Wu Ti* ruled in splendor for fifty-four years. He extended and fortified the achievements of Wên Ti; he met the challenge of the Hsiung-nu by carrying his campaigns into their home territory; he presided over China's first experimental contacts with foreign lands; and he was responsible for a 300-mile westward extension of the Great Wall, not as a barrier of defense but as an instrument of military offense. Flamboyant and luxury loving, he has often been compared, with some justice, to Louis XIV, the "Sun King" of France.

Financing the expensive projects of Wu Ti had to be linked to the economic prosperity of the empire. Wu Ti took merchants and financiers into the civil service, and with their help was able to suppress a devastating inflation that had begun in his predecessor's reign. In 136 B.C., the currency was stabilized with the issuance of copper coinage, forerunner of the hole-in-the-center "cash" that was China's basic unit of currency for centuries. Eighteen years later, the Emperor authorized a novel form of currency: the world's first paper money. To be more precise, it was leather money: foot-square pieces of white deer skin, with colored borders. The white deer were found only in the imperial hunting preserve, so counterfeiting was no problem; each "bill" was worth 40,000 copper "cash," being sold to noblemen in times of national need as a kind of forced defense loan. Taxation, too, was rigorous in Wu Ti's reign. Peasants paid their tax in the form of labor, merchants and nobles in cash or commodities.

Wu Ti continued the process of breaking up the feudal estates. His major act to effect this was the decree of 127 B.C. compelling the automatic division of a fief among the heirs of its lord. By establishing an imperial resident commissioner in each feudal domain to keep watch on the local king or marquis, Wu Ti succeeded in reducing feudalism to a matter of empty pomp. Many

---

* Often called Han Wu Ti, to distinguish him from the Emperors of later dynasties who were awarded the same posthumous title.

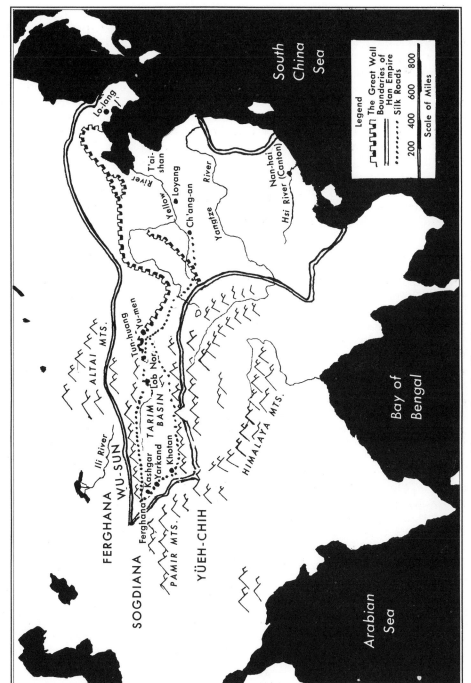

China Under the Han Dynasty, c. 100 B.C.

of the nobles were induced to commit suicide. The Emperor created a new nobility easier to manage, drawn from the ranks of "new men," upstart merchants and bureaucrats; eleven degrees of nobility were awarded, the titles being sold for the benefit of the war treasury.

Wu Ti spent freely for military adventures and for public works, wall-building and canal-building, but the budget was flexible enough to permit him to indulge his own taste for luxury. The imperial gardens and hunting preserves were vast and magnificent. Two artificial lakes served the palace for pleasure. Once trade routes to the west were established, Wu Ti imported animals and plants from the western lands, so that his palace grounds swarmed with exotic creatures. The poet Ssŭ-ma Hsiang-ju, Wu Ti's court laureate, wrote of the Empress "gazing about her from the high Orchid Terrace. Amid the perfume of cassia trees, peacocks flocked together, monkeys screamed, king-fishers gathered, and phoenixes flew about."[57]

During this splendid reign, the imperial armies marched in every direction. The chief enemy, of course, was the Hsiung-nu. Wu Ti sent prodigious expeditions, as many as 100,000 cavalrymen supported by infantry and supply trains, into the steppe. Frequently these armies met with frightful defeats. Some were totally annihilated by the highly mobile nomad warriors; others were badly whipped and came limping back through the Great Wall with heavy casualties, to the Emperor's monumental displeasure. By 127 B.C., Wu Ti's generals had mastered the technique of dealing with the nomads well enough to have driven them out of the Ordos region; in 121, General Ho Ch'ü-p'ing led 10,000 cavalrymen deep into Hsiung-nu territory and inflicted terrible losses upon the barbarians; while, in 119, General Wei Ch'ing shattered the forces of the *shan-yü* and Ho Ch'ü-p'ing pursued the fleeing nomads hundreds of miles, almost into the Gobi, before the campaign was halted. Ho Ch'ü-p'ing returned with ninety nomad chiefs as prisoners, and the power of the Hsiung-nu was crippled for many years.

Wu Ti did not object to making use of barbarian aid when he could get it. One of the prisoners brought back by Ho Ch'ü-p'ing was Chin Mi-ti, the heir apparent to the *shan-yü*. He was made a slave and sent to tend horses, but attracted the attention of the Emperor, "being eight feet in stature" (nomad princes are generally described as giants in the Chinese annals) and soon attained an influential position in the government. After the death of Wu Ti in 87 B.C., Chin Mi-ti served as guardian for the young Emperor Chao Ti.

Many of Wu Ti's generals were themselves Hsiung-nu, or else men of the northern frontier who understood Hsiung-nu warfare. Li Kuang, celebrated for his archery, came from the Shensi-Kansu border; Kung-sun Ao was a man of Ninghsia; Wei Ch'ing, one of the greatest of the generals, had been a shepherd in the steppeland as a boy, as had his nephew, Ho Ch'ü-p'ing. Kung-sun Ho, another general, was of the I-ch'u tribe of nomads, while Chao Hsin was a deserter from the Hsiung-nu who entered Chinese service. (He later was defeated and captured by his own people, and rejoined their side.) Another Han general, Chao P'o-nu, changed sides four times, deserting to the Hsiung-nu early in his career, returning to become a Chinese commander, then spending ten years as a Hsiung-nu general after his capture by the nomads, and ultimately returning to the Han banners once more.

It can be seen from this that the border situation was a fluid one. The Great Wall, clear-cut delineator that it was, failed to make the line between Chinese and nomad absolutely rigid. There was a constant exchange of loyalties, a back-and-forth flow across the Wall.

The Emperor attempted to extend Chinese civilization into the steppe as a means of stabilizing the border. It was a foredoomed project; Chinese civilization could not be exported beyond the Great Wall, as one of Wu Ti's advisers tried to point out. In Ch'in Shih Huang Ti's time, the Emperor was told, Mêng T'ien had been sent to colonize the Ordos. But the land was marshy and salt, grain had to be transported across huge distances at immense cost to feed the colonists, and there was no way to make the colonies self-sustaining. He warned that the expensive experiment could bankrupt China.

Wu Ti persisted. In 120 B.C., more than 100,000 men were sent to the Ordos. Canals were dug for irrigation, a long wall was built, farms were planted at incalculable expense. The intention was to develop a strategic bastion that would command the Mongolian heartland, and to that end a series of new walls were built outside the Great Wall, extending Chinese control a few dozen miles at a time. But the goal was an impossible one. There could be no farming in the Ordos, and turning the Chinese into stock raisers simply turned them into nomads, spurring them to drift beyond administrative control. The Yellow River, overrunning its banks in 120 B.C. drowned thousands of the settlers. Wu Ti lost interest in his Ordos colony; by 68 B.C., troops no longer patrolled the outer walls, and the Hsiung-nu moved back in.

There were other foreign adventures. From 128 to 108 B.C., Wu Ti tried to colonize Manchuria, but the effect was mainly to wreck the economies of Yen and Ch'i, the provinces bordering the new lands. The imperial armies entered Korea and established a colonial administration with headquarters near Pyŏng-yang, its control reaching as far south as Seoul. Another expeditionary force invaded the southern region around the modern Canton, and brought it under Chinese rule for the first time since the days of the First Emperor.

The most significant campaigns of Wu Ti took place in the remote west, beyond the end of the Great Wall at Kia-yü-kuan. The great western adventure began with an epic journey by a Chinese Marco Polo, and ended by bringing China almost to the back door of the Roman Empire. Legend had it that the Chou Dynasty monarch Mu Wang, who ruled about 1000 B.C., had led an army against the Jung barbarians of the west, and had gone on into Central Asia, returning eventually with four wolves and four stags, the only living creatures that he encountered on his long journey. The fabulous journey of Mu Wang, embroidered by eight hundred years of tale-spinning, may have been Wu Ti's inspiration in this new and remarkable penetration of the remote western lands. The Emperor himself was unable to undertake the expedition, but the man he sent, Chang Ch'ien, deserves to be ranked among the world's most intrepid explorers. He opened a new world for Han Dynasty China.

Seven. Westward Beyond the Great Wall

The wonderful adventure began with strife between barbarians. The Hsiung-nu had turned on their nomad neighbors to the west, the Yüeh-chih, and had driven them into hiding. The *shan-yü* of the Hsiung-nu had overcome the leader of the Yüeh-chih, and had fashioned a drinking cup from his skull. All this had happened in the time of Mao Tun, and the Yüeh-chih had taken up residence beyond the mountain barrier of the Pamirs, in the regions of Sogdiana and Bactria.

Wu Ti, when he came to the throne in 140 B.C., found reason to regret the flight of the Yüeh-chih. The sixteen-year-old Emperor reasoned that so long as the Yüeh-chih had been harrying the western flank of the Hsiung-nu, the Hsiung-nu had been less free to raid northern China. Wu Ti conceived a quixotic notion: if only the Yüeh-chih could be persuaded to return to the lands from which the Hsiung-nu had driven them, it would relieve the pressure against the Great Wall frontier of China.

He resolved to send a mission to the Yüeh-chih, wherever they might be, proposing an alliance. If the Yüeh-chih would return, China would join them in a double thrust against the common enemy, the Hsiung-nu. Chosen to head the mission was Chang Ch'ien, a native of Hanchung and a yeoman of the imperial household.

The party left in 138 B.C., numbering perhaps a hundred men in all. The route took them through Hsiung-nu territory, and hardly had they set foot beyond the Great Wall than they were captured and brought before the *shan-yü*. For ten years Chang Ch'ien remained a captive at the court of the Hsiung-nu. Eventually he managed to escape, and with curious single-mindedness immediately proceeded on his interrupted mission.

Suffering numerous trials and difficulties, he made his way to the Ili Valley, where the Yüeh-chih were said to be living. But they had migrated onward; he followed their trail to Ferghana, in what is now Russian Central Asia, only to learn that the nomads had turned southwest and were in Bactria. Here, the indefatigable wanderer caught up with them, to discover that the one-time nomads had found easy plunder and were comfortably settled, with no intention of returning to the inhospitable wastes of the steppe. Chang Ch'ien remained among them for a year, trying fruitlessly to persuade them to join Wu Ti's campaign against the Hsiung-nu. Then he turned homeward, trying to avoid the Hsiung-nu by taking the highland route through the Tangut country of Tibet. The Hsiung-nu caught him anyway, but this time were able to detain him only a year, and in 126 B.C. he reached China, accompanied by a Hsiung-nu wife whom he had acquired along the way, and by the only surviving member of his original retinue, a servant named Kan Fu. He had been gone twelve years.

Chang Ch'ien brought back no alliance. The yield of his journey was information: he brought specimens of plants and animals, accounts of the rich and powerful territories of the west, tales of wealth and luxury. He reported on possible trade routes from Szechuan in western China to India, via middlemen in Burma and Yunnan; he told the stories he had heard of India, where "the country is low, damp, and hot, and the people ride on elephants to fight in battle." Of his visit to Ta Yüan, or Ferghana, he remarked, "They have grapewine and many excellent horses. These are blood-sweating horses whose stock is the offspring of the Heavenly Horses."

A relief of the horse of T'ang T'ai Tsung. The inscription calls it his "chestnut bay warhorse." *University Museum, University of Pennsylvania*

The flood of revelations stirred Wu Ti's fertile imagination. He coveted the "blood-sweating horses" of Ferghana; he yearned for the strange animals of the far-off lands; he longed for the cunning objects made by craftsmen of those distant places. Most particularly, he saw ways to strengthen the power of the empire by opening contact with the kingdoms of the west.

One immediate result of Chang Ch'ien's return was a new Chinese attack on the Hsiung-nu. No longer tempted by the mirage of an alliance with the vanished Yüeh-chih, Wu Ti now knew he would have to depend on his own resources. Thus there followed the campaigns of Ho Ch'ü-p'ing and Wei Ch'ing, who between 124 and 119 b.c. drove the Hsiung-nu back from the line of the Great Wall deep into Mongolia, clearing the Kansu "panhandle" that soon would become the chief route from China to the west.

The heavy defeats suffered by the Hsiung-nu opened the way. Soon the ambassadors of Wu Ti were traveling along what was later known as the Old Silk Road, following the line of oases formed as the waters of melting snows ran down to the edge of the Tarim Basin.

II

Chang Ch'ien himself led one of the first of these embassies. In 115 b.c., with 300 men, he journeyed to the territory of the Wu Sun, in the Ili Valley. The Wu Sun received the Chinese hospitably enough, but they had little to offer in trade. Chang Ch'ien despatched agents onward to Ferghana, hoping to obtain some of the famous "blood-sweating horses."

These horses of Ferghana were extraordinary beasts, fierce and majestic, far superior to the stocky mounts of the nomad Hsiung-nu. Wu Ti hoped to introduce the breed to China not only for its beauty but as a major weapon against the horsemen of the north. (The "blood-sweating" description was not simply a poetic label. A tiny parasite of the animals' hides actually did cause them to seem to be sweating blood as they ran.)

The Chinese agent journeyed to Ta Yüan, or the modern Ferghana, laden with a thousand ounces of gold and even a statuette of a horse done in gold as a special gift. The people of Ferghana were unwilling to part with any of their breeding stock, and, judging that the distance separating them from China was sufficient to allow them to be defiant, refused to sell any horses at any price. The Chinese envoy, hearing this, became enraged and hammered the golden statuette into shapelessness before he strode out. Then he attempted to carry off some of the horses by force, for which he and his entourage were murdered on the frontier of Ferghana.

Several other missions were equally unsuccessful. The repeated failures to obtain the marvelous horses of Ferghana infuriated Wu Ti, who resolved to send an army of conquest to deal with the stubborn horse-breeders.

An army was despatched under Li Kuang-li in 104 b.c. It crossed the Tarim Basin and over the towering Pamirs, but the march through the difficult country exhausted the troops, and they were turned back with heavy losses at the borders of Ferghana. The angry Wu Ti refused to let Li Kuang-li and the remnants of his army re-enter China, and ordered him to remain encamped on the frontier. A second army was recruited, 60,000 men in all, and sent to Li Kuang-li in 102. This time, better prepared for the grim conditions of the march, he swept on into Ferghana and laid siege to the city of the king.

Ssŭ-ma Ch'ien's history reports that "in the city of the king of Ta Yüan there were no wells, and the people had to obtain water from a river outside. Experts in hydraulic engineering were therefore despatched to divert the course of the river so as to deprive the city of water, or to effect an opening, by sapping the foundations of the walls, through which the city might be laid open of access."[58] The water supply was cut off. Within the besieged city the people deliberated and eventually assassinated their king, sending his head to Li Kuang-li along with a declaration of willingness to surrender. As a result, the Chinese obtained "several tens of excellent horses and, besides, more than 3,000 stallions and mares of medium and inferior breeds." The horses were conveyed to Wu Ti. They became proud possessions of China thereafter; the T'ang Dynasty in particular, seven hundred years later, delighted in making porcelain statuettes of these spirited beasts.

The conquest of Ferghana in 102 B.C. left China in command of the oasis route to the west. Chang Ch'ien's twelve years of exploration, with their bountiful yield of information and scientific specimens, had spurred the Emperor to extend China's western influence by hundreds of miles, and the prancing horses of Ferghana, leaping and snorting in the imperial park at Ch'ang-an, were the visible and tangible signs of that great drive westward. Wu Ti had ruled for nearly forty years, but was only in early middle age, a man of full vigor and boundless ambition. It was necessary now to secure the great gains of the recent expeditions. The Hsiung-nu, lurking in the desert, were by no means destroyed, and they presented a constant threat to the caravans that wound westward along the Silk Road. Unable to wipe the nomads out, Wu Ti did the next best thing: he extended the Great Wall westward from Kia-yü-kuan.

III

The extension of the Wall began after the second expedition of Li Kuang-li —that is, about 100 B.C. By the time the new section was complete, it extended some 300 miles west of Kia-yü-kuan, ending near the city of Tun-huang. Beyond Tun-huang some isolated watchtowers were built, but apparently there was no attempt to continue the Wall itself into the desert.

Wu Ti's Great Wall differed in fundamental purpose from that of Ch'in Shih Huang Ti. The earlier Great Wall was intended as a defensive instrument and as a deliberate limit to China's outward expansion. As we have seen, it was also a method of sapping China's excess manpower in the period immediately after the breakdown of the feudal states. Wu Ti, however, saw the extension of the Wall as necessary to his "forward policy." The garrisons patrolling the Wall would serve to protect the Chinese caravans making their way into foreign lands. It was an outward-looking concept, quite the opposite of what the First Emperor had in mind.

The key strategic outpost of the caravan route was the new western terminus of the Great Wall, Tun-huang. This city, founded in 111 B.C., is situated at an oasis in western Kansu, along the narrow panhandle that runs between the mountains of Tibet to the south and the desert of Mongolia to the north. Tun-huang, the last town of China proper, was strongly fortified, since it controlled the access routes to Central Asia. The watchtowers, reaching out some seventy miles from the city into the desert, gave the defenders early warning of approaching difficulties from nomad raiders.

Tun-huang thus became not only the terminus of the new Great Wall but the point of embarkation for travelers on the Old Silk Road. Actually there were two silk roads leading out of Tun-huang: a northern route across the desert and the foothills of the T'ien Shan Range, and a southern route that rimmed the Tsaidam Plateau of Tibet. (A third route, beginning just west of Tun-huang at Yü-men, the "Jade Gate," ran across the desert to Loulan, a city near the lake of Lop Nor; but increasing dryness of climate forced the abandonment of this road after a time.)

The routes met again at Kashgar, more than a thousand miles from Tun-huang, and there diverged again. One led into Ferghana and on to Samarkand and Antioch in Merv (not the well-known Syrian city); another route out of Kashgar passed through Bactria, to the south. These roads now entered the country that the Chinese came to call An-sih. This was Parthia, that kingdom in eastern Iran which had recently come to power and was challenging the authority of Rome itself. The Chinese were impressed by Parthia, which they described as a huge country producing rice, wheat and grapes, where silver coins circulated, and where "they make signs on leather from side to side by way of literary record." The Chinese brought silk and other goods to Parthia, and their ambassadors returned with Parthian conjurers, the eggs of "great birds," and other novelties.

The silk route ended in Parthia so far as the Chinese were concerned. The Parthians preferred to serve as middlemen rather than letting merchants of other lands pass through their domain. Mithridates II, the great Parthian king who ruled from 124 to 88 B.C., received Chinese envoys on the one hand and ambassadors from Rome on the other, and no doubt Chinese and Romans mingled at the Parthian court, but it was impossible for Chinese to pass westward, or Romans eastward out of Parthia. The silk route itself, under Parthian auspices, continued on from Hecatompylos and Ecbatana to the twin cities of Seleucia and Ctesiphon on the Tigris just below modern Baghdad, and from there to Syria and the rest of the Near East.

There was no economic need for the Chinese to export silk. The precious fabric was largely of diplomatic value, going westward as gifts to rulers of the newly reached lands. (The secret of making silk was something that the Chinese kept to themselves as long as possible.) In Parthia and in Rome, silk garments were eagerly sought, becoming something of a craze in the time of Julius Caesar. The silk trade was a profitable one for China, bringing in return such gifts as gold, jade, fine horses, exotic delicacies like raisins, and slaves who were skilled in the arts and in the crafts. But these were matters between rulers. The real value of the silk trade to China was not in the relatively slight luxury flow out of the west, but in the general prosperity and security that resulted from regular travel through the Kansu panhandle. What had been a sparsely populated region subject to nomad raids became wealthy and populous, and the hundreds of thousands of colonists who streamed into the frontier areas to take advantage of the new channels of trade formed a powerful bulwark against the Hsiung-nu.

The garrisons along the extended Great Wall played an important part in maintaining this prosperity. The Wall was kept in good repair and the Hsiung-nu were steadily forced back for nearly a century after the conquest of Ferghana. But Wu Ti's successors gradually steered China into internal confusion, which resulted in the temporary overthrow of the Han Dynasty about the time of Christ. Order was restored, eventually, and the garrisons returned to Tun-huang, but a new period of chaos at the end of the second century of the Christian era saw the abandonment of the Kansu outposts. The descendants of barbarians took over the silk route, and the extended Great Wall was allowed to fall into disrepair.

After a while China seemed to forget that the Wall had ever reached beyond Kia-yü-kuan. Maps of the Wall once again showed it ending at Ch'in Shih Huang Ti's terminal city, and desert sand swept in to engulf Wu Ti's 300-mile extension. It remained forgotten by China and unknown to the western world until the beginning of the present century, when a Hungarian-born archaeologist rediscovered it.

This archaeologist was Mark Aurel Stein (1862–1943), who went to England to study, accepted a post in the Indian Service, and by 1900 was Inspector of Schools in the Punjab. Late in the nineteenth century such explorers as Sven Hedin had roamed Central Asia extensively, bringing back word of buried cities and caches of ancient manuscripts, and in June of 1900, Stein set out from India on an expedition of his own. Traveling eastward along the Old Silk Road, he passed through the cities of Kashgar and Khotan, and in 1901, not far from Khotan, he made important manuscript discoveries in sand-buried cities uninhabited for more than thirteen centuries.

The British Museum sponsored a second Stein expedition in 1906. After excavating once again near Khotan, he proceeded eastward to the edge of the lake of Lop Nor, to work at the site of the abandoned city of Loulan. He uncovered Chinese manuscripts on paper and silk there, halting his work when the water supply failed. After a rest, Stein set out in a northeasterly direction on February 21, 1907, through what Marco Polo had called "the desert of Lop." Stein's goal was Tun-huang.

The route took him through the "dreary, salt-encrusted shores" of a dried-up inland sea, and in the forlorn land he could not help but recall Marco Polo's description of the spirits that haunted the desert of Lop:

"When travelers are on the move by night, and one of them chances to lag behind or to fall asleep or the like, when he tries to gain his company again he will hear spirits talking, and will suppose them to be his comrades. Sometimes the spirits will call him by name; and thus shall a traveler oft-times be led astray so that he never finds his party. And in this way many have perished. Sometimes the stray traveler will hear as it were the tramp and hum of a great cavalcade of people away from the real line of road, and taking this to be their own company they will follow the sound; and when day breaks they find that a cheat has been put on them and that they are in an ill plight. Even in the daytime one hears those spirits talking. And sometimes you shall hear the sound of a variety of musical instruments, and still more commonly the sound of drums. Hence in making this journey 'tis customary for travelers to keep close together. All the animals too have bells at their necks, so that they cannot easily get astray. And at sleeping time a signal is put to show the direction of the next march. So thus it is that the desert is crossed."[59]

On March 7, the bleakness was broken by an exciting discovery: the ruins of a watchtower. Stein knew that a French diplomat named Bonin, passing this way in 1899, had seen some ruined watchtowers and even the remains of a wall running near them. Bonin had published no maps or route sketches, and Stein had to depend on luck to find the ruins.

The tower was solidly built and well preserved, fifteen feet square and about twenty-three feet high. Its hard, well-made bricks were formed of clay mixed with tamarisk branches, which Stein knew was a sign of great antiquity. Adjoining the tower on the west side was a small and badly decayed building, where Stein found a piece of wool, fragments of iron tools, and a few scraps of carved wood.

Tun-huang was only five days' march to the east, but pony fodder was running low, and Stein did not linger at the watchtower. Continuing on the next day, he came to a second tower three miles away, similar to the first. He observed a line of reed bundles cropping out of the gravel soil about sixty feet north of the tower, and, glancing eastward along the line of the reed bundles, Stein "saw the line stretching away perfectly straight towards another tower visible some three miles to the east, and assuming in the distance the form of an unmistakable wall. It was manifestly part of that early 'Chinese wall' for which M. Bonin's observation had made me look out, and a little 'prospecting' on the knoll soon revealed with clearness that I actually stood on remains of it!"[60]

Clearing away the layers of gravel and drift sand, Stein uncovered a regular wall fashioned of reed bundles placed horizontally across layers of clay mixed with gravel. Other reed bundles, bound with twists of bark, formed a facing for the wall. The bundles were about eight inches thick and eight feet long. The height of the wall, where digging had uncovered it, was about five feet.

There was no time for detailed excavation. But the first random digging turned up some rags of colored silk along the wall, and a label-like tablet of wood inscribed, in strangely archaic Chinese characters, "the clothes bag of one called Lu Ting-shih." A Chinese scholar accompanying Stein declared that the style of the writing dated back at least as far as the tenth century A.D., and probably farther, but he had no idea of its exact age.

Continuing on the track toward Tun-huang, Stein found tower after tower, with the wall cropping out here and there, in some places almost six feet high, in others ground down by erosion to a height of only inches above the gravel surface. To Stein, the wall seemed like a Roman *limes*—a wall built along a military route threatened by barbarian inroads. He knew of such

Roman *limites* as Hadrian's Wall in Northumberland, the Roman walls along the Rhine and the Danube, and others in Syria and Arabia—Chinese Walls in miniature. It was possible to follow the wall for more than fifty miles.

Stein turned southeast now and entered the walled town of Tun-huang to reprovision. On March 24, he set out for the desert again "with a dozen opium-smoking coolies, all the labor that could be raised."

Two days of searching, with icy winds sweeping down from the east, produced nothing. Stein had begun by exploring north of Tun-huang, but the wall had been obliterated there by river action. Turning east again, he found the wall once more, and was able to follow it for a distance of sixteen miles practically without a break. Here it was eight feet thick and over seven feet high. In the refuse heaps of the watchtowers, Stein discovered a number of slips of wood inscribed with Chinese characters. Many of the slips bore dates. "Our excitement was great when my Chinese secretary's decipherment showed that all these dates belonged to the first century A.D.," Stein wrote. "It thus became certain that this ruined border line was occupied already in the Former Han Dynasty's times, and that I had in my hands the oldest written Chinese documents so far recovered."[61] Quick examination showed that most of the documents were military: records of supplies, troop movements, and the like.

By April 1, the sandstorms and harsh winds forced another halt in the methodical tracing of the line of the wall, which Stein knew now to be part of the Great Wall of China. But by April 10, he was back in the field, discovering tower after tower. They were generally well preserved, twenty or twenty-four feet square at the base, tapering toward the top. He noted a lookout platform at the top of each tower, protected by a parapet. Here, signals of fire by night and smoke by day could be sent from tower to tower along the wall, exactly as had been done a thousand years earlier in Chou times.

The line of wall, Stein found, carried eastward along a succession of marshes and small lakes. Its route had been carefully chosen to take advantage of bodies of water that could serve as supplementary defenses, Stein felt, and this was confirmed when he found a document in a garrison headquarters station directing the local governor in Han days "to examine the configuration of the places. Utilizing natural obstacles, a wall is to be constructed in order to exercise control at a distance."[62]

Such documents were abundantly harvested all along the line of wall. In the dry climate of the desert, they had lain undisturbed for twenty centuries. Indeed, it seemed to Stein as he roved the dismal wasteland that time had stood still here. "Never did I realize more deeply," he wrote, "how little two thousand years mean where human activity is suspended, and even that of Nature benumbed, than when on my long reconnoitring rides the evenings found me alone at some commanding watch-station. Struck by the rays of the setting sun tower after tower, up to ten miles' distance or more, could be seen glittering as if the plaster coating which their walls had once carried were still intact. This plaster was meant, of course, to make the towers more visible from a distance. It had been frequently renewed, however, as shown by the many successive layers of white plaster which wall portions protected by debris still retained. How easy it was then to imagine that towers and wall were still guarded and that watchful eyes were scanning the deceptive depressions northward for that fleet and artful enemy, the Huns!"[63]

Arrowheads of bronze still lay near the wall and towers, testimony to ancient skirmishes. More startling to Stein was a "curiously straight furrow-like line running parallel to the wall and at a distance of about ten yards from it," visible by the slanting rays of the setting sun. "Close examination," he wrote, "showed that it was a narrow but well-defined track worn into the coarse gravel soil by the patrols who had tramped along it for centuries."

In places now, the wall rose as high as twelve feet. One completely unbroken stretch ran for more than five miles. On and on it stretched, with the watchtowers rising with monotonous regularity even where the wall itself had eroded away. A secondary wall appeared, running south from the main section; along it Stein found a massive fort with walls fifteen feet thick at the base. Where the two walls met, he came upon what must have been an important way-station during the heyday of the silk trade; it yielded strips of silk inscribed in Chinese and in the Brahmi alphabet of India, giving details of the size, weight, and place of manufacture of the bales from which they had been cut.

When he had completed his season's work along this ruined wall, Stein returned to Tun-huang, where he achieved a second major coup by gaining possession of a cache of Buddhist manuscripts dating from the eighth through eleventh centuries A.D. In time, the treasures of Stein's 1907 expedition reached European scholars, who were able to translate and date the documents found along the wall.

The Han annals declared that in 102 and 101 B.C. "military posts were established from place to place from Tun-huang westwards to the Salt Marsh." That Stein had found Wu Ti's Wall was demonstrated by the discovery of documents dated with the Chinese equivalents of 94, 96, and 100 B.C. Others bore dates corresponding to 68 B.C., to 56 B.C., and to A.D. 75. Beyond that were no fixed dates, indicating that the extension of the Great Wall had probably been abandoned not much later than 100 A.D. A third Stein expedition in 1913 and 1914 saw him following the line of the ancient wall for more than 250 miles. But there was nothing to indicate that the watchtowers had been occupied after the later days of Han. Wu Ti's dream of westward expansion had ended in drifting sand.

IV

While the great westward drive of Wu Ti was taking place, the Martial Emperor was simultaneously pressing the campaign against the Hsiung-nu. He was never able to deliver the decisive blow that would crush the nomads. They could retreat indefinitely before his armies, all the way to Siberia if they had to, and there was no way to destroy them. In 110 B.C., Wu Ti himself had led an army of 180,000 horsemen through the Great Wall to attack the barbarians in the steppe, but it turned into nothing more than a vast military parade, for the Hsiung-nu slipped into the wasteland without doing battle. In 104 B.C., divisions among the nomads allowed the Chinese to defeat them, but only a year later a Chinese army was surrounded and wiped out by barbarian attackers.

Wu Ti, a man who had little tolerance for such frustrations, could not immediately avenge that defeat, since he was then engaged in assembling the army with which Li Kuang-li would conquer Ferghana. With that operation successfully completed, the Emperor could turn to the Hsiung-nu again. In 99 B.C., General Li Ling was put at the head of a large army that was sent into the steppe. Disaster followed; Hsiung-nu warriors cut the Chinese force to tatters, and Li Ling was forced to surrender. He was taken into captivity, and his lament at life among the Hsiung-nu became a Chinese literary classic:

"All day long I see none but barbarians around me. Skins and felt protect me from wind and rain. With mutton and whey I satisfy my hunger and slake my thirst. Companions with whom to while time away, I have none. The whole country is stiff with black ice. I hear naught but the moaning of the bitter autumn blast, beneath which all vegetation has disappeared. I cannot sleep at night. I turn and listen to the distant sound of [Hsiung-nu] pipes, to the whinnying of [Hsiung-nu] steeds. . . ."[64]

Eventually Li Ling reconciled himself to life among his captors. He remained with the Hsiung-nu for twenty years, until his death, instructing the nomads in Chinese methods of war. For this he was rewarded with the gift of the *shan-yü*'s daughter as his wife. Unfortunately, when Wu Ti learned of Li Ling's treasonable defection, he had the general's Chinese wife and children, as well as his mother, put to death.

The Li Ling affair meant personal catastrophe for one important figure of Wu Ti's court on whose work we have had much occasion to draw: Ssŭ-ma Ch'ien, the Grand Historian and Astrologer to the Court.

Ssŭ-ma Ch'ien had inherited his posts from his father, Ssŭ-ma Tan, who before his death in 110 B.C. had begun a history of the Chinese from earliest times. Ssŭ-ma Ch'ien completed this work, bringing it down to the days of Wu Ti. The *Shih chi,* or *Historical Records,* is the chief source of Ch'in and early Han history. Its 130 chapters contain 700,000 Chinese characters, and, since Chinese is a concise language, that is the equivalent of a western book some fifteen times the length of the one you are now reading. Covering three thousand years, from the legendary period to the reign of Wu Ti, the *Shih chi* includes biographies of Emperors, kings, and feudal lords, essays on music, rituals, astrology, astronomy, and the calendar, and a vast mass of miscellaneous information about the Chou, Ch'in, and Han eras. This great work won Ssŭ-ma Ch'ien enormous prestige in his own day. But in 99 B.C., after the defeat and defection of Li Ling, the historian dared to defend the general before Wu Ti. The Emperor, smarting over the defeat, ordered that Ssŭ-ma Ch'ien be made a eunuch. Hardly had the mutilation been carried out than Wu Ti regretted his harsh order, and appointed Ssŭ-ma Ch'ien Minister of State by way of partial amends; but for the remaining fifteen years of his life the Grand Historian lived in withdrawal from the world.

Wu Ti's hasty temper caused him much more immediate agony a few years afterward. He had taken a concubine whom he called Kou I, and who swiftly became his favorite wife. When a son was born to her in 94 B.C., she persuaded the Emperor to name the baby as heir apparent, in place of an older son by a different wife. Kou I managed to convince Wu Ti that the heir apparent was part of a conspiracy against him, and without full investigation the Emperor had his eldest son put to death. In 88 B.C. evidence was discovered proving the innocence of the dead prince, and Kou I was herself given to the executioner. Embittered by the loss of the crown prince, Wu Ti spent the final months of his life involved with quacks and sorcerers. Like Ch'in Shih Huang Ti, he devoted a fortune to finding the elixir of life, and his quest was still short of success when death took him in 87 B.C.

Upon the death of the Martial Emperor, the throne passed to seven-year-old Liu Fu-ling, Wu Ti's son by the treacherous concubine Kou I. Wise regents —one of them the Hsiung-nu prince, Chin Mi-ti—maintained the stability of the empire during the boy's youth. Wu Ti had left a smoothly functioning realm. He had not succeeded in eradicating the Hsiung-nu, but he had successfully contained them, and the opening of the western regions had brought unparalleled prosperity. A report of the Lord Grand Secretary in 81 B.C. indicates the strength of the empire at this time:

"A piece of Chinese plain silk can be exchanged with the Hsiung-nu for articles worth several pieces of gold and thereby [we can] reduce the resources of our enemy. Mules, donkeys and camels enter the frontier in unbroken lines; horses, dapples and bays and prancing mounts come into our possession. The furs of sables, marmots, foxes and badgers, colored rugs and decorated carpets fill the imperial treasury, while jade and auspicious stones, corals and crystals, become national treasures. That is to say, foreign products keep flowing in, while our wealth is not dissipated. Novelties flowing in, the government has plenty. National wealth not being dispersed abroad, the people enjoy abundance."[65]

Wu Ti's son, who reigned as the Emperor Chao, had a short rule. He died in 74 B.C. without leaving an heir. Ho Kuang, one of the regents, put forth a nephew of the late Emperor to take the throne, but he proved worthless, and was quickly deposed. Next, Wu Ti's grandson—the son of the crown prince who had perished through Kou I's intrigue—was elevated to the throne as the Emperor Hsüan. His reign, from 73 to 49 B.C., was marked by palace skulduggery, by poisonings and plots, though the Emperor himself seems to have met a natural death.

The Han Dynasty had ruled for a century and a half. It had given China three excellent rulers, the strong men Kao Tsu and Wu Ti, and the wise, moderate Wên Ti. Now, through a cyclical process that was to become wearily familiar in China, the dynasty was declining. Weaklings were coming to the throne. China's enemies were growing stronger as the central authority of the empire slackened. Men of powerful families began to assert their independence. The dynasty itself was threatened, and its downfall seemed inevitable.

Eight. The Downfall of Han

Generation by generation, the dynasty moved toward its doom. In 48 B.C., Liu Shih came to the throne as the ninth Han Emperor, ruling as Yüan Ti. A gentle and austere man, Yüan Ti was more interested in the study of history than in the making of it; he remained aloof in the palace, diverting himself with books and music and painting, while the influence of China dwindled. An embassy came to Yüan Ti from Chi-pin, near Kashmir, a western kingdom that had not fallen under Chinese control in Wu Ti's time. The envoys from Chi-pin offered to acknowledge the sovereignty of China, but Yüan Ti, though he received them politely, simply was not interested in further westward extension of the empire. He refused the offer. When Chi-pin sent a second embassy on the same mission in the reign of Yüan Ti's son, Ch'êng Ti, the response was equally negative. "The difficulties of the road, the dangers to which it is exposed, should dismiss all idea of commerce with the Chi-pin," a minister advised Ch'êng Ti. "Besides such commerce would be of no use to our empire, since it would be confined to trade carried on by common merchants, who would be thinking only of their own advantage. If we refuse their offer of submission, moreover, they will have to protect themselves against their own neighbors without expecting help from us, and will be less likely to think of waging war elsewhere."[66]

Ostrich-in-the-sand caution was replacing the grandiose expansionist tradition of Wu Ti. The Great Wall no longer served as a base for military attacks on the Hsiung-nu; it resumed its purely defensive character.

We are told that Yüan Ti's austerity led him, at first, to take no concubines. Though it was customary for the Emperor to maintain a harem of hundreds of beauties, Yüan Ti contented himself with a single wife, the Empress Wang. Like the Empress Lü of the previous century, the Empress Wang took an active part in the government, gradually filling many of the highest posts with members of her own clan.

In time Yüan Ti agreed to replenish the imperial harem—urged, so the story goes, by a statesman who argued that the emptiness of the court was having harsh economic effects on the capital. Five hundred concubines were chosen. A certain Mao Yen-shou, who was appointed Administrator of the

Inner Courts, was given the task of painting likenesses of all five hundred girls so that the Emperor might easily be able to choose among them.

All but a few of the girls bribed Mao Yen-shou to make their portraits as flattering as possible. Those who failed to cross the Administrator's palm were depicted as plain women. One of those who objected to bribery was Chao Chün, the fairest of all the concubines, and so Mao Yen-shou's portrait of her distorted her features into ugliness, adding a mole under her right eye—an omen of misfortune. Yüan Ti, choosing his consorts on the basis of the portraits, was surprised that so plain a girl could have entered the harem at all. He ordered her transferred to an isolated pavilion, so that he would not have to look upon her even through accidental encounter.

At this time it became necessary to make the traditional gift of a Chinese princess to the *shan-yü*. There had been peace between the Chinese and the Hsiung-nu for nearly a generation; the nomads, troubled by internal conflict, had left the borders of China in peace. Thanks in part to Chinese intriguing, the Hsiung-nu had split into a southern group and a northern one, each acknowledging its own *shan-yü*. The southern Hsiung-nu were heavily under Chinese influence, receiving Chinese support in their quarrel with their northern rivals. The friendly southern *shan-yü*, Khujanga, whom the Chinese called Hu-han-hsieh, had come to the Chinese capital in 51 B.C. to swear his fealty to Yüan Ti's father, Hsüan Ti. Now, in the new reign, the alliance had been reconsecrated and was to be sealed by the gift of a princess.

Yüan Ti examined the portraits of his harem girls and selected the ugliest girl as his gift. This, of course, was Chao Chün. But when the girl was summoned to the throne room to receive her instructions, the Emperor was startled to see how beautiful she was. Appalled by the thought of parting with so fine a treasure, Yüan Ti tried to withdraw the gift, but the ambassadors of the Hsiung-nu held him to it. The girl had been promised to the *shan-yü*, and there could be no substitution at this point. Not even an imperial offer of a camel laden with gold could negotiate her repurchase.

And so Chao Chün departed for the court of the *shan-yü*. One romantic story maintains that rather than go to that bleak place the princess hurled herself into the Yellow River where it meets the Great Wall; but in fact she did go to live among the Hsiung-nu, and became their queen with the title of Hu Ning, "The Queen who brings peace to the Hsiung-nu." Her three-month journey across the treeless, wintry steppe has long served as a theme for Chinese poets and painters. In the ninth century A.D., Po Chü-i, one of China's greatest poets, wrote of the hardships of that journey and of the change they must have worked on Chao Chün's beauty:

> "Grief and pain and bitter toil have left so deep
>   a mark
> That now in the end she is very like what the
>   painter made her in his picture. . . ."[67]

The lovely princess enhanced the friendship between Emperor and *shan-yü*. Indeed, so tranquil did the relationship between Chinese and nomad become that in 33 B.C. the *shan-yü* offered to make himself responsible for the main-

Chinese collection, East Asian Library, Columbia University

tenance and defense of the western sector of the Great Wall! This strange proposal indicates that the southern Hsiung-nu had come to fear their northern and wilder cousins as much as the Chinese did; doubtless the idea was to insure a place of refuge against the outer barbarians in case of invasion, but the image of Hsiung-nu diligently repairing the Great Wall and then crowding through it in case of barbarian attack is an odd one.

The Chinese were perplexed by the offer. Certainly it would remove a burden from the imperial treasury. But it would also put the responsibility for border defense into the hands of the recent enemy, and there was no assurance that the southern Hsiung-nu would remain this friendly forever. Yüan Ti himself evidently was willing to let control of the Great Wall pass to the nomads, but one aged minister argued against it, declaring, "It is now over a century since the Great Wall was rebuilt by Wu Ti. It is not by any means a mere mud rampart. Up hill and down, it follows the natural configuration of the ground, is honeycombed with secret passages, and bristles with fortified points. Is all this vast labor to be allowed to go to rack and ruin? The more we dispense with our own defences, the more we shall be beholden to the *Shan-yü,* whose pretensions will advance in proportion. . . ."[68] He warned also that the Chinese of the border were in many cases blood relatives of the Hsiung-nu and might change their allegiance under such circumstances, and that the wild tribes of Tibet might rebel if the Chinese presence along the Wall were removed.

Considering these things, Yüan Ti refused the offer in a graceful fashion: "Know then that the Great Wall was not built so much to protect the empire against the outer world, as to protect the outer world against the over-enterprising Chinese. . . ."

The status quo remained. Within China, Yüan Ti permitted the Empress Wang to handle most of the chores of governing, and devoted himself to his concubines with increasing enthusiasm—so much so that when an eclipse of the sun was accompanied by a severe earthquake, a minister of the court named Ku Yung was bold enough to declare that the cause of the calamity was Yüan Ti's excessive attention to the ladies of the harem.

The Emperor died in 33 B.C., the year of the Hsiung-nu offer to maintain the Great Wall. The *shan-yü*, Khujanga, died two years later. Chao Chün, still only a girl, was married by Hsiung-nu custom to the new *shan-yü*, Vughturoi, and remained queen until 20 B.C. Her fate after that is uncertain; she may have been put to death by Vughturoi's successor in 18 B.C., or perhaps, as one tale has it, she died of grief when her son was killed by the new *shan-yü* in a purge of potential rivals to the title. Legend has it that she was returned to China for burial, and that the mound over her grave remains eternally green.

In China, the royal widow, the dowager Empress Wang, maintained a considerable influence during the reign of her son, the Emperor Ch'êng. The brothers of the Empress now occupied all offices of importance. Another member of the Wang clan, the nephew of the Empress, began to achieve exceptional power at this time. He was Wang Mang, born in 33 B.C., a political adventurer who briefly succeeded in driving the Han Dynasty from the throne.

II

At a time of dynastic crisis, ambitious men have frequently moved into vacuums of power. Wang Mang, energetic and able, came to maturity at a time when the imperial dynasty was at a low ebb and real authority was concentrated in the wrinkled hands of the aged dowager Empress Wang, his aunt.

Through her influence, he was appointed to high office and given titles of nobility. At seventeen, he was given the rank of marquis; ten years later, he had moved into the influential post of President of the Board of War, and was clearly the favorite of the old Empress.

The young Emperor, Ch'êng Ti, was childless. To provide an heir he adopted his wife's nephew, a boy of the Fu clan, although there were members of the imperial Liu clan who could have been chosen had they been strong enough to assert their claims. When Ch'êng Ti died in 6 B.C., the new Emperor, Ai Ti, brought his own relatives into power, at the expense both of the Wang and Liu clans. This touched off fierce palace intrigues, and Wang Mang and his relatives temporarily fell from favor. The death of Ai Ti in 1 B.C. gave Wang Mang his opportunity. Backed by the venerable Empress Wang, he put a boy of eight on the throne as the Emperor P'ing. The Fu clan was pensioned off and sent from the capital. Wang Mang, acting as regent, gave his own daughter as wife to P'ing Ti. A few years later, in A.D. 5, the Emperor died, perhaps poisoned by Wang Mang. Wang Mang now put forth as the new Emperor a baby little more than a year old, the great-grandson of Hsüan Ti. By A.D. 9, however, Wang Mang felt that the time was propitious for dethroning the boy and taking the throne himself.

Thus did a usurper push the Han Dynasty aside. A new dynastic era was proclaimed: the Hsin. Briskly and efficiently, Wang Mang established a program of reform. He broke up the large landholdings that had been assembled during forty years of weak rule, and redistributed the land to the peasants. He prohibited the widespread practice of slavery. He re-established the imperial monopoly on coinage, after decades in which private merchants had produced their own coins. To finance his reforms, Wang Mang debased the currency, ordering that all gold be turned in for bronze. He amassed an enormous hoard of gold; on his death, the imperial treasury was officially reported to hold five million ounces of the precious metal—more than the total gold supply of medieval Europe. So powerful was the drain of gold toward Wang Mang that even Rome was affected; the Emperor Tiberius (who ruled from A.D. 14 to 37) had to prohibit the wearing of silk because it meant the eastward flight of Roman gold.

Wang Mang's reforms were too harsh to be successful. After a few years he had to repeal many of them. By way of repairing the imperial prestige that had been lost through the failure of his economic program, the usurper began to foment a military adventure against the Hsiung-nu. The nomads had been quiescent for many years, and during the final chaotic decline of the Han Dynasty the rulers of China had been well content to keep on good terms with the Hsiung-nu. In 2 B.C., with Ai Ti on the throne and Wang Mang out of favor, there was some talk of launching an offensive against the barbarians, but it was quickly spiked by a court minister who advised against a proposed severing of diplomatic relations. The minister pointed out that "even Ch'in Shih Huang Ti, one of the most powerful princes who has occupied the throne, and General Mêng T'ien, the greatest soldier of his time," had never managed to shatter the power of the Hsiung-nu entirely. "This same prince thought to stop their frequent raids into our lands by constructing the Great Wall, an insufficient barrier against their incursions, which continued as before." Kao Tsu, the puissant founder of the Han Dynasty, it was further noted, had been blockaded and trapped by the Hsiung-nu, and had had to buy his freedom with tribute. Only Wu Ti, by pursuing the nomads again and again into their own deserts, had forced them to ask for peace. The minister concluded, "the Hsiung-nu are naturally belligerent, robust, and not easily exhausted. The evil they have done us, the disastrous wars we have had against them, should make us at all costs avoid finding ourselves again at odds with them. The expense of receiving their *Shan-yü*, can it be compared with the losses we would suffer if they became our enemies again?"[69]

Now, for political reasons, Wang Mang deliberately awakened the nomads. He decreed that their territory was to be a Chinese province, and ordered its partition into fifteen districts, each with its own *shan-yü*. Furthermore, he rechristened the Hsiung-nu as Hsiang-nu, a name meaning "subjugated slaves." He laid heavy taxes on the Chinese to support the cost of the vast army he was massing on the Great Wall frontier.

All this led to anger among the nomads and unrest in China. In A.D. 18 a peasant rebellion, the "Red Eyebrows" movement, sprang up and thousands of farmers marched on the capital. Wang Mang was forced to use government troops to put them down. This left the frontier army weakened and without reinforcements, so that is was easy prey for the strike-and-run attacks of the Hsiung-nu. The defenders of the Great Wall grew demoralized; Wang Mang's frontier army gave itself over to looting and rioting; thousands of soldiers simply deserted to the Hsiung-nu.

Wang Mang tried desperately to rally his supporters. He conscripted one man out of thirty throughout China and attempted to restore order in the Great Wall provinces. A Chinese historian of the next dynasty told how Wang Mang "enlisted the help of those who possessed strange arts. . . . One said he knew how to cross waters without the aid of boats or oars, so that even troops of a hundred or a thousand horse could ride over; another said that it was not necessary to maintain army grain supplies as he had a medicinal substance which would dispense with food and hunger; a third claimed to be able to fly a thousand *li* in one day and suggested that he should be sent to bring back intelligence of the movements of the Huns. Wang Mang had all these alleged methods tested without ceremony, and found that none of them were usable."[70]

The end became inevitable when descendants of the deposed Han Dynasty began to lead popular uprisings against the Emperor. The empire simply fell away from Wang Mang. An army led by Liu Hsiu, a descendant in the ninth generation from Liu Pang, invaded the capital. Wang Mang did not flee. Banking on the sanctity of his title, the Emperor donned his robes of state and mounted the throne. He was reciting the ancient writings when a soldier entered the throne room without opposition and beheaded him, in A.D. 23. His skull was an ornament of the imperial treasury for the following two hundred years.

III

The events that had followed the collapse of the Ch'in Dynasty now repeated themselves. A savage civil war broke out among the leaders of the revolt against the Emperor, and hundreds of thousands perished. After two years af anarchy, Liu Hsiu prevailed and took the throne.

Since he was of the clan of Liu, he could claim with some justice to have restored the Han Dynasty. However, he moved his capital from Ch'ang-an, which had been plundered and burned during the time of chaos, to Loyang, which had also been the later capital of the Chou kings. Thus the era after Wang Mang's brief reign is known as the Eastern Han, or Later Han, to distinguish it from the Western Han, or Earlier Han, that had come to an end in 9 A.D.

Liu Hsiu, who ruled as Kuang Wu Ti, was a strong leader, as the situation demanded. (One biographer describes him as "seven feet three inches in height,* with a fine beard and eyebrows, a prominent nose, and a large

---

* Great men of ancient China are often credited with extraordinary height by the early annalists. This may be simple exaggeration or, it has been suggested, the Han unit of measure translated as "foot" was shorter not only than our foot but than that of present-day China.

mouth."[71]) The massacres of the past few years had depopulated the country, and wholesale economic reconstruction was necessary. The revival of China under Kuang Wu Ti was a remarkable demonstration of resilience.

Most of the western territory won in Wu Ti's time had been lost through Han weakness and the confusion of Wang Mang's reign. New states had arisen in the west, strong enough both to maintain independence from China and to fend off the Hsiung-nu. The nomads themselves had encroached on China in Wang Mang's day, but had troubles of their own soon afterward. About A.D. 45, a combination of droughts and locust plagues struck the steppe, killing a large part of the Hsiung-nu livestock and crippling the strength of the nomads. The Hsiung-nu found themselves harried in the west by such newly powerful little states as Yarkand, and troubled in the east by other barbarian tribes, the Hsien-pi and the Wu Huan. At the same time, the Chinese under Kuang Wu Ti were once again strong enough to defend the Great Wall, cutting off the Hsiung-nu from the easy pickings of northern China.

Weakened and battered, the Hsiung-nu collapsed entirely about A.D. 58. Once more, they split into northern and southern wings. The southern Hsiung-nu abandoned the nomad life, settling along the Great Wall and establishing permanent trade relations with the Chinese, exchanging livestock for textiles and grain. In effect, they became subjects of China, and for the first time Chinese power was effectively extended across the Great Wall frontier into the steppe. The northern Hsiung-nu remained wild, but concentrated their attacks on Yarkand and other city-states of the west. In the east, the new barbarians, the Hsien-pi and Wu Huan, were still too sparse to create much threat for China.

The Later Han rulers managed to play off the southern Hsiung-nu against the northern nomads successfully for several decades, permitting peaceful reconstruction of Chinese power. By A.D. 73, Ming Ti, an outward-looking Emperor, revived Wu Ti's old dream of a western empire. Once more, Chinese armies struck westward beyond Kia-yü-kuan to secure the caravan route through Turkestan. Two brilliant generals, Tou Ku and Pan Ch'ao, led this new outward thrust.

Pan Ch'ao, the deputy commander, was the younger brother of the Han historian Pan Ku. Until the age of 32, he held a minor clerical post at the capital, until one day, weary of his work, he flung down his pen, exclaiming, "A hero should have other aims than these. . . . He should win renown in foreign lands, and earn for himself the honor of an earldom. He should not waste his days over pen and ink."[72] A physiognomist told him that he "had a swallow's beak and a tiger's neck;" that he "would fly and also eat meat, and be the marquis of a myriad miles away."

The mission of A.D. 73 took Pan Ch'ao to the western city-state of Shan-shan. It happened that the Hsiung-nu had sent an embassy to Shan-shan at the same time; by way of demonstrating Chinese strength, Pan Ch'ao took the blunt step of beheading the Hsiung-nu envoy and presenting the gory head to the ruler of Shan-shan. This produced an immediate willingness on the monarch's part to submit to Chinese hegemony. Next, Pan Ch'ao with thirty men bullied the city-state of Khotan into submission, and he proceeded on to Kashgar and Bactria and the surrounding areas, lopping off heads here and there and winning the allegiance of some fifty small states in the process. For this he received the rank of marquis, as the physiognomist had prophesied.

The death of Ming Ti brought an isolationist Emperor to power, Chang Ti. He left Pan Ch'ao stranded in the far west, sending neither money nor reinforcements. Nonetheless, Pan Ch'ao held on, employing a policy of "using the barbarians for attacking the barbarians," and maintained control over China's now undesired western domain. Chang Ti was succeeded in A.D. 89 by Ho Ti, whose mother was related to General Tou Ku, Pan Ch'ao's original commanding officer in the reconquest of the west. Pan Ch'ao returned to favor and led several successful campaigns against the northern Hsiung-nu. Chinese influence was extended westward beyond the Pamirs, almost to the borders of Parthia.

Had he chosen a braver man for the job, Pan Ch'ao might have succeeded in establishing contact between China and imperial Rome. In 97, he sent a mission to the far-off land the Chinese called Ta-ts'in, or Syria. His envoy, Kan Ying, was instructed to continue on to the even more remote and virtually legendary land of Rome. Kan Ying made his way through Parthia to the modern Iraq. He planned to travel by ship across the Persian Gulf to Syria, and from there perhaps would have sailed westward through the Mediterranean to Rome. But while he was still landbound in Parthia, Kan Ying lost heart. As he was about to board ship, the sailors told him, "When out at sea a multitude of things will occur to make you sigh for what you have left behind. He who occupies his business in the great waters is liable to regret and repentance for what he has undertaken. If the envoy of the Han has no father, no mother, no wife or children to pine after, then let him go to sea—not otherwise."[73] When the seamen pointed out that with unfavorable winds the westward journey might take two years, Kan Ying abandoned the project and returned to Pan Ch'ao. But for his timidity, there might have been a yellow-skinned ambassador at the court of Trajan.

IV

Despite this lamentable failure of nerve, news of China was reaching the European world. Europe was learning about China from two directions, and a result was that European geographers divided China into two separate lands, a confusion that would continue for many centuries.

One source of news of China came from Parthia and other countries along the land route west of Kia-yü-kuan. Since this was the Silk Road, Europeans began to refer to China as *Serica,* the land of the *Seres,* or silk-merchants. Meanwhile, merchant ships from Egypt and Arabia had found the sea route to China, via the Indian Ocean and the South China Sea, and were doing business with people called the *Sinae* or *Thinae.* It did not occur to westerners that the Seres and the Sinae were one and the same, and as late as the seventeenth century the distinction between China-reached-overland and China-reached-by-sea was maintained.

The earliest European reference to China dates from the time when Pan Ch'ao was conquering the western states and sending ambassadors Romeward. It is found in an anonymous book called the *Periplus of the Erythraean Sea,* written between A.D. 70 and 90. A *periplus* is the account of a voyage along the shores of a sea, while the Erythraean Sea was the modern Indian Ocean, Persian Gulf, and Red Sea. The author, a Graeco-Egyptian seafaring merchant, probably had never seen China himself, but he seems to have heard a good deal about it. This is his account:

"Behind this country [Burma] the sea comes to a termination somewhere in Thin; and in the interior of that country, quite to the north, there is a very great city called Thinae, from which raw silk and silk thread and silk stuffs are brought overland through Bactria to Barygaza, as they are on the other hand by the Ganges River to Limyrice. It is not easy, however, to get to this Thin, and few and far between are those who come from it."[74] He noted also that no one had visited the regions to the north of Thin: "Whether it be that the wintry climate and excessive cold renders it hard to penetrate them, or whether it be the result of some supernatural influence from the gods, it is the fact that they never have been explored."

Few and far between indeed were those who came from the land of Thin, and they became fewer after the retirement of Pan Ch'ao in A.D. 101. The old general, aged seventy, returned to China after an absence of nearly thirty years, and died soon after. With his passing the revival of Chinese interest in the western lands declined, and soon there began that long sleep of the western Great Wall that was ended only by Aurel Stein's explorations eighteen centuries later.

On the home front, the Chinese were enjoying a cultural renaissance. The Han period was a time of great advance in Chinese civilization, after the dark era of the warring states, the Ch'in consolidation, and the civil wars that followed, in which military necessity had hampered peacetime growth. So golden was the Han age that the Chinese often still call themselves "sons of Han."

There were new developments in science, art, literature, music, and industry. Historians such as Pan Ku flourished, building on the earlier work of Ssŭ-ma Ch'ien. The calendar was reformed. Astronomy reached a peak of attainment, so that a minister of Wang Mang's court was able to calculate the length of the solar year with remarkable accuracy at 365 and $385/1539$ days. The constellations were mapped; mathematics progressed. The new attitude toward science was indicated by the words of the astronomer Wang Ch'ung (c. 27–100), who wrote, "On an average, there is one moon eclipse in about 180 days, and a solar eclipse in about every 41 or 42 months. Eclipses are regular occurrences and are not caused by political action. All anomalies and catastrophes are of the same class and are never dependent upon political events."[75]

The inexorable pattern of the dynastic cycle developed in the Later Han as it had in the Earlier. Strong Emperors were succeeded by weak, corrupt ones; public officials succumbed to the lure of bribery; powerful families contended for greater influence. Several times, the relatives of Empresses attempted to displace the Liu clan, as had been done successfully in the time of Wang Mang. A series of child Emperors, often poisoned in boyhood, disrupted the normal line of succession and brought collateral relatives into power. Rival regents battled with each other while the Emperors grew progressively less powerful. From A.D. 150 onward, generals held the real authority. The misrule of these warlords led to peasant revolts after 184, creating a spreading anarchy.

In 190, nine-year-old Liu Hsieh became the twelfth Emperor of the Later Han Dynasty, placed on the throne by the warlord Tung Cho. Almost at once, rival generals attacked the capital. Tung Cho ordered the evacuation of Loyang, and its complete destruction. The city that had been China's capital for nearly two centuries was burned and pillaged. The government archives were largely lost, and even the tombs of the Han Emperors were looted. Rebellion became widespread. Tung Cho was assassinated in 192, after which the hapless Emperor was dragged about from place to place by the various generals who in turn took possession of him. Possession of the Emperor was all important, since the hopeful warlords wished to bring about an abdication in proper form, complete with formal transfer of the seals of office, that would permit the legitimate creation of a new dynasty.

The pitiful Liu Hsieh clung to his shaky throne for thirty years, though he never exercised any real authority. By 200, conditions had simplified so that three warlords alone challenged the central control. In the north ruled Ts'ao Ts'ao, who had possession of the Emperor; in the west was the domain of Liu Pei, who was himself of imperial blood; in the southeast was the realm of Sun Ts'e. China had already begun to divide once more into three natural geographical sections.

The end of the Han came in 220. Ts'ao Ts'ao, who had been virtual dictator of northern China for years, died. His son deposed the puppet Emperor, sending him into retirement with the title of Duke of Shan-yang. The deposed Liu Hsieh lived fourteen more years—time enough to see the China of the Han Dynasty become three separate kingdoms, and plunge into a time of troubles that would ultimately place barbarians atop the imperial throne.

Nine.
The Three Kingdoms and the Nomad Emperors

Abruptly, China had returned to the conditions of the time of warring states. The great achievement of Ch'in Shih Huang Ti had been undone. Out of the unified empire there now came the kingdoms of Wei, Shu, and Wu.

The splintering of China followed predictable lines. Ts'ao Ts'ao's son, the ruler of Wei, held control over the northern and western districts that once had been Ch'in's original domain, and also controlled the ancient eastern states of Yen and Ch'i. This was ancestral China. The Great Wall marked its northern boundary. The new kingdom of Wu was the hot, forested, rice-growing region of the Yangtze Valley, which had been late to develop but which had come to be a key economic area. Shu, in the west, was modern Szechuan, which had been added to China by the conquests of Ch'in in the fourth century B.C.

Only Liu Pei, the ruler of Shu, had any claim to legitimacy. He was a descendant of Liu Ch'i, the father of Wu Ti of the Earlier Han Dynasty. In 221, after the breakup of the Later Han Dynasty, Liu Pei proclaimed himself Emperor of Shu, and designated his dynasty as that of the Shu Han, now called Minor Han. It did not last long. In 264, Shu was absorbed by the kingdom of Wei and ceased to exist.

The kingdom of Wu was also shortlived. It was conquered by Wei in 280, thus ending the time of the Three Kingdoms. The Wei victory resulted from a policy of establishing irrigated supply bases, encircling the enemy, and starving him into submission. China was thus reunited with little real loss of manpower. The kingdom of Wei, with its capital at a rebuilt Loyang, emerged supreme, and once again the political dominance of northwestern China was established.

Ts'ao Ts'ao, who had prepared the way for the downfall of Han, had been a typical dynasty-founder, strong, determined, and ruthless. He is said to have maintained such tight discipline in his camp that when he allowed his horse to blunder into a field of grain, he sentenced himself to death under his own proclamation forbidding injury to crops. (He let his supporters persuade him to crop his hair instead of chopping off his head.) When his son,

Ts'ao P'ei, deposed the Han Emperor in 220 and proclaimed the advent of the Wei Dynasty, it seemed a certainty that China would ultimately be reunited under the reign of the clan of Ts'ao.

China was reunited, but not by a Ts'ao. A general of Wei named Ssŭ-ma Yen, a descendant of the great historian, led the army that overthrew the kingdom of Shu in 264. Encouraged by this, Ssŭ-ma Yen nudged the Wei king from his throne, proclaiming himself Emperor in his place. The new dynasty took the name of Chin, and Ssŭ-ma Yen was awarded the hallowed imperial designation of Wu Ti.

Chin Wu Ti became master of all China upon the defeat of Wu in 280. His authority never was really secure, however. Nomads were stirring in the north once more; the Hsiung-nu by this time had gone the way of the Jung and the Ti, but such tribes as the Hsien-pi and the T'o-pa were growing uncomfortably powerful. Chin Wu Ti met the challenge in traditional fashion: he rebuilt the Great Wall.

In so doing, he disregarded the words of one of his own advisers, a man named Chang Tsai. In 280, Chang Tsai had won fame for an inscription he wrote on a mountain wall, calling upon the people to "trust in virtue, not in walls." For this he received a high government post, but he soon returned to private life when he grew weary of the strain of office. Trusting less in virtue than in stout defenses, Chin Wu Ti had the western section of the Great Wall rebuilt, with watchtowers erected beyond the city of Suchow.

It was a fine gesture of defiance, but it was much too late to ward off the barbarians. During the time of the Three Kingdoms, nomad tribes had descended en masse through the Wall, which had been allowed to fall into ruins during the decline of the Han. The nomads had taken up residence in the northern provinces, establishing little principalities for themselves and ruling as an aristocracy of warriors fed by the labor of the Chinese. This arrangement had to be officially confirmed during the reign of Chin Wu Ti, who was forced to buy the allegiance of the nomad intruders by offering them titles and dignities. No less than eight princedoms had been created in the northern provinces by the time of Chin Wu Ti's death in 290.

Now the nomad pressure became irresistible. In the first century and during most of the second century, the Great Wall barrier had held firm much of the time, forcing such barbarians as the Huns to go west of China for their plunder. In that way began the great barbarian migration into Europe that culminated in the destruction of Rome, and it can be said with some accuracy that the existence of the Great Wall, by deflecting the nomads into Europe, sped the collapse of Rome. But after A.D. 300 the Great Wall ceased to be a barrier to the nomads, since the concessions made in Chin Wu Ti's time had at last given the Great Wall to the nomads.

His successors speedily made matters even worse. With stray nomad tribes raiding China at random, a Chin Emperor could think of no better way to restore order than to invite the Huns to serve as his policemen. Starting in 304, the Huns moved southward, pacifying the northern region. The Chin Emperor could well have complained, as another Emperor would declare thirteen centuries later, that he "had brought in lions to help rid himself of dogs." The Huns established themselves, remaining as conquerors instead of policemen.

Their leader was Liu Yüan-hai. As his surname indicates, he claimed descent from the imperial clan of the Han Dynasty. He insisted that he was of the line of that Han princess who had been given in marriage to the Hsiung-nu chieftain Mao Tun nearly five hundred years before, and said that by virtue of ancient treaties he was the legitimate successor to the Han, since in times of old the royal houses of China and Hsiung-nu had been like elder and younger brothers, and "when the elder brother dies, the younger succeeds."

In 304, he founded the kingdom of Han in the modern province of Shansi, and within four years proclaimed himself the first Emperor of a new Han Dynasty. This dynasty, often called the "pseudo-Han," changed its name to Chao in 319. Under its rule, the Huns gave up their old tribal structure, reorganizing themselves after the Chinese system, and began a steady advance into the territory of the Chin monarch. In 311, the capital of Loyang was invaded, and Ch'ang-an, the old Han capital, fell in 312. Four years later, the Chin Emperor fell into the hands of his Hunnish counterpart and was executed. The dynasty of the Huns was supreme in northern China.

Chin Wu Ti's futile reconstruction of the Great Wall may have had one minor consequence: the first European awareness that the Long Rampart existed. The possibility is a slim one, though. No western writer of antiquity mentions the Great Wall—at least not in any surviving account—except for a single enigmatic passage.

The reference is found in the work of the Roman historian Ammianus Marcellinus, who lived in the latter part of the fourth century A.D. In the twenty-third chapter of his *Rerum Gestarum* he described the land of the Seres, the silk-makers, as fenced round by "a circling and continuous barrier," and spoke of the Seres as dwelling "thus secure in their rich and spacious plains." The nineteenth-century geographer Sir Henry Yule, translating this passage in his monumental *Cathay and the Way Thither,* expressed doubt that Ammianus Marcellinus was actually referring to the Great Wall. Yule suggested that "he is speaking merely of an encircling rampart of lofty mountains within which the spacious and happy valley of the Seres is conceived to lie."[76] Yule to the contrary, the original Latin text uses the word *agger,* which is generally understood to mean a wall, and specifically a wall of earth. Did some traveler out of Chin China bring word to Rome of the newly rebuilt Great Wall? It was not even necessary to go that far; before turning to history, Ammianus Marcellinus had seen military action in Persia, where once Parthian kings had greeted Han ambassadors. The Roman historian may have learned of the Great Wall during that term of duty.

The remnants of the Chin court fled to the southeast and set up a capital at Nanking. The Chin Dynasty managed to survive there for more than a century, from 317 to 419. This government is known as the Eastern Chin, to distinguish it from the Western Chin, which had ruled from 265 to 316.

The Chin Dynasty's ignominious retreat left the entire Great Wall in barbarian hands. Tribe after tribe of nomads scampered through the passes of the Wall, and dynasty after barbarian dynasty held sway along the frontier.

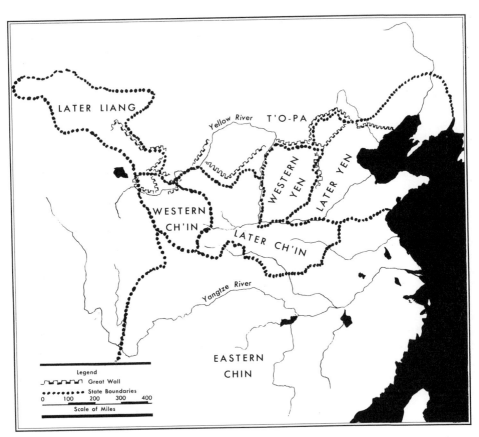

The Barbarian Dynasties, c. A.D. 390

A curious thing now occurred. The barbarians turned into Chinese themselves. Again and again, the warriors of the north pitched their tents south of the Great Wall, adopted Chinese names and Chinese customs, and slipped by easy stages into becoming true Chinese—leaving themselves vulnerable for the next wave of barbaric invaders. Meanwhile, the Chinese acquired a strong infusion of barbarian blood, so that when a "Chinese" dynasty at last ended the time of chaos centuries later, the founder of the new line was of nomad descent.

II

The helter-skelter succession of barbarian dynasties is baffling in its complexity. While the Eastern Chin Emperors held court uneasily at Nanking, no less than eighteen fugitive dynasties came and went in the north, several often existing simultaneously. The Chao Dynasty of Huns lasted twenty-five years, pushed aside finally by a different Hun family that ruled as the Later

Chao for twenty-four years more. Meanwhile, a group of exiled Chinese in Kansu and Turkestan established the so-called Early Liang Dynasty in 313, and maintained it until 376. In 351, a Tibetan general in Shensi proclaimed his own dynasty, to which he gave the exalted name of Ch'in; it lasted until 394, when it was absorbed by a dynasty of nomads that had arisen in 385, and became known as the Western Ch'in. This dynasty endured until 431. The Western Ch'in expanded out of its Kansu base to swallow up the Southern Liang Dynasty of Hsien-pi nomads, which had been founded in 397. There was a Northern Liang Dynasty too, and a Western Liang, as well as a Later Liang that flourished from 386 to 403. (And which must not be confused with an entirely different Later Liang Dynasty of the years 907–923.)

Then, too, there was a sequence of Yen Dynasties. The first of these, the Early Yen, was the product of the Hsien-pi nomads. The Yen Emperors traced their descent from Mu-jung Hui, a Hsien-pi chieftain who swore allegiance to the Chinese Chin Dynasty about A.D. 289, and died with the imperial title of duke. Mu-jung Hui was a man of extraordinary stature—the Chinese chronicler credits him with being eight feet tall—and his descendants are similarly described as giants. It was his son, Mu-jung Huang (seven feet eight inches) who named himself Prince of Yen in 337; his son Mu-jung Tsuan (eight feet two inches!) took the imperial title in 352; in 370, the Tibetan-ruled Ch'in conquered the Early Yen, but by 384 there were two new Yen states, the Later Yen in Hopei and the Western Yen in Shansi, and in 398 Mu-jung Te, youngest son of Mu-jung Huang (eight feet two inches) founded the Southern Yen Dynasty in Shantung. Eventually there was a Northern Yen Dynasty as well, in Hopei and southern Manchuria, but this was an enterprise of Chinese leaders rather than of the towering Mu-jung family.

The impression one gets from this maze of dynasties is that of chaos rampant. The impression is correct: China north of the Chin domain was a welter of tiny states, each with its own ruling dynasty and its own Emperor. Most of these were barbarian rulers—some Tibetan, some Huns, some Hsien-pi. New conquerors were on the way, though, who would sweep through the Great Wall, tumble the petty Emperors into oblivion, and establish a sound and enduring dynasty.

III

As early as the second century A.D., the nomad tribe known as the T'o-pa had drifted into the northern Chinese province of Shansi. They did not come as invaders, but rather slipped through the Great Wall in small numbers, adopting Chinese names, customs, and dress. The T'o-pa were a branch of the Hsien-pi, and they first make their appearance in official Chinese history in 275, when their prince came with other Hsien-pi chieftains to pay tribute at the court of the Chin Dynasty Emperor.

During the confusion of the late fourth century, the T'o-pa began to enter China in increasing numbers. About 385, they started to weld themselves into a coherent political group, and to challenge the supremacy of the current rulers of their district, the Western Yen. In 396, the Western Yen were defeated, and two years later the T'o-pa ruler, T'o-pa Kuei, proclaimed himself Emperor of a dynasty that he called the Wei, and which must be kept distinct from that kingdom of Wei which appeared at the end of the Han period.

The T'o-pa Wei Dynasty rapidly extended its authority, so that by 409 all of northeastern China was under Wei control. But the Wei rulers took a novel and wise approach to their Chinese subjects. The other nomad dynasties, presented with hundreds of thousands or even millions of docile peasants to rule, had tried to turn them into shepherds. Agriculture had suffered, naturally, and the resulting famines had helped to topple the barbarian masters. The T'o-pa rulers, already partly assimilated as Chinese, took every step to maintain the structure of the Chinese agricultural society. Instead of placing the conquered districts under tribal chieftains who had no understanding of their subjects, the T'o-pa restored a strong central government and staffed it with Chinese officials. Though they reserved military power for themselves, the T'o-pa relied on the Chinese bureaucracy for the job of civil government. By about 435, Wei control of northern China was so secure that a process of integration of Chinese and nomads began. The T'o-pa, who apparently had no written language of their own, adopted Chinese. Chinese were allowed to enter the army and to marry T'o-pa women. The conquerors donned the dress of their subjects, banned the use of the languages of the steppe, and gave themselves Chinese family names.

So Chinese did the T'o-pa become, in fact, that they began repairing the Great Wall to fend off their barbarian relatives of the north. Their first Emperor, T'o-pa Kuei, placed his capital at Ta-t'ung in Shensi, within the shadow of the Great Wall, as though to stress the importance of the Wall as the boundary between barbarism and civilization. His son and successor, T'o-pa Ssŭ, was the first barbarian ruler of China who felt the necessity of protecting China from other barbarians through reconstruction of the Great Wall. In 423 he built a 600-mile section of new wall following the original line of Ch'in Shih Huang Ti. This new wall stretched from Wu-yuan in Shansi eastward to Ch'ih-ch'eng in Chihli, and was specifically designed as a barrier against the raids of a new nomad tribe, the Juan-juan.

The Juan-juan, also known as the Avars, were neither Huns nor Hsien-pi. They belonged to the Mongol linguistic group, and were the first wave of the later "Tartar" invaders. Beginning about 403, they created a large empire running from the boundaries of Korea into the distant reaches of Central Asia. Beyond the Juan-juan territory, the Huns had formed a kingdom of their own called the Hsia, ruled by descendants of the old Hsiung-nu chief Mao Tun. These two nomad groups now began to harry the increasingly more Sinified Wei Emperors.

Faced with this double threat, the third T'o-pa ruler, T'o-pa Tao, continued his father's work of repairing the Great Wall. Coming to the throne in 424, he carried out a sixteen-year program of reconstruction along much of the old line of the Wall, and even added a new section intended as a direct counter to the Juan-juan threat.

There is something comic and rather touching about this. Only three generations removed from the steppe, this drinker of mare's milk had donned the yellow robe of a Son of Heaven and now solemnly went about the business of shielding his adopted country from the onslaught of the wild men of the north. T'o-pa Tao built a new loop of the Great Wall passing through Kalgan, the important marketing town north of Peking; it ran from east to west for some four hundred miles, lying seventy miles north of Ch'in Shih Huang Ti's Great Wall, which now became an inner line of defense. T'o-pa Tao also built a Long Rampart of tamped earth from north to south through Shansi to mark what was then the western border of his territory, beyond which lay the rampaging Hsia.

Surrounded though he was by these new and sturdy walls, the Wei Emperor did not depend exclusively on them for the safety of his domain. He carried the war into the steppe, leading his troops deep into nomad territory in 425, 428, 429, 443, and 448–9. Each thrust carried T'o-pa Tao's Chinese armies to the edge of the Gobi, sending the Juan-juan back in rout. Barbarian that he was, T'o-pa Tao successfully used barbarian methods of war. Rather than utilizing unwieldy masses of men who would present increasingly difficult supply problems the farther they got from the wheatfields of China, the Emperor struck with light corps of cavalry. Unhindered by baggage, the horsemen swooped down on Juan-juan encampments, taking the nomads by surprise and setting their tents ablaze before they knew what was happening. With his boldness and brilliant generalship, T'o-pa Tao disrupted the Juan-juan so thoroughly that they ceased for many years to threaten the Wei empire.

That left the T'o-pa monarchs free to look toward the as yet unconquered parts of China. In the south, there had been dynastic changes; the Eastern Chin had been overthrown in 419 by a general named Liu Yü, who claimed descent from the founder of the Han Dynasty. After deposing the last Eastern Chin Emperor, Liu Yü took the throne at Nanking and proclaimed the inauguration of the Sung Dynasty, which is always referred to as the Liu Sung to distinguish it from the much greater Sung Dynasty of six centuries later. The exiled survivors of the Chin royal family straggled northward into the T'o-pa domain, where they settled at the imperial court and campaigned aggressively for a T'o-pa "war of liberation" that would drive the Liu Sung from power in the south. For some thirty years the inconclusive struggle between T'o-pa and Liu Sung continued, both sides finding it so expensive that about 450 hostilities were dropped without significant victory for either contender.

The T'o-pa had better luck in the west. After the defeat of the Juan-juan in 429, they moved against the various small states of Kansu, bringing down in quick succession the Hsia kingdom, the Western Ch'in, the Northern Liang, and the Western Liang. The T'o-pa Wei Emperor now controlled the whole of north China, from Shantung to Kansu, and it became possible to reopen trade with the west. Caravans once again traveled the Silk Road, and Chinese merchants were seen in Turkestan and even in India. The T'o-pa at home began to affect great magnificence and love of luxury, turning their backs on their simple nomad heritage. Things Chinese were praised, the culture of the steppe was scorned, and there was much intermarriage between T'o-pa nobles and the dispossessed but highly civilized survivors of the old

Chinese aristocracy. The rough vigor of the T'o-pa conquerors was diluted with gentler Chinese strains, and after the middle of the fifth century a steady decline in T'o-pa authority began.

This process was intensified by T'o-pa Hung-yen, the sixth Wei Emperor, who began to rule in 471. He changed the family name of the imperial clan to the Chinese one of Yüan, advocated the use of the Chinese language and styles of dress by the T'o-pa, and looked upon himself as Chinese and as the legitimate ruler of all China. To symbolize this, he moved the Wei capital in 493 from Ta-t'ung in the harsh, stormswept north to Loyang, in a kinder climate. Loyang had been China's capital in Chou days and again during the Later Han, and the tradition-minded Emperor no doubt sought to establish a link between those great dynasties and his own. But the move to the south cut the T'o-pa off from their sources of power. Their herds were worthless, this far from the steppe, for what was wealth to a noble living within the Great Wall and pasturing his herds without became an expensive liability to an absentee living at the imperial court in Loyang. The move thus produced a further dilution of T'o-pa strength and created dissension among the T'o-pa families who had all along resented the increasing Sinification of the dynasty.

Shortly after the move, the Emperor decided to complete the reconstitution of ancient China by sweeping away the independent government still ruling the south. The Liu Sung Dynasty had fallen in 479, after a career of noteworthy corruption and licentiousness, and a certain general named Hsiao Tao-ch'eng had founded the Southern Ch'i Dynasty, against which the T'o-pa now mounted an assault. The attack was fiercely resisted by the Southern Ch'i, who administered such a crushing defeat in 499 that the Wei Emperor is said to have died of mortification. He was given the posthumous title of Wei Wên Ti, and his son, Yüan K'o, became the seventh Wei Emperor.

During his reign the Southern Ch'i was split by an internal dynastic struggle. The T'o-pa took advantage of this to invade the south in 501 and annex much of the Southern Ch'i territory; the following year, a member of the imperial family named Hsiao Yen removed the Southern Ch'i Emperor, seized the throne himself, and proclaimed the start of the Liang Dynasty. (A troublesome name, since it had already been used by five phantom dynasties in Kansu between 313 and 439.) Aided by members of the former Southern Ch'i Dynasty, the T'o-pa made another all-out effort to conquer the south. The Liang Emperor held firm, and in 507 the T'o-pa were thrown back with heavy losses. This defeat touched off a crisis among the T'o-pa. The T'o-pa of the Great Wall region, appalled and disgruntled by the actions of their dandified rulers, went into revolt in an attempt to reassert the old tribal virtues. In 530, this led to an uprising that swept through Shansi to the capital and culminated in a massacre of the Sinified T'o-pa nobility by the fierce tribesmen of the frontier. Those who survived fled from Loyang and the dynasty disintegrated a few years later. In 534, a group of pro-Chinese T'o-pa nobles settled in the eastern city of Yeh, and for sixteen years an impotent T'o-pa Emperor ruled over what was called the Eastern Wei Dynasty. The tougher, steppe-oriented T'o-pa moved westward to the old capital city of Ch'ang-an in Shensi and established the Western Wei Dynasty, which lasted until 557. In that year the last shred of T'o-pa supremacy was ripped away, and power passed to others. The invaders had had a long and sometimes brilliant run, lasting more than a century and a half, but the lure of Chinese culture had proven fatal to them, and they were swallowed up by their enemies.

IV

One important development of the T'o-pa era was the firm and lasting establishment of Buddhism in China. The peaceful religion of the Buddha had developed in northern India about 500 B.C. Teaching the way of moderation, Buddha advocated the Noble Eightfold Path, a program for virtuous living that led to the goal of Nirvana, a breaking of the chain of existence and a cosmic merging with the all-encompassing universe. Within two centuries, Buddhism spread through India, and was carried to Southeast Asia by Indian merchants. At the same time, it began to spread overland into Central Asia, where it took root among the Yüeh-chih, those one-time nomads who had come over the Pamirs to settle in Bactria. A Chinese chronicle of 2 B.C. tells of a Buddhist missionary from the Yüeh-chih instructing a Chinese official in Buddhist doctrine. A less reliable story claims that Buddhist priests had reached China as early as 217 B.C., at which time they were clapped into prison as vagabonds by Ch'in Shih Huang Ti.

A probably apocryphal Han Dynasty account holds that in A.D. 64 the Emperor Ming dreamed that a golden figure ten feet high and bright as the sun flew into the imperial bedchamber and declared, "My religion will spread into this land." Conferring with his ministers about this perplexing dream, Ming Ti was told of a new western religion founded by a great spirit named Fo, whose envoy the dream figure certainly must have been. Accordingly, the Emperor sent envoys westward in search of Fo, and in the realm of the Yüeh-chih they encountered a pair of Buddhist priests, whose religion seemed to coincide with that of Fo. They were persuaded to enter China, and the procession entered Loyang soon after with Buddhist images and sacred books borne on the back of a handsome white horse. Whereupon Ming Ti decreed the construction of a Buddhist monastery just outside the west gate of the capital, calling it the Monastery of the White Horse. Whether or not there is any substance to the tale, it is certain that about A.D. 65 a Buddhist colony existed in what is now northern Kiangsu (near the mouth of the Yangtze) at the court of Ming Ti's brother, the King of Ch'u, and that the monastery of the story actually was built.

A Parthian prince whom the Chinese called An Shih-kao was the next important figure in Chinese Buddhism. He entered China to settle at Loyang between 148 and 170, and was active as a translator of Buddhist texts and a propagator of Buddhist tenets. In 166, the Han Emperor agreed to erect a Buddhist temple in the palace, but he tempered his enthusiasm by adding shrines for the legendary Yellow Emperor, Huang Ti, and for Lao-tzu, the legendary founder of the important Chinese religion of Taoism.

Buddhist missionaries from the west continued to enter China during the troubled times of the third century. Weary of political strife, disappointed by the traditional faiths of the country, the Chinese were ripe for conversion. The most devout of the Chinese Buddhists felt it incumbent upon them to make pilgrimages to the sacred places of Buddhism in India, and so began a long and remarkable series of overland treks that took the place of the earlier silk commerce in linking China with the west.

The first known Buddhist pilgrim left China in A.D. 259; by 790, when the movement lost its force, there had been 186 recorded pilgrimages to India. Only forty-two of the Chinese pilgrims reached India safely, carried out their studies, and returned to their native land. Their roads were the old silk routes, now neglected and dangerous. As in Han days, Tun-huang was the place where they left China behind; they journeyed some 300 miles out into the desert, then chose between the southern and the northern roads around the wasteland of the Tarim Basin. The southern route went via Khotan and Yarkand into India, the northern through the oases of Karashahr and Kucha to Kashgar. A pilgrim might travel 10,000 miles in his round trip, much or all of it on foot.

One of the most celebrated of the Buddhist pilgrims was Fa-hsien, who passed through Tun-huang in 399. At that time, as we learn from Fa-hsien's account, "the frontier is held by the military for a distance of 80 li from east to west, and 40 li from north to south"—but this was before the T'o-pa conquest of Kansu, so the soldiers must have been those of one of the petty tribal states that flourished then on the western border. Fa-hsien's account continues: "The Governor of Tun-huang, by name Li Hao, gave [us] all necessaries for crossing the desert of Gobi. In this desert there are a great many evil spirits and also hot winds; those who encounter them perish to a man. There are neither birds above nor beasts below. Gazing on all sides as far as the eye can reach in order to mark the track, no guidance is to be obtained save from the rotting bones of dead men, which point the way."[77]

The last watchtowers of the Great Wall vanished in the east. The pilgrims made their way across the haunted desert to Karashahr, thence to Khotan, and on into India after six years of travail, of which 259 days had been spent actually on the march, the rest in obtaining provisions and resting at oases along the route. Fa-hsien passed six years in India, from 405 to 411, collecting and copying the sacred texts of various Buddhist schools. His return voyage was made by sea; taking passage via Ceylon and Java, he landed at Shantung after a storm-tossed voyage said to have lasted 330 days, and finally reached Ch'ang-an in 414, with his books and relics miraculously still intact. Evidently he found the T'o-pa environment a chilly one, for by 416 he moved on to Nanking, the capital of the Eastern Chin Dynasty, and there compiled his famous memoir of his fifteen-year journey, graphically describing the places he had visited, the hardships he had suffered, and the legends he had heard.

T'o-pa enthusiasm for Buddhism blew hot and cold. The first Wei Emperors found the new religion useful, since it preached humility and peacefulness, and might further the docility of the conquered Chinese. As invaders, they had no loyalty to Confucianism, the quasi-religious philosophy that most Chinese professed, and in fact they preferred to push Confucianism aside as a

A seated Maitreya from Lung-mên.
*University Museum, University of
Pennsylvania*

possible seed of loyalist Chinese revolution. An early nomad Emperor declared, "We were born out of the marches. . . . Buddha, being a barbarian
god, is the one we should worship." But in 439 the Wei Emperor T'o-pa Tao
became converted to Taoism, a religion much infested with mysticism and
alchemy, and five years later he proclaimed it the official Chinese religion.
This led to a fierce persecution of the Chinese Buddhists in the following
year, which continued until his death in 452. Under his successors, Buddhism
was granted tolerance once more, and by about 500 it had become the most
powerful religious movement in both northern and southern China.

Pilgrim after pilgrim left Tun-huang for the western regions. That remote
outpost at the end of the Great Wall returned to an importance it had not
had since the mighty days of the Han. When Tun-huang fell into the hands
of the Wei Dynasty midway through the fifth century, the town was rebuilt
and fortified anew, and work was begun on an astonishing artistic effort: the
Caves of the Thousand Buddhas at Tun-huang. In a soft formation of con-
glomerate rock and clay twelve miles from the Tun-huang oasis, generations
of artisans hollowed out honeycomb grottoes which they filled with statues

of the Buddha. Some shrines had colossal Buddhas ninety feet high; others were tiny. Legions of Buddhist monks took up residence there. Today, in a cliff face a mile and a quarter long from north to south, there are 480 caves, which have been extensively explored by Aurel Stein and later archaeologists.

Two other important Buddhist sites also date from Wei Dynasty times. At Yün-kang, near the original Wei capital of Ta-t'ung, the Emperor permitted monks to excavate five caves in a mountain ridge and carve a statue of Buddha in each. The five Buddhas, which ranged in height from 46 to 54 feet, were carved about 460. Thirty-seven more shrines followed at Yün-kang; here, just within the Great Wall, the nomad rulers sponsored a towering artistic achievement, and Buddhist sculptors lovingly crafted devotional statues that combined techniques of Indian and classical Chinese sculpture in a strange and wonderful synthesis. The long-faced, slim-necked Buddhas of Yün-kang have an air of timeless tranquility that belies the troubled era in which they were carved.

When the Wei dynasty made its ill-advised southward move to the new capital at Loyang, more Buddhist shrines were carved in the sandstone hills overlooking the River I, at Lung-mên. From 495 on, the sculptors toiled at the "Dragon Gate" outside Loyang, and the caves there are a museum of changing styles, since the building of the shrines went on for several centuries, long after the T'o-pa monarchs had been driven from the land. The sculpture of the Wei era, as seen in the caves of Tun-huang, Yün-kang, and Lung-mên, stands as a strange and wonderful monument to a time of barbarian rule.

V

The splitting of the Wei Dynasty into eastern and western branches in 534 marked the end of T'o-pa power in China. At Yeh, a puppet T'o-pa ruler held the Eastern Wei throne under the control of Kao Huan, a Chinese who may have been of Hsien-pi descent. After a wobbly rule of sixteen years the powerless Emperor was pushed aside by a son of Kao Huan named Kao Huang, who founded a dynasty that he styled the Northern Ch'i. And in the west, at Ch'ang-an, another puppet T'o-pa Emperor reigned as monarch of the Western Wei under the domination of Yü-wen T'ai, a man of Shansi who traced his descent from the Hsiung-nu. The Western Wei was permitted to survive from 535 to 557, when Yü-wen T'ai died. As had happened so often, the heirs of the man who had been content to manipulate a puppet Emperor chose to take the throne for themselves. Yü-wen T'ai's son, Yü-wen Chüo, thrust the Western Wei Emperor aside and proclaimed the advent of the Northern Chou Dynasty in 557. He was promptly put to death by his uncle, Yü-wen Hu, who put the second son of Yü-wen T'ai on the throne, but found it necessary to assassinate him in 560. A third brother became Emperor, bided his time until 567, and put the murderous regent Yü-wen Hu to death in this manner, as described in the *Chinese Biographical Dictionary of* H. A. Giles:

"At length, his yoke becoming intolerable, the young Emperor summoned him [Yü-wen Hu], and asked him to reprove the Empress Dowager for her habits of drinking, producing at the same time some wine as proof of her delinquencies. This Yü-wen Hu at once proceeded to do; and while he was occupied in lecturing her Majesty, the Emperor suddenly hit him a heavy blow from behind with a jade sceptre and felled him to the ground. His body was carried out and decapitated, and his sons were put to death."[78]

These Northern Chou Emperors were plainly nothing but murderous rogues, and their contemporaries of the Northern Ch'i were no better. Their accomplishments were few. The Northern Chou Emperors concerned themselves with returning to the customs of their nomad forebears, giving up their Chinese names for barbarian ones, restoring Hsien-pi and T'o-pa customs and tribal structure, and repudiating the use of the Chinese language. This attempt to step two centuries into the past was no more successful among the Northern Chou than it has been elsewhere in history. The Northern Chou state tumbled swiftly into chaos. In the east, the Northern Ch'i, being basically a Chinese dynasty, occupied itself after the Chinese manner by building ramparts. It strengthened the Wei wall in Shansi, that north–south loop that now warded off the Northern Chou. And in 555, the Northern Ch'i began building a new wall 300 miles long, running from Peking to the old T'o-pa capital at Ta-t'ung. Supposedly, 1,800,000 men were assigned to the labor battalions that built this wall, an unlikely figure in view of the chaotic political situation that prevailed. However, the architects of the Northern Ch'i built well; parts of their Great Wall north of Peking were incorporated into the refurbished Long Rampart of the Ming Dynasty nine centuries later, and still exist, probably the oldest sections now extant of the eastern limb of the Great Wall.

While rascals ruled briefly in the north, dynasties almost as ephemeral flitted by in the south. The Liang, which had swept away the Southern Ch'i Dynasty in 502, had watched with quiet pleasure as its bitter northern enemy, the Wei, shattered in 534. The Liang Emperor, who bore the familiar name of Wu Ti, devoted himself to literature and to Buddhism, and paid little heed to political matters once the T'o-pa threat was removed. After the downfall of the Wei, a northern general named Hou Ching began to negotiate with the Liang, with the thought of setting up a northern state under his own control. The ruler of the Northern Ch'i state, troubled by Hou Ching's plans, warned the Liang Emperor to have nothing to do with him. While Liang hesitated, Hou Ching marched south in 548, and, aided by a treacherous Liang prince, invaded the southern capital in 549 and executed Liang Wu Ti after a reign of 47 years. The customary routine followed: Hou Ching put his Liang puppet on the throne for a short while, deposed him in less than two years, and became Emperor himself.

This event was notable for just one reason. Hou Ching was a T'o-pa, and it marked the first time that a northern barbarian had come into possession of the throne of southern China. The far-off Great Wall looked more futile than ever, now that a T'o-pa general wore imperial yellow in Nanking. But Hou Ching's backing melted away, and in 552 the Chinese drove him out. The Liang Dynasty returned, at least in name, but by 557 it was overthrown by a general named Ch'ên Pa-hsien, who founded the Ch'ên Dynasty.

By this time, much of southern China had fallen into the hands of the new Northern Chou state, and the process of conquest continued steadily. A Northern Chou army captured the territory around the modern Hankow, and a feudal state subject to Northern Chou was set up there, under a Northern Chou prince who called his line Later Liang—the second of the three Chinese dynasties to bear that designation. The feeble Ch'ên Dynasty was left with nothing more than the lower Yangtze Valley.

Beyond the Great Wall, still another nomad tribe was coming to power in the Mongolian steppe, that spawning ground of conquerors. The Juan-juan, who had menaced northern China on and off since about 403, were overthrown by a subject tribe in 551, and were driven out of Asia, migrating eventually across the Urals in 558 and terrorizing the Danube regions seven years later. The subject tribe that touched off this rebellion and sent nomads spinning into Europe was the T'u-chüeh, as they were known in Chinese. The Juan-juan called them the Türküt. Herewith the Turks make their first appearance in recorded history.

The T'u-chüeh, once their Juan-juan masters were in flight, set about the task of welding together an empire of their own. Within a decade and a half they had assembled a vast domain covering all northern Asia, embracing Mongolia, Turkestan, and Afghanistan. Ambassadors of the T'u-chüeh appeared at the courts of Byzantium and Persia, and were received with trepidation by the Northern Chou Emperor at Ch'ang-an. He was hardly in a position to snub this new colossus of the north, and the Son of Heaven, himself not too many generations descended from the steppe, took on a pose of humility when the Turkish envoys swaggered into his realm.

The T'u-chüeh promised to help the Northern Chou conquer their eastern rivals, the Northern Ch'i. Armed mainly with this assurance, the Northern Chou opened an offensive against the Northern Ch'i in 563, but the Turkish reinforcements failed to materialize, and Chou suffered defeat. Soon afterward, the T'u-chüeh raided the eastern state separately, while at the same time inroads were made on Ch'i by the forces of the Ch'ên Dynasty in the south. Harried on all sides, the Northern Ch'i state fell before a Chou attack in 577. Once more, northern China had a single master.

Not, however, a very powerful one. The Northern Chou Emperor ruled from Shantung to Kansu, but he ruled by grace of the T'u-chüeh, and it seemed to be only a matter of time before the Turks added China to their mushrooming empire. For once, the inevitable failed to occur. Unexpectedly, China cast off the barbarian yoke that had oppressed it for three centuries. The Turks were held back. Once again the Great Wall became a meaningful boundary, penning back the barbarian tide and delineating the frontier of a resurgent China.

China's rebirth began in that abode of vipers, the court of Northern Chou. The family of Yü-wen still held the throne there. Yü-wen Yung, he who had clubbed his treacherous uncle down with a jade sceptre, died in 578, a year after his conquest of Northern Ch'i. He was succeeded by his son, a worthless and incapable ruler, who turned the day-by-day responsibility of government over to one Yang Chien, his chief minister.

Yang Chien was Chinese, claiming descent from a Han Dynasty philosopher named Yang Chên, called the Confucius of the West. By marriage he was linked to the Huns; his son married a girl of the old Hsiung-nu royal family, and his daughter was the bride of the Northern Chou Emperor Hsüan, who had T'o-pa blood. When Hsüan Ti died in 580, Yang Chien awarded himself the title of Grand Chancellor. The next year he slew the boy ruler, Ching Ti, along with fifty-nine princes of the blood, and announced himself to be the first Emperor of the Sui Dynasty, with the imperial title of Wên Ti.

As China went through the vulnerability of a dynastic change, it would have been an auspicious moment for the T'u-chüeh to come pouring across the Great Wall and conquer. But the T'u-chüeh were preoccupied by internal strife. Their unwieldy empire, too hastily joined, broke in half in 582 when a powerful tribal leader named Tardu made himself khan, or ruler, of the western Turks. Before the T'u-chüeh could recover from their split, Yang Chien, as Sui Wên Ti, had an unbreakable grip on China. In the grand manner of such earlier empire builders as Ch'in Shih Huang Ti and Liu Pang, the new Emperor established a strong central government and made his writ law in every part of China. With his control of the north secure, Yang Chien marched south in 587 and his army engulfed the feudal state of the Later Liang; the following year he crossed the Yangtze and invaded the capital of the Ch'ên Emperor, who offered no resistance whatever. By 589, Yang Chien ruled over much the same vast empire that had first been put together by Ch'in Shih Huang Ti.

By cunning manipulations he managed to keep the two factions of the T'u-chüeh at odds. But by 585 the khan of the western Turks, the violent, turbulent Tardu, whom Yang Chien had encouraged in his rebellion against the eastern branch of the Turks, suddenly became altogether too dangerous and turned against China. Yang Chien was able to keep the Turks out of China, but he lost no time in strengthening the Great Wall. He commanded that the Wall be repaired—the sixth time since Han Wu Ti's day that a full-scale reconstruction had been ordered—and also had the Wall extended. Yang Chien's addition to the Great Wall cut diagonally across the loop of the Yellow River, leaving the Ordos mostly in Turkish possession, and ran some two hundred miles west of the river. Thirty thousand men were assigned to this task in 585, and during the remaining years of Yang Chien's reign there was constant work on the northern fortifications. That and a shrewd policy of spurring the rivalries of the different Turkish factions held the barbarians at bay. Tardu defeated the eastern Turks in 601 and threatened the Sui Dynasty's western capital at Ch'ang-an, but he fell from power two years later and the Turks underwent further division that reduced their power. The Chinese formed an alliance with the eastern Turks and another with the westernmost branch; the central faction that had arisen in 603, seeing itself outflanked, chose to make peace with China rather than to follow Tardu's wild course.

There was strife within the Chinese imperial family as well. Yang Chien quarreled with his eldest son, the heir apparent, and set him aside in favor of his younger brother Kuang. Kuang immediately slew his deposed brother to forestall his reinstatement. In 604 Yang Chien himself died quite suddenly, perhaps also a victim of Kuang's ambition. One story has it that the imperial prince was seen thrusting a dagger into the heart of a clay image on which Yang Chien's name had been written. Others hint darkly of poison.

The new Emperor styled himself Yang Ti. Short of Ch'in Shih Huang Ti, he has been the most vigorously damned of all China's Emperors, and for many of the same reasons. Like the First Emperor, Yang Ti lived in great splendor; like him, he channeled the resources of a newly united empire into massive public works projects; like him, he failed to create a lasting dynasty. That last similarity is perhaps the most cogent reason for the bad reputation Yang Ti has earned. Just as the historians of Han blackened the name of Ch'in Shih Huang Ti, so did the historians of T'ang limn Yang Ti in villainous guise.

II

Villain or hero, Yang Ti accomplished much. He strengthened the internal administration of the empire, ended the persecution of the Buddhists that had sprung up again in 574, and defended the borders successfully against the barbarians. He overhauled the sketchy system of water transport that linked the Huang Ho and the Yangtze, turning it into the famous Grand Canal. And had the Great Wall not already existed, Yang Ti would certainly have conceived it. As it was, he had to be content with rebuilding it.

Those were his public achievements. For his own pleasure, he built a new capital at Yangchow, the inland port near the mouth of the Yangtze, though he had two other capitals in the north that a more modest ruler might have found sufficient. Ch'ang-an, which had been his father's capital, may have had too many sinister memories for Yang Ti, so he lent his favor to the eastern capital at Loyang. He built an immense palace there on the shores of an artificial lake in which rose three islands a hundred feet high. Sixteen villas for his sixteen favorite wives lined the banks of the river that fed the artificial lake. A park some seventy miles around surrounded the entire imperial compound. Along the road from Ch'ang-an to Loyang, Yang Ti constructed forty palaces so that he might rest in comfort while traveling from one northern capital to the other. When the southern capital was built, Yang Ti journeyed there for the first time at the head of a flotilla of "dragon-boats" that formed a line of vessels nearly a hundred miles in length along the Yangtze.

He understood the ways of opulence. When the leaves fell in the imperial park at autumn time, Yang Ti had them replaced by artificial ones of silk. In the imperial lake there drifted artificial lotus flowers, also silken. To provide down for his cushions and to decorate the gowns of the royal concubines, thousands of birds were slain, supposedly so many that whole provinces of China were stripped of their winged population for generations.

The people groaned under Yang Ti's extravagances, but they groaned even more beneath the lashes of his overseers. The Grand Canal was begun in the reign of Yang Chien, who recognized the need for an inland waterway that would transport food from the fertile south to the politically supreme north. An existing small canal linking the Yangtze to the Huai River was enlarged to a width of forty paces, with roads constructed along both banks and planted with elms and willows. In 605, Yang Ti added a canal from the Yellow River to the Huai, and three years later constructed another from the Yellow River to the Peking area, in order to supply his troops with grain during an attempted (and disastrous) invasion of Korea. By 610 the first Grand Canal of China was complete. It began in Ch'ang-an, ran eastward through Loyang, trending southeast toward the third capital at Yangchow, and continued southward to Hangchow. Thus the rich rice lands of the Yangtze delta were linked by water to the important capital cities of the north, and a steady flow of tribute, in the form of food, was assured. The armies defending the northern border along the Great Wall now could count on full granaries at all times.

This monument to Yang Ti's political shrewdness and impulse toward grandeur could only have been constructed at a time of powerful central authority. An anonymous book of the Sui period, the *K'ai Ho Chi*, or *Record of the Opening of the Canal*, translates the effort into terms of manpower. Some 5,500,000 workers were conscripted for the building of the Grand Canal, in some areas including every commoner between the ages of fifteen and fifty. They worked under the supervision of 50,000 overseers. Every fifth family of the land was compelled to contribute one member to aid in the supply and preparation of food for the workers. Those who resisted the conscription were "punished by flogging and neck-weights." Over two million men were said to have been "lost," a figure that probably includes those who fled from the labor gangs as well as those who died on the job. The value of the Grand

Canal became evident during the T'ang Dynasty of the following century; millions of tons of rice were transported northward each year by about 735, and by the end of the eighth century nine-tenths of the cost of government was being met by the "taxes" of rice produced by the people of the lower Yangtze.

Yang Ti put his northern subjects to work on the Great Wall while the southern ones slaved on the Grand Canal. In 607 and 608 he added a new section of Wall east of the upper loop of the Huang Ho, and completed the extension that his father had begun west of the river. A contemporary report says that a million men worked on the Wall for ten days in the summer of 607, and that half of them died—though here again the runaways may have been included with the casualties.

The second Sui Emperor was building for the centuries ahead. He gave China a canal system it desperately needed, and he restored the Great Wall to a condition of strength from the sea to the western curve of the Huang Ho, keeping the barbarians safely in check. These were great deeds; but they put an unbearable strain on the people compelled to take part in their performance. Yang Ti lost the allegiance of his empire. The cruelty and personal extravagance of the Sui regime led to dissension and the threat of revolution. Ignoring the portents, Yang Ti launched one more bold project and at last overreached himself. In 614, he attempted to invade Korea for the fourth time, and for the fourth time was thrown back with staggering losses.

The eastern Turks, quiescent too long, chose this time to attack. Yang Ti met their thrust with an army weakened by the Korean fiasco, and found himself trapped at Yenmên in Shansi. For a full month in 615 the Turkish khan held the Emperor bottled up. Revolution broke out the moment Yang Ti's contact with the empire was severed by the Turkish siege. With the Emperor penned against the Great Wall, insurrections began in many parts of China, and in the anarchy that ensued the Sui Dynasty was swept to destruction after thirty-six years of supremacy. A Chinese scholar writing ten centuries later commented that Yang Ti had "shortened the life of his dynasty by a number of years, but benefited posterity unto ten thousand generations. He ruled without benevolence, but his rule is to be credited with enduring accomplishments."[79]

III

Ch'in Shih Huang Ti, a hated ruler, had built the Great Wall and had left a heritage of chaos, out of which emerged the powerful Han Dynasty that led China to greatness. Yang Ti, nearly as unpopular as the First Emperor, had built the Grand Canal and had yielded to anarchy, out of which arose another splendid and enduring dynasty, the T'ang. The irony of the T'ang conquest is that the family that took China to the most brilliant three centuries of its history was partly of Turkish descent. The Great Wall still existed, stronger than ever. The new dynasty was indubitably Chinese in custom, language, and tradition. Yet not too many generations behind the magnificence of the T'ang lay the heritage of the horsemen of the steppe.

Their rise began with Yang Ti's embarrassment at Yenmên. The story goes that the besieged Sui Emperor was saved only by a trick: the dowager queen of the T'u-chüeh, a Chinese princess by birth, put an end to the siege by spreading a false rumor among her people that the Uighurs, outer barbarians of the north, were attacking Turkish land. The T'u-chüeh prepared to withdraw. At the same time, a meager Chinese army led by a sixteen-year-old officer named Li Shih-min was coming to the Emperor's rescue, and by dint of loud beating of drums and wild waving of banners managed to look like an imposing force, thus hastening the Turkish retreat.

Yang Ti was free, but disorder was general, and no less than seven rival Emperors had proclaimed themselves in various parts of the country. Yang Ti's strength evidently deserted him. Instead of meeting the challenge of the insurrectionists, he returned to his southern capital at Yangchow and shut himself in his magnificent palace, living in debauchery while he awaited the end. In the north, at Ch'ang-an, a new family raised its banner in 617. It was headed by Li Yüan, a nobleman who was related to Yang Ti but who also had Turkish ancestry. The real power of the new faction was in the hands of his son, Li Shih-min, the youthful soldier who had gone to the defense of Yang Ti at the siege of Yenmên two years before.

The forces of Li Yüan took Ch'ang-an in 617. The following April, Yang Ti was assassinated in his Yangchow palace by Yü-wen Hua-chi, a scion of the bloodthirsty family that once had called itself the Northern Chou Dynasty. In the familiar tradition, Li Yüan set up a puppet Emperor of the Sui house, a grandson of Yang Chien, who speedily abdicated in Li Yüan's favor. In the summer of 618 Li Yüan proclaimed the founding of the T'ang Dynasty.

His reign was short, merely a prelude for that of his son. Li Yüan built on the foundations of the Sui, restoring the authority of the central government by 623. The bureaucracy was reformed and some of the great estates were broken up. Li Yüan's program of reform had immediate results; the resilient Chinese economy began to recover with unusual speed from the strains placed upon it during Yang Ti's reign and the anarchy that had followed. In 626, Li Yüan abdicated in favor of his son, Li Shih-min, who had cleared a path to the throne by assassinating two of his brothers.

The new Emperor, who is known to history as T'ai Tsung, may well have been the most able man ever to hold the Chinese throne. His reign of twenty-three years was a time of unparalleled brilliance and glory. Internal rebellion was suppressed and enemies beyond the Great Wall were crushed. The harsh Sui laws gave way to a gentler, more moderate penal code. Governing through an expanded civil service chosen once more by competitive examination, T'ai Tsung and his successors achieved an unusual degree of control over their far-flung empire. A T'ang innovation was the system of post stations at ten-mile intervals along every major road and waterway radiating from the capital at Ch'ang-an. These post stations served as hostelries for government officials as they traveled on tours of inspection through the provinces, making possible frequent and intensive supervision even in the most remote places.

T'ai Tsung's attitude toward the Great Wall was new in Chinese history too. Walls, he said, promoted a false sense of security. The proper strategy was to carry the war to the enemy. When a general named Li Chi led a successful campaign against the Turks and brought them to heel, T'ai Tsung declared, "You are a more efficient Great Wall than that built by Yang Ti." He put an end to the regular inspection and repair of the Great Wall that had been so important to Yang Ti. Yet even for T'ai Tsung the Wall retained its subtler purpose, that of confining the Chinese and keeping valuable manpower from straying into nomad ways. T'ai Tsung ordered that no Chinese was to cross the Great Wall and leave the country without official permission. In 629, a young Chinese Buddhist priest named Hsüan-tsang applied for such permission in order to make the traditional pilgrimage to the shrines of India, but his requests were pigeonholed by T'ang bureaucrats and he received no answer. Finally, Hsüan-tsang slipped through the Wall at night, after being fired upon by the archers on guard, and made his way to India by the northern route. He traveled for sixteen years, visiting every part of India and such adjoining points as Nepal and Ceylon, and returned to China in 645 after a journey of some 20,000 miles. Though he had been compelled to leave secretly, Hsüan-tsang was welcomed as the celebrity he had now become; an official party met him outside the Great Wall and conducted him to T'ai Tsung, who greeted him with respect and requested him to write an account of his travels. Hsüan-tsang's memoirs, a masterpiece of travel literature, inspired many other Chinese to venture abroad, and soon the prohibition against foreign travel was lifted and Chinese adventurers were en route to such unlikely parts of the world as Syria and Africa.

T'ai Tsung dealt decisively with the barbarians north of the Great Wall. After resisting Turkish thrusts early in his reign, he carried the war into the steppe in 630, trouncing the eastern Turks soundly and compelling them to acknowledge him as their khan. Until 682, the Turkish chieftains acknowledged the supremacy of the Emperor at Ch'ang-an. A Turkish inscription of the year 732, found in 1889 on the eastern bank of the Orkhon River some thirty miles from the ruins of the ancient capital of the T'u-chüeh, states that "the sons of nobles became slaves of the Chinese people, and their pure daughters serfs. The Turkish nobles abandoned their Turkish titles, and, receiving Chinese titles of dignitaries in China, submitted to the Chinese khan, and for fifty years gave him their service and their strength."[80]

T'ai Tsung swept a path through the western Turks between 641 and 648, opening the way for renewed Chinese travel to India and Persia. A new and possibly dangerous foe had meanwhile appeared in the mountainous western land of Tibet, where nomadic tribesmen had been consolidated into an aggressive nation under the first Tibetan king, Sron-bcan-sgan-po. By way of announcing his arrival in Asian politics, the Tibetan monarch asked T'ai Tsung for the hand of a Chinese princess in marriage. This was refused, and the Tibetans invaded China. T'ai Tsung turned the invaders back in 641, then sent the Princess Wên-ch'êng to Tibet as Sron-bcan-sgan-po's bride, insuring peace in that quarter.

The dream of Korean conquest, which had been the undoing of Yang Ti, seems to have plagued T'ai Tsung as well. In 645, a Chinese army was massacred near Pyŏng-yang, and, stung by his only important defeat, T'ai Tsung did not press the attack again before his death in 649. Under his son and successor, Kao Tsung, who ruled until 683, Korea finally came under Chinese sway.

Kao Tsung's reign was a time of gathering hostility beyond China's borders. Tibet, in the youth of its nationhood, pressed northward on China in the vicinity of the Tarim Basin, and in 678 inflicted a severe defeat on a Chinese army. Through persevering diplomacy, the Chinese managed to divide the Tibetans and to break up their realm in 699, but they remained a threat until then. The Turks, too, gathered power in the late seventh century, after a defeat in 657 that sent Turkish hordes fleeing across Russia into Hungary.

The grandeur of the early T'ang gradually gave way toward the end of Kao Tsung's rule. Indeed, the dynasty suffered a brief collapse that paralleled in some ways Empress Lü's usurpation of power in the time of the Han. Kao Tsung had raised his favorite concubine to high position as the Empress Wu.

This remarkable woman had joined the harem of T'ai Tsung in 637, at the age of twelve. Upon that Emperor's death twelve years later she had retired into a Buddhist nunnery, but returned to the court in the reign of his son Kao Tsung.

She displaced Kao Tsung's first Empress by strangling her own baby and blaming the crime on the Emperor's consort. The Empress was deposed in 655, but when the new Empress Wu found that Kao Tsung still thought fondly of her predecessor, she had her fallen rival's hands and feet cut off. Kao Tsung, awed by his ferocious mate, allowed her an ever greater share of the imperial responsibilities; in 674 she awarded herself the title of the Divine Empress, and the following year Kao Tsung nearly resolved to abdicate in her favor. He was little more than a puppet from then till his death in 683. Afterward, she ruled through nominal monarchs for five years; in 688, two princes of the Li family rebelled against her, which provided her with a pretext for slaying most of the royal clan. In 690, she deposed the current puppet Emperor and took the throne herself—the only time in Chinese history that a woman has been supreme ruler. To mark her ascendancy she announced the end of the T'ang Dynasty, and proclaimed the initiation of a new dynasty which she styled Chou.

This meant little enough to the peasants tilling the fields, but it stunned the educated men, to whom the dynastic line was the thread that gave the nation its historical continuity. The venomous Empress had further shocks in store. She moved the capital from Ch'ang-an to Loyang, cutting off the power base of the T'ang nobility. For much the same reason she embraced Buddhism enthusiastically, attempting to make it the state religion. Quietly, the T'ang nobility conspired against her, and in 705, when the eighty-year-old Empress lay ill, she was forced to abdicate in favor of Li Hsien, Kao Tsung's first successor, who had been deposed by her twenty years before. The arrogant old lady—who had refused to let anyone say that she was as fair as a lily or a rose, insisting that they declare that the lily or the rose was as fair as her Majesty—went into retirement.

The coup restored the T'ang line, but the restored Emperor was dominated by his own consort, the Empress Wei, who at length poisoned him in 710 and tried to seize the throne. The late Emperor's nephew, Li Lung-chi, led the opposition; the Empress Wei and her supporters were slain, and the father of Li Lung-chi became Emperor. (He had ruled before, from 684 to 690, as the puppet of Empress Wu.) Within two years, he abdicated in favor of Li Lung-chi, who was known during his reign as Hsüan Tsung ("Mysterious Ancestor") and also as Ming Huang ("Enlightened Emperor"). The dynastic crisis was over. Hsüan Tsung's rule of more than half a century saw a return to the earlier T'ang glory.

IV

Culturally, the T'ang epoch was a glittering one, and never more so than in the reign of Hsüan Tsung. Ch'ang-an, the capital, became a cosmopolitan center for travelers from many lands. In that magnificent city, which in T'ang days occupied a rectangle of thirty square miles and had a population of more

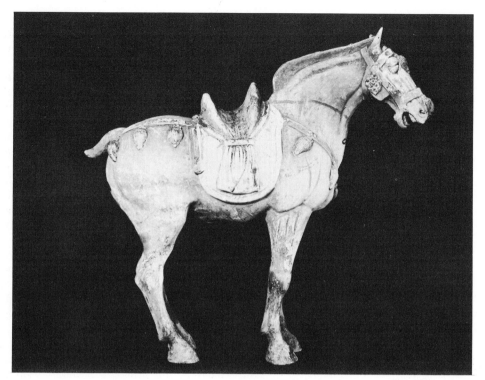

A magnificent T'ang horse of unglazed pottery.   *University Museum,*
University of Pennsylvania

than a million, there could be found Arabs, Persians, and Syrians, Koreans and Japanese, Tibetans and Khotanese. The collapse of the Persian Sassanid Dynasty under Arab attack in 674 had brought a flood of Persian refugees to China, and with them many new techniques of art. Ambassadors from India and Byzantium opened trade routes from China to the west. The powerful new empire of the Arabs sent merchants to trade in the South China ports, and by the ninth century hundreds of thousands of Moslems had taken up permanent residence in such cities as Canton and Hangchow. The multitude of foreigners transformed Chinese culture, making it a blend of all that was novel and attractive from India westward to the fringes of barbarian-dominated Europe. While the western world labored through the Dark Ages, T'ang China emitted blinding light.

It was a golden age of art and poetry. Such T'ang poets as Li Po (701–762) and Po Chü-i (772–846) made indelible literary contributions. Porcelain, now fully developed for the first time, came into glorious perfection. T'ang craftsmen modeled in porcelain the fierce, snorting horses that must have been of the blood-sweating Ferghana line, and produced the sumptuous and shining vases in glowing greens and oranges that made T'ang kilns famous from India to Cairo. A T'ang poet tells how the potters of his day "despoiled the thousand peaks of their colors." The caliphs of Baghdad were eager customers for T'ang export ware. Painters, too, achieved wonders, and many of the strange, violently colored T'ang paintings have survived to this day for our present delight.

The T'ang period gave birth to printing, centuries before Gutenberg. Movable type was impractical with a written language that required a font of thousands of characters; the Chinese carved wooden blocks as the "plates" for their books. The process was first used in the early seventh century; by 770 it had spread to Japan, where an Empress used it to produce a million-copy edition of a Buddhist charm. The oldest surviving Chinese book is a Buddhist text dating from 868, which Aurel Stein found in a cave at Tun-huang.

Another T'ang innovation was shorthand. An Arab work of the tenth century, the *Index of the Sciences* of al-Warraq of Baghdad, tells this story concerning the ninth-century Arab physician and alchemist, Rhazes, who said:

"A Chinese scholar came to my house, and remained in the town [probably Baghdad] about a year. In five months he learnt to speak and write Arabic, attaining indeed eloquence in speech and calligraphy in writing. When he decided to return to his country, he said to me a month or so beforehand, 'I am about to leave. I would be very glad if someone would dictate to me the sixteen books of Galen before I go.' I told him that he had not sufficient time to copy more than a small part of it, but he said, 'I beg you to give me all your time until I go, and to dictate to me as rapidly as possible. You will see that I shall write faster than you can dictate.' So together with one of my students we read Galen to him as fast as we could, but he wrote still faster. We did not believe that he was getting it correctly until we made a collation and found it exact throughout. I asked him how this could be, and he said, 'We have in our country a way of writing which we call shorthand, and this is what you see. When we wish to write very fast we use this style, and then afterwards transcribe it into the ordinary characters at will.' But he added that an intelligent man who learns quickly cannot master this script in under twenty years."[81]

The concept of fingerprinting also has a T'ang pedigree. The thirteenth-century Arab historian Rashid-ud-din wrote that in China, "when any contract is entered into," it was usual "for the outline of the fingers of the parties to be traced upon the document. For experience shows that no two individuals have fingers precisely alike."[82] The practice was ancient in Rashid-ud-din's day, evidently, for three documents of the T'ang era, dated 782 and 786, bear fingerprints and a notation to the effect that "prints of the fingers have been put on as a distinctive mark."

V

T'ang magnificence reached its peak about 750, late in the long reign of Hsüan Tsung. When the collapse came, it was with terrifying suddenness. The Emperor had surrounded himself with a brilliant court of poets, musicians, and scholars, spending his days in revelry and his nights in the arms of the famous concubine Yang Kuei-fei, while enemies gathered beyond the Chinese borders. The Uighurs, fiercest of the Turkish tribes, conquered Mongolia in 745 and once more presented a united and hostile front along China's weakest section of the Great Wall, the Ordos loop. To the east, in what is now called Manchuria, a nomad tribe called the Khitan was moving southward along the Liao River, and in 751 defeated the foreign-born Chinese general An Lu-shan west of that river in Jehol.

In the west, the Arabs were eying the Chinese subject states of Ferghana, Tashkent, Bokhara, and Samarkand. A prince of Tashkent invited the Arabs to free the land west of the Pamirs from Chinese domination, and the Battle of the Talas River in 751 saw the annihilation of 50,000 Chinese soldiers by Arabs. The whole Turkestan region fell into Arab control, and Islam replaced Buddhism as the religion of this key area, China's sole link to the western world. Tibet, strong once more, entered into negotiations with the Arabs to form an anti-Chinese alliance. The Korean-born general Kao Hsien-chih made an epic march across the Pamirs in 747 to break up this Arab-Tibetan coalition, but it was the last important T'ang victory; four years later he was the defeated general at the Talas River, the decisive battle that cracked the T'ang military machine.

The outlying territories of the empire broke away: first the Thai states in the south, then Korea. And while Tibetan, Arab, Uighur, Khitan, Korean, and Thai all bit into the empire from its borders, revolt struck at its heart. In 755 General An Lu-shan, a man of partly Turkish origin, rose against the Emperor and marched on Ch'ang-an with 200,000 men. The aged Hsüan Tsung fled into Szechuan, after seeing the seductive concubine Yang Kuei-fei strangled before his eyes. He abdicated in 756, giving the throne to his son Li Ting. The new Emperor, calling himself Su Tsung, retreated into Shensi and then crossed the Great Wall into Turkish territory, where he was somehow able to enlist the aid of Arab and Uighur regiments. Inspired Chinese generalship carried these foreign troops onward to Ch'ang-an, and in a great battle in 757 An Lu-shan was slain and Su Tsung restored to his empire.

But the dynasty had received its mortal wound, and only its dogged vitality kept it writhing in uncertain life for another century and a half. Su Tsung's empire was not that which his father had known. Turkish armies roamed China; An Lu-shan and his generals had been more Turkish than Chinese by descent and orientation, while the Uighur soldiers who saved the T'ang Emperor were nothing but Turks. The Uighurs, having whipped the rebels, now turned on the city of Loyang and sacked it, forcing Su Tsung to buy them off with 10,000 rolls of silk and the promise of an annual tribute of 20,000 rolls more. Never in the six years of his reign did Su Tsung have his barbarian allies under full control.

When the Emperor died in 762, the Uighur khan attempted to make himself ruler over China. While he advanced from the north, Tibetan armies entered China from the west, captured Ch'ang-an, and burned the city. The Tibetan incursion led the Uighurs to change their plans; they struck an alliance with the eighth T'ang Emperor, Li Yü, and helped him drive the Tibetans out. China became virtually a protectorate of the Uighurs. Nomad chieftains thronged the Chinese cities, demanding that they be maintained at government expense, and compelling the Chinese to buy horses from them at exorbitant prices. The Chinese, who had little use for the Uighur steeds, paid for them with bales of fine silk.

The cycle ground onward toward its obvious climax. One weak Emperor followed another. Eunuchs and Empresses vied for power at the court, while such feeble-minded Emperors as Li Hêng and Li Shên met their deaths through drinking poisonous concoctions fondly hoped to be elixirs of immortality. With Korea, Turkestan, Manchuria, and the southern provinces lopped away, China shrank back toward its pre-T'ang scope. In time, the domineering Uighurs broke up through that plague of the steppe, tribal rivalry, but other Turks, the Sha-t'o, replaced them as overlords of China. In eastern China, a series of revolts occurred after 860, led by a Shantung merchant, Huang Ch'ao. He captured Ch'ang-an in 880, putting the eighteenth T'ang Emperor, Li Yen, to flight and proclaiming a dynasty of his own; but three years later Sha-t'o troops captured and slew him, putting the puppet Emperor back on the throne.

Li Yen was succeeded in 888 by the clever and ambitious Li Chieh, who sought· some way of driving the Uighur masters out and restoring Chinese sovereignty. His first task, though, was to get rid of the clique of eunuchs who had taken so much of the imperial power into their own hands. In this he had little success. His reign was complicated by rivalry between his Sha-t'o protector, Li K'o-yung, and a Chinese rebel named Chu Ch'üan-chung, who had inherited the supporters of Huang Ch'ao. In 890, these two began civil war, Chu Ch'üan-chung based in the eastern plains and his rival in Shansi. The governors of the western province of Szechuan and the southeastern one of Chekiang took the opportunity to secede and name themselves as Emperors of new dynasties.

The T'ang Emperor backed Li K'o-yung, having no other choice. But he was forced to flee from the capital in 896. Soon after, he fell into the hands of Chu Ch'üan-chung, who slaughtered the entire court, sparing only the Emperor himself. Since Ch'ang-an had been sacked once more during the uprisings, the captive Emperor was taken to Loyang, where in 904 Chu found an excuse for putting him to death.

The Emperor's son, Li Chu, became the twentieth (and last) T'ang Emperor. The dynasty's long agony ended in 906, when Chu Ch'üan-chung forced Li Chu to abdicate. The rebel Chu now became the Emperor Chu Wen, of the Later Liang Dynasty. China was about to enter a new era of chaos, which its historians came to call the Five Dynasties period; before order could be restored, six decades later, the northern provinces lay under barbarian domination. The Great Wall would not be an instrument of Chinese policy again for almost four hundred years.

Eleven. Divided China

The tone of the new era is best captured by a résumé of the career of one Fêng Tao (881–954), a bureaucrat born in eastern China. He entered the service of a nobleman called the Prince of Chin in Shansi, during the Later Liang Dynasty. When the Prince of Chin proclaimed himself first Emperor of the Later T'ang Dynasty in 923, Fêng Tao received the post of Secretary of the Board of Revenue. During the reign of the second Later T'ang Emperor, a rebel leader named Ts'ung Ko captured the capital, whereupon Fêng Tao hastened to take service with him. Shortly afterward, Ts'ung Ko was crushed by the man who in 936 founded the Later Chin Dynasty, and the flexible Fêng Tao transferred his allegiance to the new monarch. In time, the Khitan of Manchuria knocked down the Later Chin, and Fêng Tao presented himself at the court of the Khitan sovereign, saying that he had "no home, no army, and very little brains"; he was named Grand Tutor to the Heir Apparent. But when the Later Han Dynasty was established in 947, Fêng Tao left his nomad patrons to enter Chinese service once more. Four years later, the Later Han succumbed to the forces of the Later Chou, and . . . yes, Fêng Tao found a niche in the Later Chou civil service. All told he served ten sovereigns of four Chinese and one nomad dynasties, within a span of thirty years.

The political history of this time of disturbance does not call for detailed analysis. Not only were there five dynasties in the north, but there were ten more in the south, which, however, were never recognized as "official" by Chinese historians. One such historian, Ou-yang Hsiu (1007–1072) began his account of the Five Dynasties period with the word, "Alas!", and that perhaps sums it up neatly.

The family of the bandit Chu Ch'üan-chung set the capital of their dynasty, the Later Liang, at Kaifeng in 907. Meanwhile the Sha-t'o general, Li K'o-yung, maintained an opposition in the west. When one of Chu's sons assassinated him in 912, there were defections from the Later Liang forces to those of Li K'o-yung, but it was not until 923 that the son of the Sha-t'o leader was able to remove the Later Liang entirely and proclaim the Later T'ang.

Despite its name, this was a Turkish dynasty, which bore the old T'ang clan name of Li only because it had been honorarily awarded to Li K'o-yung by the T'ang Emperor in 869. A cadre of 100,000 Turkish tribesmen formed the ruling class, but most of them were little more than shepherds, and a handful of Sha-t'o chieftains governed the country with the aid of a large force of native Chinese civil servants like the aforementioned Fêng Tao. It was, surprisingly, a time of cultural progress; in 932, the Emperor Ming ordered the printing of the Confucian canon of texts, a task that occupied twenty-one years and produced 130 volumes. Buddhist studies also benefited, leading eventually to the printing of a 5,048-volume collection of Buddhist scriptures later in the century.

The throne changed hands briskly in the Later T'ang. The dynasty's founder was assassinated by an actor "upon whom he had conferred a high post" in 925; his adopted brother ruled until 933 as Ming Ti, apparently dying naturally, and was succeeded by his son, who was assassinated almost immediately by Li Ts'ung-ko, an adopted son. This fourth Later T'ang Emperor ruled for two years, perishing when a Khitan army invaded the capital. He set fire to his palace and died in the flames along with his imperial treasures.

The throne went to his son-in-law, a Sha-t'o Turk named Shih Chiang-t'ang, who had prudently allied himself with the Khitan. The price of Khitan support was most of northeastern China; Hopei, the province that includes Peking, fell into Khitan hands, as did northern Shansi. This gave the Manchurian Khitan control over the best preserved section of the Great Wall, which had long since ceased to be a barrier against nomad invasions.

The Later Chin Dynasty, as this new Sha-t'o line called itself, made its capital at Kaifeng. The Sha-t'o nobles, themselves more barbarian than not, urged the Emperor to make war against the Khitan, but he hesitated, and while he hesitated the Khitan nibbled away at his shrinking domain.

A witness to this moment of Chinese weakness was an Arab traveler, Abu Dulaf Mis'ar Ibn Muhalhil, who was residing at the court of the Moslem ruler of Bokhara about 940 when ambassadors arrived from China to negotiate a marriage between the Chinese Emperor's daughter and the Bokharan crown prince. Ibn Muhalhil took the opportunity to journey into China the following year, accompanying the ambassadors on their return trip. Some fragments of his narrative, possibly spurious, have survived as quotations in the works of thirteeenth-century Arab geographers. They detail his eastward progress through Turkestan, until finally he came to the "Halting-place of the Gate"—presumably the Great Wall—"in a sandy region." This was probably Yü-men. At the Halting-place of the Gate is stationed an officer of the King of China, the Arab account relates, and "anyone desiring to enter China from the Turkish countries or elsewhere must ask leave here."[83] After being entertained for three days at Chinese expense, Ibn Muhalhil and the ambassadors were allowed to depart.

In time they came to the "Valley of the Halting-place" (Tun-huang), where once again they had to ask leave to enter, and where they again spent three days at the "king's expense." The valley, described as "one of the pleasantest and fairest regions of God's earth," was almost certainly Tun-huang, and Ibn Muhalhil there passed through the Great Wall of China, which he does not describe, and into the realm of the Later Chin.

II

The Khitan were growing increasingly eager to make themselves masters of all China. In 947, they left their Chinese base at Peking, moved south, and sacked the Later Chin capital at Kaifeng, putting an end to the dynasty. The Khitan ruler proclaimed himself Emperor of China as head of the Liao Dynasty, taking the name from the Manchurian river that ran through the original heart of the Khitan lands. The proud Sha-t'o nobles refused to recognize this new dynasty; under a Turkish general, Liu Chih-yüan, they established the proudly named but pitifully weak Later Han Dynasty in the northwest. It lasted only four years, surviving as long as it did merely because the Khitan happened to be rent by an inner dynastic struggle at the time.

A court revolt took the life of the second Later Han Emperor in 951. A Chinese general, Kuo Wei, founded the Later Chou Dynasty, the fifth and last of that trying era. It lasted only a fews years, eking out an uneasy existence in a China largely dominated by the Khitan. The dynasty collapsed in 960, and in the same year another Chinese general, Chao K'uang-yin, inaugurated a new and more lasting line. His dynasty, the Sung, is one of China's most famous. But in its 319 years the Sung never had possession of the Great Wall area; so we must look now toward those who did, the Khitan.

They were of the Tatar stock, probably descended from the Hsien-pi and T'o-pa. Their home territory was southern Manchuria and eastern Mongolia; on east and west they were flanked by nomads of different linguistic groups, the Tungusic Jurchen in Manchuria and the Turkish Uighurs on the Mongolian steppe. Because of their geographical location, the Khitan economy was a mixed one, depending on pastoral nomadism in the western part of the tribal territory, on hunting and fishing in the east. There was some rough agriculture among the Khitan, the main crop being millet, but their wealth was measured in terms of sheep and horses long after their conquest of northern China.

Khitan power dated from 907, when a tribal chieftain known in Chinese records as Yeh-lü A-pao-chi founded a confederation reminiscent of the old Hsiung-nu league of more than a thousand years before. After serving as elective chief for several three-year terms, according to nomad custom, A-pao-chi fought off the claims of his brothers and set up a dynasty with his son recognized as heir apparent. The core of his strength was a cavalry of mounted archers, mobile and fierce. He established an elite guard of some two thousand men, called an *ordo;* Europeans later applied the word "horde" to such aggregations when Mongol *ordos* began to invade the west. (The desert area known as the Ordos derives its name from the same word.) Eventually twelve *ordos* made up the Khitan striking force, a fearsome cavalry of some 70,000 armored horsemen.

An almost mechanical precision of organization marked the Khitan expansion. Tactics of ambush combined with siege techniques gave them victory after victory. They moved down through Liao-tung, scattering a rival nomad tribe called the P'o-hai. In the autumn of 908, only a year after A-pao-chi's accession, the Khitan had moved southward to the vicinity of Shanhaikuan, the eastern terminus of the Great Wall. The weak Later Liang Dynasty that had just begun to rule in China offered little resistance to the Khitan advance. By way of consolidating their new holdings, the Khitan did something amusingly unprecedented: to quote from their official annals, "On the first day *chi-hai* of the tenth month . . . the Great Wall was extended to the sea-mouth of Chên-tung."[84] Which is to say—topsy-turvy as it sounds—that the barbarian horde built an eastward prong of the Great Wall from Shanhaikuan to the mouth of the Liao River as a defense against the *Chinese* to the south!

The second Khitan Emperor carried the advance into China. In 926, the Khitan plunged deep into Hopei. Ten years later, as we have seen, they were instrumental in establishing the Later Chin Dynasty, and their puppet Emperor presented them, by way of tribute, with sixteen border prefectures around Peking in northern Hopei and around Ta-t'ung (the old T'o-pa capital) in northern Shansi.

The Long Rampart of the Great Wall now bisected Khitan territory. They chose Peking as their southern capital—the first time that city played an important role in Chinese history—and retained the city of Shan-ching as their supreme capital north of the Great Wall. (The name *Peking* means "Northern Capital," and so the Khitan did not call it that. They referred to it as *Nan-ching*, which is to say, "Southern Capital," but it should not be confused with the well-known Nanking in southern China, a "Southern Capital" of later days.*)

The Later Chin Dynasty was rash enough to defy its Khitan protectors in 946. Invasion followed; the capital was taken and the entire Later Chin court, along with "artisans, maps and registers, astronomical charts, classics cut in stone, bronze statues, water clocks, musical treatises and instruments, armor, and so forth," was led off into captivity in eastern Mongolia. In 947 the Khitan claimed the Chinese throne for themselves under the dynastic name of Liao. Two weak Chinese dynasties, the Later Han and the Later Chou, managed to hold out until 960 in the west, but in that year China was partitioned, the Khitan taking control of the entire north and the new Sung Dynasty ruling in the south.

The Liao Dynasty maintained a dual state, with separate prime ministers and administrators in the districts north and south of the Great Wall. North of the Wall, the Liao kept tribal ways; the conquered area of China proper was governed through a wholly different bureaucracy staffed largely by Chinese civil servants. To oversee this unwieldy realm, the Liao Emperor traveled a circuit from capital to capital; there were five in all, one at Peking, one at Ta-t'ung, and three north of the Wall.

---

* A more common name for Peking at that time was Yenching—a pre-Khitan name that remained in use until the Mongol conquest of the thirteenth century.

The Liao rulers never really grasped the nature of the Chinese agricultural system. The Chinese peasant worked a small plot of land, cultivating it intensively and requiring defense against those polar threats, drought and flood. To guard against flood, the state had to build embankments; to ward off drought, irrigation canals were vital. The Liao, only dimly comprehending this, built no new dikes and no new canals during their two hundred years of rule, and the existing waterworks gradually deteriorated in the absence of any governmental move to maintain them.

In some ways, however, the Liao accepted transfusions of Chinese customs. Having no written language of their own, they adapted Chinese script, though in the west they also made use of the simpler Uighur alphabet. They devoted some attention to Confucianism, Buddhism, and Taoism, though their religious devotion was lukewarm in all creeds. They permitted publication and circulation of such Chinese historical works as those of Ssŭ-ma Ch'ien and Pan Ku.

The Liao struggled continually to keep from being swallowed up by Chinese culture. China had eventually engulfed the T'o-pa, the Huns, the Sha-t'o, and many another nomad conqueror. A creeping Sinification began to possess the Khitan almost as soon as they moved south of the Great Wall: Khitan officials in China were allowed to take Chinese wives, and by 983 Chinese clothes were being worn by Khitan nobles on high ceremonial occasions; the dragon, a Chinese emblem, was accepted on a basis of equality with such Khitan emblems as the sun, the mountains, and the moon; by 1055 the Khitan were well on their way toward absorption into China, spurring the Liao Emperor of that time to take countermeasures. When a Khitan noble permitted his son to take the examination for entry into the Chinese civil service, he was severely beaten and further sternly punished. An imperial decree in 1070 restated the concept of basic difference between Khitan and Chinese culture, adding that Khitan attainments were in every way the equal of Chinese. By that time, though, the nomad vigor of the Khitan had been seriously compromised by Chinese infiltration. Within two generations more, the Liao Dynasty was cast down by nomads of a purer strain, and the conquest of China proceeded anew.

III

When the Khitan came to power in China in 947, the southern part of the sundered empire was in fragments. The death of the Later Chou Emperor in 959 accelerated the onset of chaos. With a boy of the Chou line nominally occupying the throne, real power went to a general named Chao K'uang-yin, who was raised to the imperial yellow in 960 much in the manner of the later Roman Emperors, by army acclamation.

The founder of the new Sung Dynasty took the name of T'ai Tsu, "Grand Ancestor." (His brother, who succeeded him in 976 and completed the work he had begun, called himself T'ai Tsung.) Instead of attempting to challenge the powerful Khitan in the north, T'ai Tsu concentrated on uniting the small states of the south behind his banner. This project occupied him and his successor for eighteen years. By 979, the last secessionist state had been crushed, and the authority of the central government was restored, though the border provinces of the north remained in barbarian possession. Tolerant and benevolent, T'ai Tsu was lenient toward the leaders of the breakaway states. He placed his own chief generals in minor positions where they could not foment new rebellions, and gradually reconstituted the T'ang civil service. The best military units were transferred to Kaifeng, the capital, thereby strengthening the power of the new dynasty.

With unity a fact, the second Sung Emperor, T'ai Tsung, embarked on the hopeless task of driving the Khitan back through the Great Wall. He was hampered in this because the plains region of the north, where horses for the Chinese army had been bred and trained, was in Khitan hands. A weak cavalry could never hope to defeat the Khitan. The Sung army was badly beaten in 986, and occasional skirmishes during the next two decades invariably resulted in Sung defeat. The Khitan in 1004 penetrated as far south as the Chinese capital, and the desperate Sung Emperor halted them only with the promise of heavy tribute. Beginning in 1005, the Sung paid an annual bribe of 100,000 ounces of silver and 200,000 pieces of silk. In 1041, a seminomadic Tibetan tribe, the Tangut, invaded Sung territory and was thrown back with the help of the Khitan, who as a fee for their services raised the annual tribute to 200,000 ounces of silver and 300,000 pieces of silk. Then, in 1043, the Tangut again entered China, discovered the tribute game for themselves, and exacted a price of 1,000,000 strings of copper cash, 100,000 pieces of silk, and 40,000 pounds of tea. During this period of tribute-paying, Sung relations with the Khitan Liao Emperor were courteous, in the manner of vassal to master; Sung pride none the less smoldered, so that when an amiable Liao Emperor sent his portrait to his Sung counterpart in 1054, declaring, "We now desire to see his portrait," none was forthcoming, and the southern monarch sent his likeness only when asked again, years later, by the next Liao ruler.

Though Sung China was militarily weak and hemmed in on all sides by greedy and powerful barbarians, it was not an unsuccessful era. The unity of the truncated empire was maintained, dynastic crises were few, and a devoted civil service kept the governmental machinery running smoothly. In the arts, too, China flourished. The lyric poetry that had been a glory of the T'ang gave way to learned works of prose on themes of history, philosophy, economy, and natural science. The flamboyance and color of T'ang painting and porcelain yielded to a more mature technique, austere and even somber. Sung scrolls, with their dark and misty representations of mountainous northern landscapes, are generally regarded as the finest of Chinese paintings, while the slender, monochromatic Sung porcelains have a resonant inner simplicity that modern tastes prefer to the exuberant gaudiness of the T'ang pieces.

The Sung economy was a thriving one. By 1100, there were at least five cities with populations of more than a million. Waterways and flood-control dikes were built; one great sea wall running northward from Hangchow spanned 180 miles. Where the T'ang peasants had sat upon the floor and the upper classes on raised platforms, the men of Sung now used chairs.

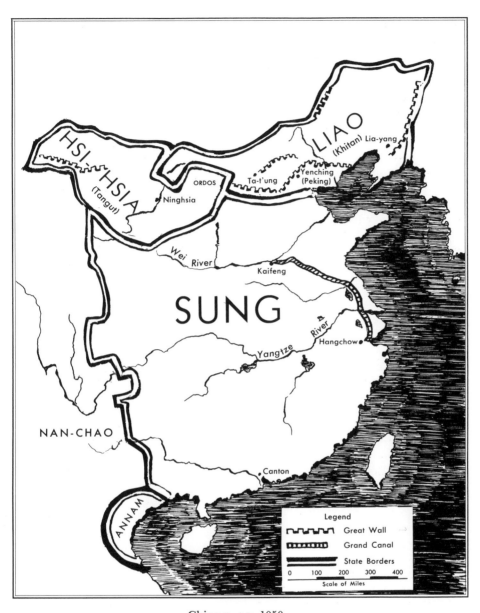

China c. A.D. 1050

Sung homes were luxurious and large, with carefully cultivated gardens. A common beverage was tea, which had been known in China since at least the third century A.D., though it had not been widely used until T'ang times. In the Sung, tea became a prized article of commerce, and Arab merchants, visiting the southern Chinese ports in great numbers, sampled the new beverage with interest. It did not, however, reach Europe until the seventeenth century. As late as the sixteenth, a Dominican friar serving in China, Gaspar da Cruz, was able to speak of tea in these terms of strangeness:

"Whatsoever person or persons come to any man's house of quality, he hath a custom to offer him in a fine basket one Porcelain, or as many as the persons are, with a kind of drink which they call Cha, which is somewhat bitter, red, and medicinal, which they are wont to make of a certain concoction of herbs somewhat bitter: with this they welcome commonly all manner of persons that they do respect, be they strangers or be they not; to me they offered it many times."[85]

Another Sung development was paper money. Copper cash were too bulky for easy transfer, and there was no coinage of precious metals. Han Wu Ti had met this problem by issuing his leather money in 118 B.C.; by 811, the T'ang had issued drafts reimbursable at the capital, and under the Sung these drafts became a common means of exchange. True paper currency was issued by private bankers, in the form of certificates of deposit that passed from hand to hand and were redeemable at the bank for a three per cent service charge. In 1024, the Sung government took these private issues over, converting them into the first truly official paper money the world had seen. They were issued in denominations of 200 to 1,000 cash, and were redeemable at the same service charge; the government backed them at the outset by reserves of copper coins, at a rate of about 29,000 cash for each 100,000 cash worth of notes, but eventually the backing was withdrawn. In later dynasties the paper currency was inflated into worthlessness, setting a pattern that would be repeated in many lands over many centuries.

Despite their obvious military weakness, the Sung Emperors never abandoned the dream of recapturing the north. The Great Wall loomed on the horizon as the symbol of all that had been Chinese strength, and the thought that the Long Rampart passed wholly through barbarian territory rankled in Sung bosoms. Chao Hsu, the sixth Sung Emperor, was particularly eager to lead an army of conquest northward. Ruling as Shên Tsung ("Inspired Ancestor") from 1067 to 1085, he appointed as his Prime Minister a strong-willed reformer, Wang An-shih, who set about the perennially necessary job of breaking up landed estates, regulating prices, and reorganizing the tax structure so that more revenue would reach the imperial treasury and less would be diverted into the coffers of the large landowners. Such reforms were required regularly because of an inherent flaw in the Chinese governmental system. The bureaucracy could only be drawn from the rich gentry, since long years of study were required to become literate and to pass the civil service examinations, and no peasant could hope to support himself while undergoing this rigorous course of study. Therefore it became customary for each landowning family to designate one son in every generation for the civil service. The government thus had to be entrusted to a breed of scholar gentry, whose loyalty could all too easily be subverted by family ties.

Wang An-shih cleaned house with a vengeance, and naturally met powerful opposition from the vested interests; he was attacked in bitter terms oddly reminiscent of those aimed at Franklin Delano Roosevelt in the early years of the New Deal. Eventually the landowners forced the minister from power in 1076 and undid his reforms, but not before enough money had been raised to finance several military adventures.

Strangely, Shên Tsung attempted to "prepare" for his war with the Khitan by fighting several smaller wars first. He sent armies against the Tibetan tribes, against the aborigines of the remote southwest, and elsewhere, squandering men and money for little strategic return. By 1074, he felt the time had come to attack the major enemy. He began by building a Sung "Great Wall" along his northern frontier—not of brick and stone, but of elm and willow trees, which hopefully would impede the charging Khitan cavalry. Bothered by this and by the massing of Sung troops along the border, the Liao Emperor sent an embassy to the Sung capital demanding destruction of the new border fortifications. Wang An-shih's enemies, accusing him of being a "warmonger," used this as a lever to pry him from office soon afterward.

The elaborate Sung defenses—three million trees planted along a frontier of almost 300 miles, and backed by a network of canals, ditches, and artificial lakes—failed to stop the Khitan troops when the attack came. They broke through the outer defenses, though they were stopped by the walled cities to the south, and by the "porcupine" of last-ditch Sung defenders.

But something had happened to Khitan momentum. Newer nomad tribes had grown strong on the Liao borders, and Sung, though unable to press an attack, was able to mount a powerful defense. In 1077, the Khitan began to build a border wall along their southern frontier, just as they had done in 908 when their domain ended in Liao-tung. Then they had been consolidating before further leaps; now they refused to leap at all. In the words of a Chinese chronicler of several centuries later: "Surrounded on the four sides by militant peoples, [Liao] crouched in their midst like a tiger whom no one dared to challenge."[86] The crouching tiger added another wall in the north, running through Mongolia well beyond the old Great Wall line, and fortified also the west, while looking worriedly eastward toward the unexpectedly troublesome Koreans. The time was ripe for a Sung reconquest of the north, but that never occurred. Instead, new barbarians took an even deeper bite from the Chinese homeland, after slaying the toothless Khitan tiger.

IV

Two other nomad states had arisen during the heyday of the Liao Dynasty. In the west, a Tibetan people called the Tangut had fashioned a kingdom in Kansu, known as the Hsi-Hsia. Their capital was at Ninghsia, a Yellow River city on the flank of the Mongolian steppe. As early as 990, the Khitan recognized them as rightful rulers of the region around the western end of the Great Wall. For many years, the Tangut paid tribute to the Sung, but in 1038 they declared their independence, and, as we have seen, within a few years were on the receiving end of Sung tribute. The Tangut had a mixed economy, agricultural in the oases, nomadic in the desert, with some reliance on trade as well. For many years they retained their independence, a thorn in the side of both the Liao and the Sung, both of whose downfalls they survived. Culturally they were open to influence from many sides; Buddhism was the state religion, and religious texts in Chinese, Tibetan, Uighur, and various other languages were printed and widely distributed.

The other new nomad state was that of the Jurchen, a Manchurian people who came out of the forests of the far north. Linguistically they were of the Tungusic family—that is, their language stemmed from that of the ancient Tung-hu nomads; while the Mongolian Khitan were of Hsiung-nu ancestry. At the beginning of the eleventh century, the height of Khitan power, the Jurchen were half-savage woodsmen with only a rudimentary tribal structure, and they were subjugated as vassals of the Khitan. But as the Khitan star waned, that of the Jurchen grew more brilliant. A powerful leader named A-ku-ta arose among them.

Crisis developed in 1112. T'ien-tsu, the Liao Emperor, was presiding over the traditional First Fish Feast at a winter camp in Manchuria. Around him were ranged the nobles of the court; before him were his guests, the tribal chieftains of the Jurchen, among them A-ku-ta. The wine-bowl passed again and again; the Liao Emperor and his nobles grew tipsy. Then, according to the official history of the Liao Dynasty, "When the serving of the wine reached a certain point, the Emperor mounted his carriage and ordered all the chieftains one after the other to get up and dance. A-ku-ta alone refused on the grounds of inability. He was ordered repeatedly but refused to the end."[87]

A-ku-ta's stubborn refusal was more than simply a breach of court etiquette. It sounded the first trumpet call to revolution. In 1115, A-ku-ta rose in revolt, calling upon the Jurchen to rally behind him. He seized the eastern capital of the Khitan, and then the supreme capital of Shan-ching. The Liao power began to crumble. A famine in 1118, brought on by the careless Khitan policy of allowing dikes and irrigation canals to fall into disrepair, sped the Liao collapse. The dynastic history has this grim entry for that year: "The people stripped the bark from elm trees and ate it. Later men even ate each other."[88] The Liao Emperor, as ignorant of Chinese ways as the first of his line had been two hundred years before, was puzzled by the starvation ravaging the farmers of the wheat-growing country. Milk was still plentiful, and the barbarian ruler asked, with an innocence that summons up another famous question of the French Revolution, "Why don't they eat curds?" The Chinese, he might have known, had a deep-seated revulsion to any milk product, in contrast to the people of the steppe; they preferred cannibalism, evidently, to dining on nomad fare.

The breakup was rapid. By 1121, almost half the Liao empire was in Jurchen hands; the Emperor fled westward in 1122, putting his son to death on a rumor of treason which later proved false. In the same year, A-ku-ta took the title of Emperor himself, calling his dynasty the Chin, or "golden." The Liao Emperor's second son took charge of the fleeing Khitan forces, but he died late in 1123 after having deposed his father. The next year, a Khitan of the imperial family named Yeh-lü Ta-shih led a small band of his people westward into central Asia, where they were welcomed by the Uighurs and eventually established a new empire called Kara-Khitai (Black Khitai, or Western Liao), which came to occupy a great deal of territory on both sides of the Pamirs. Those Khitan who did not join that migration were hunted down by the warriors of the new Chin Dynasty, and by 1125 the complete destruction of the Liao had been accomplished.

V

The Sung Emperor, watching the annihilation of the Khitan foe, unwisely tried to turn the situation to his own advantage. The reigning monarch was Hui Tsung ("Excellent Ancestor"), who had come to the throne in 1100. In 1122, he sent an army to join the Jurchen forces, who had no need of Sung assistance in the rout of Liao. After the Liao catastrophe, the Jurchen tossed the Sung six prefectures around Peking as a reward for their feeble aid. Hui Tsung protested sharply, whereupon the irritated barbarians marched south into the Sung domain. The Emperor sought to bribe them to go back, but the treasury was empty, and his only recourse was quick abdication. His son, the ninth Sung Emperor, had no way to check the Jurchen hordes, and in 1126 they captured the Sung capital, Kaifeng, along with Chao Huan, the new Emperor, and his father. The entire imperial court, numbering three thousand in all, was carried off beyond the Great Wall as prisoners of the Chin.

A brother of the captive Sung Emperor fled southward across the Yangtze River to safety, settling for a while at Yangchow and proclaiming himself to be Kao Tsung ("High Ancestor"), the first Emperor of the Southern Sung Dynasty. In 1129, Chin forces pushed him further to the south, and by 1138 he had established what he hopefully called a "temporary capital" at Lin-an, the modern Hangchow. The forces of Chin found it difficult to continue their offensive into this part of China, for the many rivers and canals of the south hampered their cavalry thrusts, and by 1141 the Sung Emperor negotiated a treaty of peace with the northern conquerors. A new boundary was set, which the Sung agreed not to fortify; it was stipulated that the Sung empire was vassal to the Chin, and that an annual tribute of silver and silk would be paid.

The shrunken Southern Sung empire included only central and southern China. The new Emperors were generally weak and ineffectual men. Yet the Chin never were able to conquer their southern neighbors, and, indeed, after 1165 the Sung tribute was reduced and the status of outright vassalage was dropped. The Southern Sung empire prospered in its new boundary; the wealth of the rice fields no longer was dissipated in hopeless military ventures, and the new capital, which Marco Polo called Quinsay, grew so grand that even in its decay, after the collapse of the dynasty, it struck

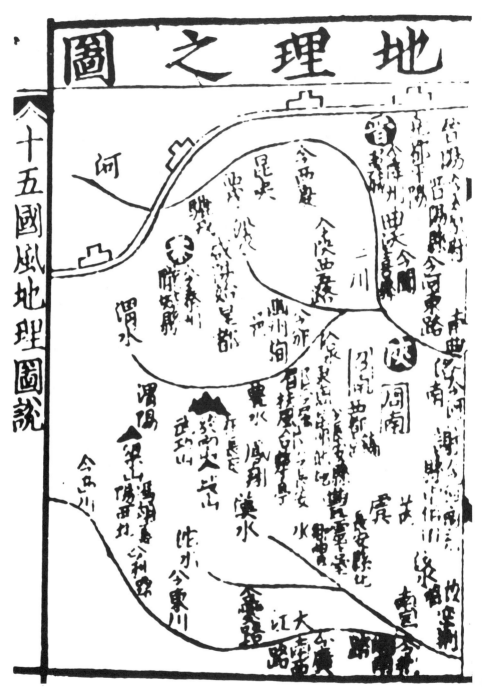

A map of West China, published around A.D. 1155 and showing the Great Wall.
Cambridge University Press

that cosmopolitan of Venice as "beyond dispute the finest and noblest city in the world."

With the north closed off, China for the first time began to look outward along the sea. A Sung navy grew from 11 squadrons and 3,000 men in 1130 to 20 squadrons and 52,000 men by 1237. The vast Chinese ships which we know as "junks" began to be seen plying the coastal routes to India and beyond, as well as the open-sea lanes to Arabia. As one Chinese historian wrote in 1178, "The ships which sail the Southern Sea and south of it are like houses. When their sails are spread they are like great clouds in the sky. Their rudders are several tens of feet long. A single ship carries several hundred men. It has stored on board a year's supply of grain."[89] Foreign trade flourished: Chinese junks went to Japan, to Indochina, to Bengal, to the African coasts. Arabian and Persian vessels, which had first begun to visit Chinese ports in T'ang times, became fewer as the bulk of traffic went to the junks. From foreign lands came wondrous imports: rhinoceros horns from Indochina, ivory from India and Africa, incense, camphor, pearls, crystal, coral, agate, sandalwood and aloe, all pouring in as Chinese silks and porcelain went out.

Warfare was enlivened by the invention of gunpowder. It had first been used in China about 1044; primitive bombs and grenades were employed in the struggle against the invading Jurchen in 1126 and again in 1161, and the Jurchen in turn learned the secret of explosives and began to use them against the Mongolian foes who were starting to tread on them from the rear.

Sung poets, understandably, devoted much attention to lamenting the lost lands. Comfortable in their warm cities, they mourned the loss of the cold north. Tai Fu-ku, writing at the end of the thirteenth century, spoke for his whole nation when he declared:

> How bitterly I wish that mountains blocked my wandering
> gaze,
> For northwards, far as eye can reach, our conquered
> land seems endless.[90]

Twelve. The Mongol Hordes

In the middle of the thirteenth century, the English monk Matthew of Paris* made this entry in his historical chronicle, under the heading *Anno 1240:*

"The detestable people of Satan, to wit, an infinite number of Tartars, brake forth from their mountain-compassed and rock-defended region, like devils loosed out of Hell (that they may well be called Tartarians, as Tartareans) and like grasshoppers covering the face of the earth, spoiling the eastern confines with fire and sword, ruining cities, cutting up woods, rooting up vineyards, killing the people both of city and country. . . . They are rather monsters than men, thirsting and drinking blood, tearing and devouring the flesh of dogs and men; clothed with ox-hides, armed with iron plates; in stature thick and short, well set, strong in body; in war invincible, in labor infatigable. . . ."[91]

Matthew Paris wrote at a time when all Europe shivered under the Mongol threat. They had come out of the steppes of Asia and had speared deep into Europe, reaching Poland, Hungary, and the Danube Valley by 1241 before casually abandoning their drive and retreating undefeated. They called themselves Tatars, which to men like Matthew of Paris suggested a natural pun, *Tartars,* or beings out of Tartarus, a medieval name for Hell. The pun passed into the languages of Europe; as "Tartars" men knew them and men dreaded them. But long before the western world had reason to fear the Mongol hordes, the horsemen of the steppe had sharpened their teeth on the flanks of China. Once again, wild men broke through the Great Wall. But this time the nomads did something none of their forebears had achieved: they made themselves lords of all China, from the Great Wall to the torrid jungles of the south.

As late as the middle of the twelfth century, the Tatar tribesmen who would form the Mongol empire lived a simple nomadic life deep in barbarian country. Those on the fringe of the Siberian forest were hunters and fishers, but most of the Mongol-speaking tribesmen were nomads of the open steppe, living in small family groups, each family occupying a *yurt,* or tent of felt. They drifted from pasture to pasture as the needs of their herds required. Fam-

---

* Also known as Mathew Paris.

ily clans tended to move together during these seasonal migrations, forming a larger tribal unit. The society was a fluid one; adoption from clan to clan was common. So was petty warfare between clans, and between tribes.

About the year 1167, a Mongol child was born in a camp on the banks of the Amur River, and named Temujin. His father, Yesukai, was a tribal chieftain of great valor, and the shaman of the tribe diplomatically predicted that the child would become a mighty warrior. Legend has it that when he was only nine, Temujin could ride a speeding horse without using the reins, showering arrows unerringly in all directions. When he was thirteen, his father died; Temujin was unable to assert his claim to the chieftainship, and years of intrigue and warfare followed before he came into his heritage. Gradually he mastered the art of tribal politics, building through cunning, strength, and treachery a position of authority first in his own tribe, then in many tribes. By 1204, Temujin could count himself master of all the nomad tribes of Mongolia.

That status was confirmed two years later at a *khuriltai,* or meeting of all tribes, on the Kerulen River. By common agreement, Temujin was chosen as the first *khaghan,* or king, of the Mongols. They acclaimed him as Genghis Khan, which meant something like "Universal Ruler," or "King of Kings." Legend has it that when the ceremony took place a stone lying near the assemblage broke open of its own accord, revealing a seal of carved jade, which became the emblem of royal authority among the Mongols thereafter.

Genghis Khan, then about forty years old, proved a superb organizer of men. He shaped the scattered tribes into a political unit, building upward from family to clan, from clan to tribe, from tribe to larger groups, all encompassed in one empire with a divinely-appointed khan, himself, as its leader. He laid down codes of laws, both civil and criminal, and insured their enforcement. The useful Uighur alphabet was borrowed to provide the Mongols with a written language. Genghis Khan and his successors never hesitated to make use of the accomplishments of other peoples; he took Uighur Turks into his administration, and Moslems from Bokhara and points west, and later, as we will see, a Christian family from Venice served a Mongol khan in high office.

Having forged a state, Genghis turned it to military purposes immediately. The first objective was conquest of the Tangut kingdom of Hsi-Hsia, in Kansu. The Mongols swept down on it in 1205, and within four years Tangut power was broken, though the final subjugation did not occur until 1227. And in 1211, Genghis Khan looked southward across the Great Wall, at that immemorial target of nomad conquerors, China.

II

China on the eve of Mongol conquest was still a divided land. In the south was the prosperous, populous Southern Sung realm; from the Yangtze north to the Great Wall and beyond, the masters were the Jurchen Chin Dynasty.

The Jurchen had been in control since 1125, when they had annihilated the Khitan. The Manchurian conquerors had not shown any superior virtues during their stewardship over north China; they were gruff, simple-minded warriors who were content to drain the wealth of China so long as it was there to be drained. They had beaten the Khitan with a mixed army of Jurchen, Chinese, and renegade Khitan, but before long most of the non-Jurchen elements were purged from their positions of authority. The Jurchen attempted to keep aloof from the people they ruled. They had their own language and script, which were used alongside Chinese in all official documents, and Jurchen customs were staunchly maintained and even, for a while, forced on the Chinese, who were ordered to take Jurchen names and wear Jurchen clothes and Jurchen-style haircuts. Eventually this practice began to reverse itself as China started to ingest this new overlord; by 1187, the Chin Emperor was compelled to decree punishments for Jurchen who had taken Chinese surnames or wore Chinese clothes, and he found it necessary to reprimand a courtier who bowed in the Chinese fashion.

As Mongol strength began to assert itself north of the Chin empire late in the twelfth century, worried Chin Emperors sought ways to protect their territory. One method was to build walls. The Jurchen strengthened the Great Wall; but that rampart ran through the middle of their domain, and could only serve as an inner line of defense. Farther north, the Jurchen rebuilt a wall that the Khitan had originally erected as a defense against *them*. They added a new outer loop, five hundred miles long, reaching as far north as the 48th parallel in some places. In the west, the Jurchen built a wall parallel to and north of the Great Wall, beyond the loop of the Huang Ho.

Then they braced themselves for the onslaught.

The Mongol horde of Genghis Khan, having dealt with the Hsi-Hsia kingdom, advanced toward Jurchen-occupied China. That word "horde," though, summons up a wholly inaccurate image of Mongol forces as numerous, to use Matthew of Paris' simile, as "grasshoppers covering the face of the earth." As has been seen, "horde" is derived from the Mongol word *ordo,* meaning no more than an elite cavalry force. The Mongol armies were never large, though their numbers were multiplied by the terrified imagination of their victims. At the height of his power, Genghis Khan never commanded more than about 250,000 men, of whom about half were Mongols and the rest allies such as the Uighurs. The whole Mongol population was probably no greater than one or two million; the Chinese at that time already numbered more than a hundred million.

The Mongol war machine depended on speed and valor, not on numbers. The leather-clad horsemen, born to the saddle, could ride for days at a time, changing horses without halting. During the invasion of Hungary a Mongol army covered 270 miles in three days, an awesome feat to the men of the thirteenth century. Mongol discipline was formidable. When food ran low, the soldiers got along with mare's milk, or, failing that, even the blood of their horses—according to the feverish chroniclers of their advance, at any rate. In battle, they sallied forth in flying columns, encircling their foes and pressing them inward, ringing them into a panicky herd that could be easily routed. The Mongol bows could slay at two hundred yards' distance. A favorite tactic was the feigned retreat, tempting the enemy to pursue; at the right moment the Mongols would wheel and charge their astonished pursuers. "In this sort of warfare," observed Marco Polo, "the adversary imagines he has gained a victory, when in fact he has lost the battle." Terror was another Mongol weapon: they put whole cities to the sword, not out of innate cruelty as Europeans thought, but for propaganda purposes; enemies who were shivering at the mere rumor of Mongol ferocity were half beaten before the first blow was struck. As conquerors, however, the Mongols proved to be far less bestial than their advance reputation had led men to think. They were, in fact, tolerant and just rulers, however fierce they were in conquest.

When Genghis Khan began his invasion of China in 1211, he conceived it as a war of liberation. He was going to drive out the Jurchen, ancient oppressors of his own people, rather than to conquer the Chinese. The risks were great. His newly constructed empire would crumble at once if he suffered a defeat so far from his Mongolian base. He assembled all the forces at his command for the desperate attempt.

Scouts preceded the main army, fanning out over a wide territory. The Mongol troops covered the 450 miles from the Kerulen River to the Jurchen frontier of China quickly, crossing the mountains and the eastern Gobi without losing a man. Each rider had one or more spare mounts; cattle followed along, a food supply on hooves.

Genghis Khan's logical goal was the Chin capital, Yenching, the modern Peking. The Great Wall was at its strongest here in the mountainous country of eastern China. Two walls, from thirty to sixty miles apart, guarded the approach to Yenching, while the city itself was surrounded by formidable walls that made the Great Wall itself look fragile by comparison. Under the Liao Dynasty, the city had been the southern capital, and had been stoutly walled, but the Chin rulers had enlarged the capital's fortifications with extravagance born of fear. Walls forty feet high, topped with hundreds of watchtowers, ringed the capital. A triple line of moats afforded more protection. Finally, the city was flanked by four massive walled forts, each a mile square, with its own array of towers, moats, granaries, and arsenals.

The Mongols easily broke through the outer loops of the Great Wall. But the inner defenses proved more stubborn. Again and again the Mongols hurled themselves at the gate of the Wall at Chüyungkuan, north of the capital, only to be thrown back. The fortress held. In 1212 the Mongols retreated.

A secondary Mongol army, 120 miles to the west, had had better luck. The Wall in Shansi was guarded by a tribe of Jurchen vassals, the Ongut. The practice of hiring mercenaries to defend the Wall was proven unwise once again; the Ongut, seeing the shape of future events, surrendered to the Mongols without a battle, and opened the Great Wall. The invaders irrupted into the rich province of Shansi.

The imperial Chin troops, who had been guarding the passes north of the capital, hastily turned westward and took the mountainous roads into Shansi to stem the Mongol tide. Genghis' strategic skill proved too much for them. The Chin troops were caught between two arms of the Mongol force, and the densely packed infantrymen were slain by thousands in a rain of Mongol arrows. The heart of the Chin army was sundered.

Genghis now circled back, hoping once more to penetrate the Great Wall north of the capital now that the ranks of the defenders had been thinned. In September of 1213, Mongol armies pounded against the gate at Chüyung-kuan a second time. The gate held. The Wall had been newly fortified with outer trenches and earthworks; the gate itself had been sealed with iron, one story said, so that it could not be opened even from within.

The siege went on fruitlessly for a month. Then Genghis sent a smaller force commanded by one of his sons to challenge the Great Wall pass at Tzuchingkuan, southwest of the capital. The unexpected thrust succeeded; the Mongol horsemen broke into the plain within the Wall, stormed the fortress at Chüyungkuan from the southern side, and opened the gate to the main army waiting without.

The way to the capital was open. But when the Mongols pulled up before the walls of Yenching in 1214, they were aghast at the scope of the task that still awaited them. Who could scale such walls? Who could cross such moats? From the four corners of the city, defenders showered down missiles and crude bombs. For the first time, Genghis began to comprehend the magnitude of China. He had sent one army through the Wall in the west, and it now held the province of Shansi. After almost three years of siege, he had managed to enter this eastern province, Hopei. But there were a dozen such provinces, each with its walled cities. How could those cities be taken? Could China ever be conquered? And, if it could, how could his little band of Mongols ever govern such a vast and populous land?

The khan hesitated. Two thrusts against the city wall of the capital were repulsed. Perhaps it would be best to settle for what had already been con-quered, Genghis thought. Rather than commence a siege that could last for years, he made plans to withdraw. At this point the Chin Emperor ill-advisedly sent an envoy to Genghis, asking what the khan's intentions were. The envoy, as it happened, was a Khitan in the service of the Jurchen, and he let it be known that, while the capital was impregnable at the moment, there was the strong possibility of an internal uprising against the Jurchen, who were hated by their Chinese and Khitan subjects.

Genghis noted that for future reference. For the present, he took advantage of the Chin Emperor's willingness to buy peace. The khan accepted an im-perial princess, five hundred Chinese conçubines, and a tribute of horses, gold, silver, and silk, as the price of retreating beyond the Great Wall.

The following May—1215—the uprising came. There was strife within the capital, and traitors handed the mighty city over to the Mongols. The mag-nificent capital was looted and burned, and its inhabitants were slain by the thousands, by way of serving notice on China's other walled cities. The Chin Emperor, Wan-yen Hsün, fled with his court to Kaifeng, once the Sung cap-ital. All of China north of the Huang Ho fell into Mongol hands. Far to the south, the Southern Sung Emperor rejoiced at the downfall of the Jurchen, and made bold enough to withhold the annual tribute that had been paid to the Chin monarch for almost a century. In the twelfth century, a Sung ruler had welcomed the Jurchen as liberators who would drive out the Khitan. Now, the Mongols were hailed in the same way—and with the same ultimate result, since eventually they would devour the Sung domain. But the Sung did not expect that, in 1215. There was still the torso of the Jurchen realm as a buffer between the Sung and the Mongols. Besides, barbarians never had invaded the south before, so why should they do it now? They had no use for such hot, swampy country.

Genghis Khan, surveying the smoldering ruins of Yenching, pondered the next course to take. Continue south, root out the Jurchen, capture all of China? Or turn to other conquests elsewhere? There were many possibilities.

There was also the problem of what to do with conquered northern China, with its wheat fields and its teeming peasantry. One of the khan's advisers had a simple suggestion: "Although you have now conquered the men of Han, they are no use to us; it would be better to kill them all and turn their lands back to pasture so that we can feed our beasts on it." The khan seemed to agree; it appeared that three thousand years of Chinese civilization would be swept away and the steppe extended hundreds of miles south of the Great Wall.

But among Genghis Khan's retinue was one Yeh-lü Ch'u-ts'ai, a descendant of the old Khitan royal house of Liao. He had served in the Jurchen bureaucracy, and was captured by the Mongols when Yenching fell. Described traditionally as "eight feet tall, with a splendid beard and a voice like thunder,"[92] the noble Khitan was taken before Genghis, who remarked, "You are a Khitan. I sent my generals to take vengeance upon your enemies, the Chin."

To this Yeh-lü Ch'u-ts'ai replied, "My father and I have both served the Chin; how can they be my enemies?"

The forthright answer so impressed Genghis that he took the Khitan prince into his service, giving him the nickname of "Longbeard." Though of nomad descent, Yeh-lü Ch'u-ts'ai had been born in China and understood the dynamics of the Chinese economy more profoundly than his imperial ancestors ever had. When Genghis Khan proposed to turn all northern China into a vast pasture, the Khitan attacked the idea in these words:

"Now that you have conquered everywhere under Heaven and all the riches of the four seas, you can have everything you want, but you have not organized it. You should set up taxation on land and merchants, and should make profits on wine, salt, iron, and the produce of the mountains and marshes. In this way in a single year you will obtain 500,000 ounces of silver, 80,000 rolls of silk, and 400,000 piculs* of grain. How can you say that the Chinese people are no use to you?"[93]

The advice seemed sound. Genghis gave orders that the government of China be organized along traditional lines, and that nothing be done to hamper Chinese productivity. He did not attempt to press his conquest of China further at this point. There was trouble in the far west, where the Tangut of Hsi-Hsia were stirring again, and where the Black Khitai kingdom

---

* The picul was equal to 133 pounds.

founded by fugitive Khitan a hundred years earlier was making menacing gestures. In 1219, Genghis left a lieutenant in charge of occupied China, and led his armies westward.

III

The land of the Black Khitai was the first to fall. Instead of turning immediately to deal with the Tangut, Genghis continued marching westward, and by 1221 had conquered the Turkish state of Khorezm, in what is now Russian Turkestan. The rich oasis cities of Bokhara and Samarkand thus were annexed by the Mongols, and Turkish tribes were incorporated into the Mongol hordes. The invaders forged onward to Persia and even to the Crimea, and Genghis was contemplating an invasion of India as well. But, one tale reports, Genghis had just entered the mountains of Tibet when a strange one-horned beast came toward him, knelt, and declared, "Prince! Return whence you came!"

The faithful Yeh-lü Ch'u-ts'ai told the khan that the unicorn's warning should not be disregarded. "It is a gentle animal, with a horror of slaughter," he said. "Your Majesty has now been at war in these kingdoms for four years. It may be that Heaven has seen enough of bloodshed and has sent this creature to warn us to retire."[94] Genghis bowed to the advice. Late in 1224 he swung round and marched against the Tangut.

The conquest of the Hsi-Hsia kingdom occupied him until the summer of 1227, and the great khan died just before the final victory. In his sixty years he had welded nomad tribes into an empire that swept across Asia from the Islamic states of the west to the sea in the east. He died in the Ordos country, probably of natural causes (though his death now is cobwebbed by a hundred conflicting legends) and was taken north into the steppe for burial.

His third son, Ogödai, succeeded him. In 1230, he returned to China, giving Yeh-lü Ch'u-ts'ai the assignment of putting together a Chinese civil service. The Mongols now proceeded to clear away the remains of the Jurchen realm. Aided by the blithely heedless Sung Emperor, who was fashioning his own doom, Ogödai attacked the Chin capital at Kaifeng, trapping the last Chin Emperor in 1234 and forcing him to take his own life. The Jurchen were gone. China was divided between the Mongols and the Sung.

Cautiously, the Mongols tested Sung strength. They knew that they would have to fight on unfamiliar terrain, not well suited for their style of attack. One Mongol army moved along the Yellow River; another stabbed into the Sung province of Szechuan, to encircle the western rim of the Sung empire. But the Mongols went no further, at that time, and might never have tried to take the south at all had not the Sung goaded them into doing so.

Mongol forces also were spreading out over western Asia. The sons of Genghis each had an army to command, and conquest was proceeding on four fronts at once. Ogödai, the *khaghan* or Great Khan, ruled in China. His nephew Batu, grandson of Genghis, led the army known as the Golden Horde into Europe in 1236; these were the Tartars described by Matthew of Paris, the ones so terrifying to the western world. Batu's armies crossed the Volga, burned Moscow, took Kiev, flooded into Poland and Hungary by 1241. A third Mongol horde was ravaging Persia and Mesopotamia under Chagadai, another son of Genghis. A fourth was attacking Korea.

All Mongol conquest came to a halt in 1241 with the death of Ogödai. A new Great Khan had to be chosen, and all the Mongol princes had to participate in the *khuriltai*. Batu abruptly ended his invasion of Europe and headed for the homeland, to the endless astonishment of the Europeans, who were helpless before him and fully expected to see the entire continent conquered by the irresistible horde.

Ogödai's son Kuyuk was elected Great Khan, after considerable politicking among the sons and grandsons of Genghis. The Mongols returned to the attack after their long interlude of politics. When Kuyuk died, his cousin Mangu replaced him, and by 1259, the year of Mangu's death, the Mongols held the grandest empire the world had ever known, an awesome territory stretching from the Yellow River to the banks of the Danube, and from Siberia to the Persian Gulf.

The changes in Mongol leadership had given the Sung time to fortify their defenses. With the election of Mangu as Great Khan in 1251, the Mongol drive into southern China resumed, and this time it did not falter, stubborn as the Sung fortifications were to prove.

IV

The Southern Sung Emperors were foolish men, but their nation was rich and strong. The Huai and Han Rivers protected the northern border of Southern Sung China, with mountains and chains of fortresses providing an inner line of defense. To the east was the ocean, to the west the savage mountains of Tibet.

Encouraged by these natural barriers, the Sung stupidly and suicidally mounted an offensive against the Mongols. Capable Sung generals took a few towns from the enemy, rousing false hopes. Thwarted in their first attempts at a frontal attack, the Mongols moved to the flank, conquering the non-Chinese kingdom of Nan-chao in modern Yunnan, southwest of the Sung domain, in 1253. But little further progress was made for years after that.

Mangu Khan died in 1259. Once again, the Mongol princes vied for power, and the high prize went to the thirty-five-year-old Kublai, who was leading the attack against Sung China. Kublai was the nephew of Ogödai, and the grandson of Genghis Khan. His elder brother was Mangu, the preceding Great Khan. When word of Mangu's death reached Kublai in China, he hurried across the Great Wall into Mongolia, since by Mongol law all the princes of Genghis' line had to gather to choose the new khan. Several of the princes did not bother to attend the *khuriltai*. Kublai's cousin Bereke, then engaged in carving out a Russian empire for himself as successor to his late brother Batu, had no real interest in who ruled the homeland. And Kublai's brother Hulagu, having just captured Baghdad and overthrown the Caliphate, was kept from returning by an uprising led by the Sultan of Egypt.

The Mongol chieftains gathered before Kublai himself could arrive. They did not trust him, for he had spent most of his life in China and had acquired Chinese ways. Hastily, the chiefs named Kublai's youngest brother, Arik-buga, as the new Great Khan.

Kublai took drastic measures. He held a *khuriltai* of his own at a place called Shang-tu, the Xanadu of Coleridge, not far north of the Great Wall. There he persuaded his close relatives and his generals to elect him Great Khan. It was an election of dubious legality, but he made it stick through force; he invaded the Mongol capital of Karakorum, starved it out, drove Arik-buga into the Mongolian desert, and forced him to surrender.

With that done, and with another claimant disposed of by 1264, Kublai Khan was free to complete the conquest of China. The main invasion route lay along the Han River, guarded by twin cities at Hsiang-yang. From 1268 to 1273, Mongol forces laid siege, with both sides employing big catapults and explosive bombs. Mongol artillery brought the fortress to surrender, finally. The invaders reached the Yangtze and began to move along the river.

Kublai meanwhile had chosen Peking as his southern capital. In 1271, he proclaimed himself Emperor of China, calling his dynasty the Yüan, meaning "The First Beginning," or "The Origin." Genghis Khan, as founder of the dynasty, was posthumously awarded the imperial title of T'ai Tsu, "Grand Progenitor." Kublai himself is known in Chinese annals as Shih Tsu, "Regenerating Progenitor." Since Peking had been sacked by Genghis in 1215, it was necessary to rebuild it, Kublai choosing a site just to the north of the ruins of the Chin Dynasty's city of Yenching. The new city, which was called in Chinese Tai-tu, was known to the Mongols as Khan-baliq, "City of the Khan." This was transformed into Cambaluc in Marco Polo's account. When he came to China later in Kublai's reign, Marco was awed by Cambaluc, describing it in these terms:

"The streets are so wide and straight that you can see right along them from one gate to another. And up and down the city there are beautiful palaces and many great and fine houses in great number. All the plots of ground on which the houses are built are four-square, and laid out in straight lines. . . . Each square plot is encompassed by handsome streets for traffic; and thus the whole city is arranged in squares just like a chessboard, and disposed in a manner so perfect and masterly that it is impossible to give a description that would do it justice."[95]

The Mongol khan was now Son of Heaven as well, a development Genghis could hardly have anticipated as he stared at the wall of the Jurchen capital in 1215. The elimination of the Sung Dynasty followed in short order. Chao Ch'i, the sixth Southern Sung Emperor, died in 1274 and the throne passed to his three-year-old son, with the dowager Empress as regent. At once the Mongols invaded Sung territory in great force, and many cities opened their gates. Nanking was abandoned; Hangchow, the capital, was besieged. When a group of Mongol ambassadors was murdered while negotiating for peace, the last hope of Sung survival was lost. The war had shifted to the sea now; a great naval battle near Chinkiang crippled the Sung forces, and in 1276 the capital surrendered. The boy Emperor was sent to Cambaluc as a prisoner, and died in Mongolia the following year.

Another son of Chao Ch'i, a boy of eight, escaped and was named Emperor by the remaining Sung faction. Taking to the sea under cover of fog, he made his way southward from port to port, pursued by the Mongol fleet. For two years this ghostly Sung court eluded capture, but a typhoon sent the Emperor to his death at sea in 1278.

One last son of Chao Ch'i was enthroned by the Sung diehards. The Emperor's partisans still numbered about 20,000, with a thousand ships to their fleet; southwest of Canton, these ships took formation in a compact group as a kind of floating fortress and held out for a month, their numbers thinned by Mongol artillery and by Chinese defections. At last, in 1279, only sixteen Sung ships remained. The Mongols closed in. A loyal minister, taking the eight-year-old Emperor on his back, leaped into the sea, and the dynasty came to an ignominious end. China belonged to Kublai Khan. For the first time in history, men from beyond the Great Wall were masters of the entire realm.

V

A great empire had fallen to the Mongols, and they had made it the crowning gem of an even greater one. Inevitably, the huge Mongol realm began to split into separate khanates as the outlying princes went their own way, but all the rulers were of one family, and all acknowledged, however loosely, the supremacy of Kublai over the others. The Great Khan himself, from his two capitals at Cambaluc and Shang-tu, ruled all of China, Korea, Mongolia, Manchuria, and Tibet, with Burma, Java, and Indochina paying tribute. The sons of Chagadai ruled the Chagadai Khanate in Central Asia, Turkestan, and Afghanistan. Hulagu's descendants established the Persian Ilkhanate, embracing Persia, Asia Minor, and much of the Near East. The Kipchak Khanate, or the Golden Horde, held Russia and Siberia.

In governing China, Kublai did his best to avoid reviving the Chinese bureaucracy of the scholar gentry. The Chinese civil servants had smothered one barbarian conqueror after another by forcing them into a state of dependence; when tax revenues had to be collected through a native bureaucracy making use of a written language so complex that, as Owen Lattimore says, "it was virtually a professional secret," the nomad masters had found themselves at the mercy of their own subjects. Kublai recognized that China could be administered only through a large corps of civil servants. But he staffed his bureaucracy with outsiders: Uighur Turks, who had become Christians and who used a simple alphabetic script, and Moslems from the western lands, whose languages, Turkish, Persian, and Arabic, were more accessible than Chinese. Few official documents were written in Chinese, and it would appear that Marco Polo, who remained in China 27 years, had little knowledge of the Chinese language and was able to get along with Mongol or Persian, or possibly both.

Kublai Khan has gone into history as an enlightened ruler. This is chiefly the doing of Marco Polo, who admired the Emperor inordinately and said so in a book that has never lacked for readers. Certainly Kublai's tolerance of all religions—and most particularly, of Christianity—made him seem an unusual sort of Oriental despot. Actually, his accomplishments were considerable. He fostered the arts and the sciences, gathering scholars, painters, architects, and engineers at Cambaluc. He built an observatory, and sponsored a calendar reform. Foreign trade was encouraged, and commerce was aided by a unified nation-wide system of paper currency. Buddhist, Taoist, Moslem, and Christian temples flourished side by side. The Mongols themselves seemed to regard all religions as equally valid, though gradually they came under the sway of the debased Tibetan form of Buddhism known as Lamaism, which ultimately helped to bring about their downfall.

The wise and benevolent Kublai was charitable; an edict of 1271 established a system of public hospitals and orphanages, and Marco Polo declares that the Emperor distributed alms to 30,000 paupers a day. Some of the discredited "socialist" reforms of Wang An-shih were revived, and state granaries were constructed to store food that could be distributed in years of crop failure.

Now that divided China was whole again, the Grand Canal was restored. The original T'ang Grand Canal had carried food from the south to the capital at Ch'ang-an, but now the political center of China had shifted eastward to Cambaluc, which is to say Peking, and the Grand Canal was extended northward to serve the new capital. Along the stone embankments of the canal ran a paved road, eleven hundred miles long, from Hangchow to Peking.

It is easy to be fond of Kublai Khan, but the fact remains that China did not prosper under Mongol rule. The first issue of Mongol paper money, that of 1260, had to be called in in 1287 and exchanged for new notes on a 1 for 5 basis, and again in 1309 there was a 1 for 5 exchange, meaning a twenty-five-fold depreciation in the paper currency over half a century. The Mongols and their foreign-born administrators did a poor job of maintaining the flood control systems, so that famine was common and the peasantry suffered bitterly; the population of China declined from one hundred million in 1125 to forty-five million two hundred years later, and of that number seven and a half million were officially listed as "starving." Only the landlords and the governors grew fat. For all his talk of Kublai's enlightened rule, Marco Polo nevertheless observed that in every province "there were many disloyal and seditious persons, at all times disposed to break out in rebellion," and Mongol garrisons were kept outside every large city to preserve the peace.

One cause of this discontent was Kublai's employment of foreigners. Marco noted that the Chinese "detested the Great Khan's rule because he set over them governors who were Tartars, or still more frequently Saracens, and these they could not endure, for they were treated by them just like slaves." But the most famous of those foreign officials was Marco Polo himself, whose travels lasted longer than those of Odysseus, and bear much the same fascination.

Thirteen.
White Faces in the Yellow Realm

The century of Mongol rule opened China to the west as never before. A single empire ran the length of Asia, and Europe, beginning to recover from the shocks inflicted by Batu from 1236 to 1241, realized that it was now possible to travel through that vast empire under Mongol protection. Europeans began to travel to the fabled land called Cathay. Some took the hard way through South Russia and the steppe; others crossed the Black Sea and followed the line of oases of the Old Silk Road; others came by sea, through the Indian Ocean and around Southeast Asia to Canton, while some went by sea to Syria and overland via Baghdad the rest of the way.

The motive for much of this travel was trade, but there was another reason for European interest in Asia. This was the time of the Crusades, and Arabs and Turks menaced the Christian nations of Europe. The Mongols, Europe had learned, had no particular religion of their own; some said that they might even be Christians of a sort. At any rate, they were not Moslems. If they could be shielded from Islam and converted to Christianity, it might be possible to put Mongols to work in the campaign against the Turks. A Europe that had cowered before the Mongols a generation ago now saw them as potential Christians and potential allies.

These hopes were not entirely fanciful. As early as 625, Christian missionaries of the Nestorian sect had reached China, and had been received in friendly manner by T'ang T'ai Tsung. Reportedly the Emperor declared, "The Way has more than one name. There is more than one sage. . . . This religion does good to all men. Let it be preached freely in our empire." Nestorian Christian churches had kept a foothold in China ever since. Kublai Khan's mother, indeed, had been a Nestorian. To Catholics, of course, the Nestorians were heretics, but at least they were worshipers of Christ.

In 1245 Pope Innocent IV sent Friar John of Plano Carpini on the first mission to the Mongols. The sturdy friar entered the Golden Horde's camp on the Volga, was received by Batu, went eastward with him to Karakorum, and was present at the enthronement of the Great Khan Kuyuk in 1246. He reported that the Mongols were neither hostile nor friendly to Christianity.

When asked if he were a Christian, Kuyuk replied coolly, "God knows. And if the Pope also wishes to know he had better come and see."

A few years later, King Louis IX of France, seeking aid from the Mongols for a crusading campaign, sent another monk across the world: the fat, hearty Franciscan Friar William of Rubruck, who also called upon Batu first, and was taken on a long and exhausting journey to see the incumbent Great Khan, Mangu. The friar traveled a long way, making some shrewd observations about the Chinese written and spoken language, and noting that Cathay was probably the same as the silk-producing land that the ancient Greek and Roman geographers had called Serica, the country of the Seres. He had harsh words for the Nestorians, declaring that they "know nothing. They say their offices, and have sacred books in Syrian, but they do not know the language and they are utterly depraved." His meeting with Mangu was unsuccessful; the Great Khan was tipsy, and so was his interpreter, and little was achieved. Not for a generation more did missionaries journey toward Cathay, and now it was the turn of the merchants.

II

Of all the cities of thirteenth-century Europe, the proudest and most splendid was Venice. Venetian merchants went everywhere. Venetian galleys kept the sea free of pirates. Every crusader had to pass eastward through Venice, parting with much of his gold on the way. The tolls of Europe made Venice rich, and the Venetians ran the Crusades like a private business enterprise.

Two outlying exponents of Venetian commerce were the brothers Niccolo and Maffeo Polo, jewelers, who owned a house in the Italian commercial colony at Soldaia, on the Black Sea. In 1260, after a trading mission to Byzantium, they set off on horseback to pay their respects to, and perhaps do some business with, the new khan of the Golden Horde: Batu's successor, Bereke. He welcomed them cordially, there was an exchange of gifts, and the Polos spent a year at his court. When war broke out between Bereke and his cousin Hulagu, the Polos quickly left the zone of hostilities, but decided to go eastward into Mongol territory instead of returning home. For three years they were held in Bokhara by the unsafe conditions of the caravan route; then came an opportunity to travel still further east in the company of an embassy from Hulagu to the newly crowned Great Khan, Kublai.

In time they arrived at Kublai's capital. The Great Khan "was greatly pleased at their arrival," according to their kinsman Marco's account. He questioned them at length about the customs of Europe, and sent them back to their own land with a request to the Pope. Kublai wanted "some hundred wise men learned in the law of Christ" to teach and preach to his Mongols, and also some holy oil from the lamp in the sacred sepulchre at Jerusalem. Three more years passed before the Polos reached the Mediterranean. At Acre, in 1269, they learned that the Pope had just died, and they decided to go home to Venice to await the election of a new Pope.

Papal politics were intricate in those days. Two years went by without an election. The brothers decided to return to Kublai without further wait, and took with them Niccolo's son, seventeen-year-old Marco. Soon after they set out, they heard of the election of Pope Gregory X; they went to him, explained Kublai's request, and were given two Dominican friars (not the hundred Kublai had wanted) and rich gifts for the khan.

The two Dominican friars, easily frightened, soon turned back. The three Polos pressed on, past Mount Ararat in Armenia, through Baghdad and Mosul, through the salt deserts of Persia, into the icy reaches of the Pamirs, and over the "roof of the world" to the oasis cities of Kashgar, Yarkand, and Khotan. Then came the thirty-day journey across the Gobi, the demon-ridden desert whose terrors and phantoms Marco described in a passage quoted above. Then they attained the Tangut country, skirted the steppe, and were greeted somewhere on China's borders by envoys of the Great Khan, who was by now also the Chinese Emperor. No doubt they passed through the Great Wall at Kia-yü-kuan, though Marco says not a word about it. It was May of 1275. They had journeyed for three and a half years.

At last they reached Shang-tu, where Kublai Khan had a stately pleasure-dome decreed. The Emperor greeted them in his sumptuous summer palace, and Marco's long service began. The boy was enrolled among the attendants of Kublai, and spent long hours telling the khan tales of the customs of Europe. In time, Kublai appointed the young Venetian as a roving ambassador, who went from city to city collecting information about Chinese ways to feed Kublai's insatiable craving for knowledge. Marco passed through Shansi, Shensi, and Szechuan; he trekked along the Tibetan frontier and went to Yunnan, and thence to northern Burma. He went by sea to southern India; he spent three years among the Tangut and three more as governor of the huge city of Yangchow; he dwelled a while at the old Mongol capital of Karakorum. Wherever he went, he kept his eyes sharp, and many years later, in 1298, a hack writer named Rustichello helped him put it all into a book while both were prisoners of the Genoese, Marco having returned to Europe three years before.

The result was imperishable. Marco Polo told Europe the story of Cathay, and found generations of readers—one of them a Genoese named Christopher Columbus, who scribbled notes in the margin of a copy of Marco Polo's book that still exists, and eventually went off in search of Cathay himself.

III

The origin of the name Cathay can detain us a moment here. It derives from the word *Khitai,* which is what Moslem historians called the Liao empire of the Khitan. The Khitan vanished after 1125, but the name somehow lingered on; the Russians to this day call China *Khitai.* Friar John of Plano Carpini spoke of Kitaia; William of Rubruck referred to Cataya, or Cathaia, and by Marco Polo's day the name had become fixed as Cathay.

It did not apply to all of China. The old Sung domain, which was in the throes of conquest when Marco reached Shang-tu in 1275, is called *Manji* or *Manzi* in Marco's text. The name was derived from an old north Chinese nickname for the southerners: *man-tzu,* "southern ruffians." Marco Polo also occasionally referred to the southern land as *Chin* or *Sin*, and later European geographers transformed that into China. No one seemed aware that Cathay and China were two names for the same land for several centuries. Cathay was reached overland, China by sea, and those who went to one did not seem to comprehend the nature of the other. Finally, at the end of the sixteenth century, Jesuit priests in the Orient sent back word that China and Cathay were identical. But the fallacy endured a while longer. An Icelandic sailor named Jon Olafsson, who visited the Indies though not China in the middle of the seventeenth century, was capable of making this statement as late as 1661:

"China is a very large and powerful land: to the south of it is India, to the west Tartary, from which it is separated by high mountains and a long wall, said to be 1,000 miles long, which stands between Cathay and China."[96]

Marco Polo visited both Cathay and China, and his failure to say a word about the Great Wall is one of the perplexing things about his narrative. A nineteenth-century scholar, the Archimandrite Palladius, argued that the wall had fallen into such disrepair in Marco's time that it hardly existed, and so escaped his notice: "The Wall as we know it, with its grandiose battlements and embrasures, is due to the work of the Ming, who all the time had to fight the Mongols."[97] But we know that Genghis Khan found the Wall in good repair when he assailed it in 1211–15, and there is no reason to believe that it had crumbled away in the space of less than a century, or that the Mongols had gone to the trouble of tearing it down. Marco Polo failed to mention a number of significant facts about China, such as the custom of binding women's feet, and that of drinking tea. Sir George Staunton, a member of the Macartney expedition to China at the end of the eighteenth century (of which more later), explained Marco's failure to mention the Wall by working out a fanciful and implausible route for him, southeastward from Samarkand across the River Ganges to Bengal, and thence south of the mountains of Tibet and into China. This route would indeed have brought Marco to China without encountering the Great Wall, but it does not fit at all with what Marco tells us of his route, which clearly skirted the Gobi and brought him in the customary way, along the Kansu panhandle. Beyond doubt Marco Polo saw the Wall, just as he drank tea, met women with bound feet, and observed other Chinese customs that he neglected to describe. Perhaps he simply neglected to put everything down. It is said that many of his friends thought he had exaggerated the wonders of Cathay, and that, when on his deathbed, they asked him "to correct the book, by removing everything that went beyond the facts. To which his reply was that he had not told *one half* of what he had really seen."[98] The Great Wall may have been in that undescribed half.

What Marco did describe was impressive enough. He dwelled long on Kublai himself, who was "very shapely in all his limbs," having "a becoming amount of flesh," being "neither tall nor short, but of a middle height." The Emperor's complexion was "white and red, the eyes black and fine, the nose well formed and well set on. He has four wives, whom he retains permanently as his legitimate consorts."

The palace at Cambaluc awed the Venetian, with good reason. He tells us, "You must know that it is the greatest palace that ever was. The hall of the palace is so large that it could easily dine 6,000 people; and it is quite a marvel to see how many rooms there are besides. The building is altogether so vast, so rich and so beautiful, that no man on earth could design anything superior to it. The outside of the roof also is all colors with vermilion and yellow and green and blue and other hues, which are fixed with a varnish so fine and exquisite that they shine like crystal. . . ."[99]

Marco's pages shine like crystal too, with the reflected opulence of Kublai Khan. His famous descriptions of the splendors of Cambaluc and the differently splendid cities of the newly conquered south need no further quotation here. Several curious passages do, however, and bring us to a strange myth of the medieval world: the Wall of Gog and Magog, built by Alexander the Great.

Marco makes two separate references to the components of this myth. Passing through Georgia, in the Caucasus, he speaks of the legendary campaigns of Alexander the Great, and says, "I should let you know that Alexander had a tower and fortress built here, so that the natives could not sally out to attack him. This was called the Iron Gates. It is the place where the *Alexander Book* relates that he shut in the Tartars between two mountains. In fact they were not Tartars, but people called Comanians and various other races besides, because there were no Tartars at that time."[100]

The other reference deals with Mongolia, and says nothing about walls: "This is the place which we call in our language Gog and Magog; the natives call it Ung and Mungul. Each of these two provinces was inhabited by a separate race: in Ung lived the Gog, in Mungul the Tartars."[101]

Alexander's wall in the Caucasus; Gog and Magog in Mongolia—clear enough to Marco. It was less clear to others, who had managed to befuddle the issue so that Alexander's (mythical) wall became a barrier against the (mythical) tribes of Gog and Magog. That wall now was identified with the Great Wall of China. The western world, when it learned of the Great Wall, moved Alexander's wall into China and accepted the Mongols as Gog and Magog. Some unraveling of the snarled legends is required here.

IV

Gog and Magog are Biblical names. In *Genesis*, x, 2, we are told that Magog was one of the sons of Japheth. In *Ezekiel*, xxxviii, occurs the line, "And the word of the Lord came unto me, saying, Son of man, set thy face toward Gog, of the land of Magog, the prince of Rosh, Meshech, and Tubal."

Ezekiel delivers himself of a grim prophecy concerning Gog a few lines on: "And thou [Gog] shalt come from thy place out of the uttermost parts of the north, thou and many peoples with thee, all of them riding upon horses, a great company and a mighty army. . . . Surely in that day there shall be a great shaking in the land of Israel; so that the fishes of the sea, and the fowls of the heaven, and the beasts of the field, and all creeping things that creep upon the earth, shall shake at my presence, and the mountains shall be thrown down, and the steep places shall fall, and every wall shall fall to the ground."

There is a New Testament citation too, *Revelation,* xx, 7–8: "And when the thousand years are finished, Satan shall be loosed out of his prison, and shall come forth to deceive the nations which are in the four corners of the earth, Gog and Magog, to gather them together to the war; the number of whom is as the sand of the sea."

Ezekiel wrote about 600 B.C., and what he meant by Gog and Magog is a debatable matter. Perhaps his lines echoed some tradition of the invasion of the Cimmerians, a barbaric northern people who invaded the Near East about 700 B.C., or of the Scythians, who came a generation later. Nearly a thousand years went by, and new barbarians descended. They were the Huns, the displaced Hsiung-nu who were deflected by the Great Wall of China, kept going west into Russia, and eventually tumbled down on the Roman world, wreaking havoc everywhere. A particularly terrifying Hun invasion in 395 saw the barbarian tribes breaking out of the Caucasus to ravage the Christian Byzantine Empire, the eastern half of the sundered Roman world. It must have seemed then as if the prophecies of Ezekiel had come true, and that Gog and Magog were loosed upon the world.

There was an entirely different cycle of legends dealing with Alexander the Great, adding a whole series of fanciful achievements to the remarkable things Alexander really did. One bit of embroidery that may have been woven about the third century A.D. was the notion, cited above by Marco Polo, that Alexander built a wall between two mountains in the Caucasus to keep the barbarians back. The irruption of the Huns in 395 completed the equation: Alexander had built a wall in the Caucasus to hold back Gog and Magog.

By the sixth century A.D., this had been embodied in various manuscripts, of which the earliest known is the Syrian *Christian Legend Concerning Alexander,* probably written in 514. In this tale, Alexander leads his troops into the high mountains of the Caucasus, and discovers that beyond the highest mountain of all dwells a savage and barbaric tribe. Questioning a native of the place, Alexander asks, "Who are the nations within this mountain upon which we are looking?"

"They are Huns," is the reply.

"Who are their kings?" Alexander asks.

And he is told, "Gog and Magog and Nawal the kings of the sons of Japhet; and Gig and Teamron [and ten more], these are the kings of the Huns."

Turning now to his troops, Alexander asks, "Do you desire that we should do something wonderful in this land?" And the legend continues:

"They said to him, 'As thy majesty commands we will do.' The king said, 'Let us make a gate of brass and close up this breach.' His troops said, 'As thy majesty commands we will do.' And Alexander commanded and fetched three thousand smiths, workers in iron, and three thousand men, workers in brass. And they put down brass and iron, and kneaded it as a man kneads when he works clay. Then they brought it and made a gate, the length of which was twelve cubits and its breadth eight cubits. And he made a lower threshold from mountain to mountain, the length of which was twelve cubits;

and he hammered it into the rocks of the mountains, and it was fixed in with brass and iron."[102] Having done this, Alexander caused an inscription to be engraved on the gate, to the effect that at the end of eight hundred and twenty-six years the Huns would break forth and "make the earth tremble," and that at the conclusion of nine hundred and forty years "the world shall come to an end by the command of God."

The legend took root. Other authors altered it in various ways, adding a Hun king or two, putting ever more lofty speeches into Alexander's mouth, but always maintaining the idea that Alexander's wall against Gog and Magog, which is to say the Huns, was in the Caucasus, in the vicinity of the Caspian Sea—a long way from China. One such later author was the one who produced the fanciful tale of Alexander that goes by the name of Pseudo-Callisthenes, because it is credited apocryphally to Callisthenes, a companion of Alexander. This is the *Alexander Book* to which Marco Polo refers—a favorite romance of the Middle Ages.

The story also planted itself, strangely, in the Koran. When Mohammed and his followers compiled the Moslem scripture in the seventh century, some-one bodily lifted the tale from one of the Syrian manuscripts and inserted it in the section known as "The Cave," giving Alexander the Arabic name of Dhu'l-Qarneyn, "the two-horned one," derived from yet another legend. This is the version in the Koran:

93. Then he followed a road.

94. Till, when he came between the two mountains, he found upon their hither side a folk that scarce could understand a saying.

95. They said: O Dhu'l-Qarneyn! Lo! Gog and Magog are spoiling the land. So may we pay thee tribute on condition that thou set a barrier between us and them?

96. He said: That wherein my Lord hath established me is better (than your tribute). Do but help me with strength (of men), I will set between you and them a bank.

97. Give me pieces of iron—till, when he had levelled up (the gap) between the cliffs, he said: Blow!—till, when he had made it a fire, he said: Bring me molten copper to pour thereon.

98. And (Gog and Magog) were not able to surmount, nor could they pierce (it).[103]

What is most curious about this Koranic account is that its author must certainly have known that there was a genuine wall in the Caucasus, built not by Alexander but rather, quite recently, by the Persian King Anushirvan, in whose reign Mohammed was born.

Anushirvan's wall was at Derbend, right on the Caspian's western shore. It was build around A.D. 542, and was generally known as the Iron Gate. Since it dated from a generation after the Syrian Alexander story, there was no rea-son for anyone to think that it had been built by Alexander about 330 B.C. Certainly Mohammed did not think so. But in Europe, those who heard of the Iron Gate of Derbend and knew the tale of Alexander's wall in the Cau-casus eventually merged the two, robbing Anushirvan of credit and dubbing his wall "The Iron Gate of Alexander."

Later Christian travelers followed this tradition. We have already noted Marco Polo's reference; many others could be cited, such as that of William of Rubruck, who also talked of "Porta Ferrea, or the Iron Gate, now called Derbend, which Alexander built to exclude the barbarous nations out of Persia."[104]

The Moslems knew well enough that the wall at Derbend was Anushirvan's, not Alexander's. But where, then, was the wall of which the Koran spoke? In the ninth century, one Caliph of Baghdad was troubled enough by that question to send out an expedition—which may well have reached the Great Wall of China.

He was Wathiq-bi'llah, who began his short reign as Commander of the Faithful in 842. Though something less than a successful monarch, Wathiq was a man of inquiring mind, particularly given to the exploration of certain romantic myths. As soon as he became Caliph, for example, he sent the astronomer Mohammed ben Musa in search of the Seven Sleepers of Ephesus, the legendary Christian youths who supposedly entered a Syrian cave in A.D. 250 to avoid persecution, fell into a miraculous sleep, and awoke from time to time thereafter to utter prophecies. The astronomer sent by Wathiq was shown certain undecayed corpses in a cave at Arabissus, and accepted them as the remains of the Seven Sleepers.

A few years later, Wathiq sent another man known as Sallam the Interpreter to find Alexander's wall. An Islamic prince of Armenia had done the same in the middle of the seventh century, and, so the unlikely story had it, the wall was eventually found deep in Asia, bearing inscribed upon it the passage from the Koran quoted above. This tale was probably known to Wathiq. The story of Wathiq's expedition is related in the writings of an Arab geographer and historian, Ibn Khurdadbih, whose account dates from 846. According to this narrative, the Caliph Wathiq had dreamed that the wall built by Dhu'l-Qarneyn (Alexander) against Gog and Magog had opened—a serious matter, since it meant the imminent end of the world. Troubled, Wathiq summoned a man called Sallam the Interpreter, who spoke thirty languages.

"I wish you to go out to the Rampart," the Caliph said, "that you may actually see it, and bring me news of it."[105]

He furnished Sallam with a company of fifty strong men, and gave him fifty thousand gold pieces for expenses, and provided food for a year. "And he ordered felt cloaks covered with morocco leather to be made for the men. And he had saddle-cloths of fur, and wooden stirrups made for them. He gave [Sallam] two hundred mules to carry the provisions and water."

The expedition set out from Samarra, in Iraq, and journeyed through Armenia and into the land of the Alans, a mountain folk, and eastward to the country of the Khazars. At a place called Ika, they first saw the mountains of the land of Gog and Magog, and were told by the people that Alexander had camped there long before. Three days' journey further on, the Arabs reached "a lofty mountain on which was a fortress," and looked out toward Alexander's wall. Ibn Khurdadbih gives Sallam's account:

"And the Rampart which Dhu'l-Qarneyn built is in a broad opening between two mountains, the breadth of which is two hundred cubits. That was the road through which they [Gog and Magog] issued and spread over the earth.

"And he dug the foundation of it to the depth of thirty cubits, and built it of iron and copper until it reached to the surface of the ground. Then he raised two side pillars near to the mountains on both sides of the opening twenty-five cubits broad and fifty cubits high. . . . The whole was built with iron bricks covered with copper, each a cubit and a half by a cubit and a half, and four finger-breadths high." Sallam described the gate as having a bolt, "seven cubits long and a fathom round, which two men could not draw." There was also an immense lock, from which hung a key a cubit and a half long. Adjoining the gate were two huge fortresses.

The wall was in perfect repair but for one crack as thin as a thread. Sallam scraped some rust from this crack to show to the Caliph. Upon asking the men of the fortress, "Have you seen anyone of Gog and Magog," he was told that giants were often seen on the mountains within the wall. Satisfied, Sallam departed, and Ibn Khurdadbih says that he returned to the Caliph in twelve months and some days, having made the outbound journey to the wall in sixteen months.

Whether the wall Sallam reached was the Great Wall of China has been a point of contention among geographers ever since. The twentieth-century view seems to be that the entire story is a fable, or else that Sallam reached some other wall somewhere in Turkestan. I prefer to agree with the nineteenth-century Dutch scholar, M. J. de Goeje, who thought that Sallam's wall was the Great Wall. It does not seem likely that he could have reached Kia-yü-kuan, which was thought to be the western terminus of the Wall until Aurel Stein rediscovered the Han extension in 1907. It could very well be that the Arab party did reach the Wall at Tun-huang, which was still being maintained in T'ang times. Ibn Khurdadbih mentions that one of the first towns Sallam came to on his return journey was Al-Lub; Marco Polo called the desert surrounding Tun-huang the "Desert of Lop," and the lake of Lop Nor or Lob Nor is not far from the last watchtower of the Tun-huang limb of the Great Wall.

Whatever the truth of Sallam's expedition the fact is indisputable that Moslem geographers began to place Alexander's wall in China, and to identify it with the Great Wall, news of which had long since reached them. Thus the geographer Abulfeda (1273–1331) writes, "The Ocean turns northward along the east of China, and then expands in the same direction till it passes China, and comes opposite to the Rampart of Yajuj and Majuj." And Ibn Battuta, a rollicking, globe-trotting Arab from Tangier, who spent twenty-eight years roaming the world, covering 75,000 miles and acquiring more wives than even the Prophet thought wise, makes an even more explicit identification of the Great Wall as the wall against Gog and Magog. Ibn Battuta set out for China in 1342, accompanying an embassy from the Sultan of Delhi, whom he had served for eight years. Shipwrecked en route, the durable Arab spent a year and a half in the Maldive Islands (where he was made a judge), then visited Ceylon, Bengal, and the Malay Archipelago, and finally got to China in 1347, late in the period of Mongol rule.

Ibn Battuta reported that "China is the safest as well as the pleasantest of all the regions on the earth for a traveller. You may travel the whole nine months' journey to which the empire extends without the slightest cause for fear, even if you have treasure in your charge."[106] However, he entered China from the seaward side, and his travels took him only through the port cities of the south. The accuracy of his observations is rendered doubtful by his remark that "Beyond this city of Sin-ul-Sin [Canton] there are no other cities, whether of infidels or Musulmans," which leads us to wonder if he had ever heard of majestic Cambaluc in the north. He goes on to comment that "Between it [Canton] and the Rampart, or Great Wall of Gog and Magog, there is a space of sixty days' journey as I was told. This territory is occupied by wandering tribes of heathen, who eat such people as they can catch, and for this reason no one enters their country or attempts to travel there. I saw nobody in this city who had been to the Great Wall, or who knew anybody who had been there."[107]

Perhaps if Ibn Battuta had ventured north of Canton, he would have brought back more exact information about the Great Wall. But its identification with Alexander's wall was now complete, so far as Moslems were concerned. In the west, there was still an element of haziness, some writers (like Marco Polo and William of Rubruck) declaring Alexander's wall to be that built by Anushirvan at Derbend, and others now placing it in China. The celebrated map of 1375 known as the Catalan Map, compiled in Barcelona and based mainly on Marco Polo's written account, pushes the Great Wall into the remote northeastern corner of Asia, with an inscription indicating that it shuts up the tribes of Gog and Magog. But the mountains surrounding Gog and Magog on that map are called the *Caspis* Mountains, showing that the map-maker had some lingering feeling that Alexander's wall really ought to be in the vicinity of the Caspian, at Derbend, and not off somewhere in the wild reaches of China. Gog and Magog remained on maps of China for centuries; Mercator put them there in 1569 (though he had them up by the Arctic circle, far north of the Great Wall, which he also charted).

V

Marco Polo and the elder Polos had difficulties escaping from Kublai Khan's benevolent presence. He found them so useful and diverting that he kept them in Cathay, loading them with wealth and honor but refusing to grant their wish to let them visit their native city once again. Seventeen years had passed since their arrival at Kublai's court.

An opportunity to depart occurred in 1292. Some years before, Argun, the Mongol Khan of Persia, had lost his favorite wife, and he had sent ambassadors to Cambaluc to obtain a new bride from the same Mongol tribe. The ambassadors feared to return to Persia via the overland route, because of military uncertainties along the way, but they feared equally to journey by sea, and so they remained at Kublai's court until they discovered that there were three foreigners in the service of the Great Khan who were experienced seamen. Argun's ambassadors begged Kublai to let them have the Polos as guides and companions for their return voyage.

Kublai reluctantly agreed. Early in 1292, the expedition set out from a Chinese port in fourteen huge junks. Aboard were Marco, his father and uncle, the envoys of the Persian khan, and the princess, a lovely girl of seventeen. (One version of Marco's account says that they also took a Sung princess who had been captured and reared by Kublai's queen.) The journey was a slow one; by the time the party reached Persia, two years later, two of the three Persian envoys had died en route. The Persian khan had died in the meanwhile also; the Mongol princess was handed over to the young new khan, and the Polos remained for nine months at the Persian court. While they were there, news came of the death of Kublai Khan, at eighty. The entire vast Mongol empire mourned, and with good reason, for it would never have so wise a leader again. Continuing onward, the Polos reached Venice at the end of 1295. They had been gone more than twenty years, and, it is said, no one recognized them at first. In time they proved their identity, and invited all their kinsmen to a sumptuous banquet. Then—the story comes from Ramusio, the Italian who edited the text of Marco's narrative in the fifteenth century—they donned coarse coats of Mongol make at the banquet table, and, rising grandly, they ripped open the seams and the linings, "upon which there poured forth a great quantity of precious stones, rubies, sapphires, carbuncles, diamonds, and emeralds, which had been sewn into each coat with great care, so that nobody could have suspected that anything was there. . . . The exhibition of such an extraordinary and infinite treasure of jewels and precious stones, which covered the table, once more filled all present with such astonishment that they were dumb and almost beside themselves with surprise: and they at once recognized those honored and venerated gentlemen . . . whom at first they had doubted, and received them with the greatest honor and reverence."[108]

After three years of regaling Venice with his boundless (and probably half-believed) tales of Mongol magnificence, Marco went to sea again, as commander of a galley in Venice's long-running naval war with Genoa. He was captured and flung into prison to our everlasting benefit, for there he met the journeyman romancer Rustichello, who collaborated with him on the book of his travels. He was released after a year, and returned to Venice, where he lived in wealth and honor until his death in 1324.

VI

Kublai's grandson Timur was now Great Khan of the Mongols, and Emperor in Cathay. The Mongol khans of the western realms paid lip service to him as their supreme monarch, but the empire of Genghis was well on its way to dissolution, and Timur Khan's power in fact extended only to the borders of his Chinese dominion. He was a pious Mongol, of sorts, who reintroduced the worship of Confucius, fostered the cultivation of music and poetry, and presided over the development of a new Chinese art form, the prose novel. As a gesture toward reform, Timur dispensed with the services of 18,000 bureaucrats who had been accused of exploiting the people.

He was tolerant toward Christianity. To his court in 1295 had come Friar John of Montecorvino, of the same Franciscan order as those earlier travelers,

John of Plano Carpino and William of Rubruck. At the age of fifty, John of Montecorvino had left Italy to become papal legate to India and China; he labored alone at the court of Cathay for eleven years, establishing a Roman Catholic church and weaning converts away from Nestorian Christianity and the pagan creeds. In 1307, Pope Clement V rewarded him with the resounding title of Archbishop of Cambaluc. In a letter that he sent from Cambaluc in 1307, the Archbishop reported, "I have built a church in the city of Cambaliech, in which the king has his chief residence. This I completed six years ago; and I have built a bell-tower to it, and put three bells in it. I have baptized there, as well as I can estimate, up to this time some 6,000 persons. . . . And I am often still engaged in baptizing.

"Also I have gradually bought one hundred fifty boys, the children of pagan parents, and of ages varying from seven to eleven, who have never learned any religion. These boys I have baptized, and I have taught them Greek and Latin after our manner. . . . Eleven of the boys already know our service, and form a choir and take their weekly turn of duty as they do in convents, whether I am there or not. . . . His Majesty the Emperor moreover delights much to hear them chanting."[109]

Timur Khan died in that year, and in the next twenty-five years no less than six Emperors of the Yüan Dynasty briefly occupied the increasingly shaky Mongol throne. The Emperors had lost control of China; the foreign bureaucrats were hated, the native ones were unreliable, and the administration crumbled with awesome speed. Archbishop John labored on through the time of gathering chaos, lamenting, "I myself am grown old and gray, more with toil and trouble than with years." More Catholic priests, all Franciscans, came to aid him in China, such as Odoric of Pordenone, who visited much of Asia en route and left a travel book nearly as fascinating as Marco Polo's. Friar Odoric witnessed the notable scene of the Mongol Great Khan kissing the cross before Archbishop John. The saintly Archbishop died in 1328. Eventually his place was taken by the last great Christian missionary to Mongol China, Friar John of Marignolli, who served at Cambaluc from 1342 to 1346.

The merchants were still coming, too. They generally took the overland route from Tana on the Black Sea, traveling in safety from the domain of one Mongol prince to the next—for, however much they might quarrel among themselves, the khans were of one family, and a kind of *pax mongolica* prevailed, keeping the roads open most of the time. Thus Francis Balducci Pegolotti of Florence, who wrote a handbook of travel information for the use of merchants about 1340, could remark, "The road you travel from Tana to Cathay is perfectly safe, whether by day or night, according to what merchants say who have used it."

But darkness was descending. Tohan Timur, the tenth Emperor of the Mongol line, ruled a paralyzed land. The Chinese were rising to throw off the barbarian yoke. The rebellion came; the Mongols fled. All China was Chinese again, for the first time since the great days of the T'ang, and suddenly a silken curtain hard as steel closed off the borders. The foreigners left. The missions were closed. The Great Wall was again the chief symbol of China's outlook on the world.

Fourteen.
The Ming Dynasty

The new dynasty followed the familiar Chinese dynastic pattern. It rose in a time of chaos, founded by a strong man who wished to rectify the wrongs of the previous monarchs as well as to possess power. An initial period of consolidation and organization gave way to a time of vigorous expansion and construction, which in turn put a strain on the national resources that led to gradual decay. The weak, dissolute Emperors that always seemed to come to the throne in the second century of a dynasty aided the process of collapse, making necessary an eventual period of reform, followed by renewed mal-administration and the inevitable toppling of the dynasty.

The strong man who initiated the dynasty was Chu Yüan-chang, born in 1328 to a peasant family. Strikingly ugly, with a snoutlike face that brought him the whispered nickname of "Pig Emperor," he spent a hard, lonely child-hood, and after a famine had left him without family he entered a Buddhist monastery. As the Mongol regime began to fall apart, Chu joined a Chinese rebel army, and by 1356 he had risen to be general, and captured Nanking as the Chinese began to push the Mongols northward.

The barbarian overlords had never been popular in China, and their num-bers were so few that a mass civil uprising, with peasants assassinating the foreign bureaucrats all over the empire, nearly wiped them out. A steady re-treat toward the Great Wall marked the last years of Mongol rule. By 1368, they had been driven from Peking, and two years later the last Mongol Em-peror died at Genghis' old capital of Karakorum, removing the symbol of Mongol authority. A year later, the Mongols had been chased entirely out of China; the panicky descendants of the warriors of Genghis fled like sheep be-fore the onrushing Chinese armies.

After the capture of Peking in 1368, Chu Yüan-chang named himself the first Emperor of the Ming ("Brilliant") Dynasty. In proper Chinese tradition, his successors gave him a posthumous title chosen from the small group of usual names, in this case T'ai Tsu ("Grand Progenitor") which had also been given to Genghis Khan and to the first Sung Emperor, among others. But Ming T'ai Tsu is also—and better—known by his "year period," Hung-wu, which

Ming Dynasty China

meant "Vast Military Power." All previous Chinese Emperors had designated various "year periods" throughout their reign, changing the names as the fancy pleased them. At the outset of the Ming, the custom was altered, so that the Emperor kept the same "year period" through his entire reign. Ming Emperors, and those of the Ch'ing Dynasty that followed, are generally spoken of by these secondary titles. Thus we call the founder of the Ming Hung-wu. In all accuracy, we should say "The Emperor of the Hung-wu period, or "The Hung-wu Emperor," but it is simpler to call him "Hung-wu" and let the rest be understood.

Hung-wu was a capable administrator, intelligent, foresighted, clever, above all a superb politician. To him fell the dynasty-founder's task of reorganizing a government that had come to pieces, and this he did with a vengeance;

"subversives" and "collaborators" were rooted out vigorously, and thousands perished in the purges, many of them innocent. The harsh background of Hung-wu's own life, and perhaps his great ugliness, made him irascible, suspicious, and in his later years almost pathologically violent. He grew despotic, condemning his subordinates to terrible tortures for petty offenses, and in 1380 abolished the prime ministership and the central chancellery, thereby removing much of the machinery by which an Emperor could reach down to the lower regions of the bureaucracy. His attempt at one-man government led to the formation of unofficial governing bodies within the court, one composed of the Emperor's secretaries, the other a league of court eunuchs. In later reigns, the secretaries took on an institutional role as a kind of "kitchen cabinet," while the eunuchs eventually came to dominate the Emperors completely.

The first Ming Emperor chose Nanking, the center of population and wealth, as his capital. There he reigned until 1398; at his death, he named his grandson as his successor, having outlived his eldest son. "For thirty-one years," Hung-wu wrote in his final testament, "I have labored to discharge Heaven's will, tormented by worries and fears, without relaxing for a day."

The new Emperor's rule was short. Civil war broke out between the monarch and his ambitious uncle, Chu Ti. The latter, who bore the title of Prince of Yen (the area around modern Peking), resented having been passed over in the line of succession; he was the fourth son of Hung-wu. The new Emperor tried to mollify him by making him administrator of northern China, but Chu Ti launched a war from his northern base, defeated the loyalist forces of the north in a series of bloody battles, and marched southward toward the capital. In 1403 he crossed the Yangtze and entered the capital. Hui Ti, the young Emperor, disappeared in the confusion and was never seen again, though in after years various pretenders appeared, claiming to be the deposed Emperor, and won fairly widespread backing for their short-lived revolts.

Chu Ti took the throne at the age of forty-three. His imperial title was T'ai Tsung, but he is always known by his reign title of Yung-lo ("Perpetual Happiness"). Though he began his rule under the cloud of his usurpation, Yung-lo was a powerful and effective ruler, who strengthened the country, kept the Mongols at bay, and earned a glorious place in Chinese annals.

II

One of the monuments of Yung-lo's reign is a scholarly one: the world's vastest encyclopedia, a compilation that is to the *Encyclopaedia Britannica* as the Great Wall of China is to a garden hedge. Yung-lo's reign had commenced with an anti-intellectual act for which he was much criticized; the scholar and poet Fang Hsiao-ju, tutor to the overthrown Emperor Hui Ti, refused to serve the usurper, and Yung-lo had him cut to pieces in the market place, his family exterminated, and his philosophical writings burned. Perhaps in atonement for this harsh deed, Yung-lo ordered, several months later, an enormous compilation of all knowledge into one book of many volumes.

Commissioned in 1403, the great work was completed in five years by a staff consisting of five chief directors, twenty subdirectors, and some 2,100 subordinates. Known as the *Yung-lo Ta-tien,* the encyclopedia comprised 11,095 bound volumes containing 22,877 chapters, plus an extensive index. Each volume was half an inch thick, one foot eight inches high, and one foot broad. Piled one atop the other, they would have made a stack 460 feet in height.

There were 917,480 pages, each produced by hand, for the work was considered too bulky to print. Whole books were copied straight into the encyclopedia, being borrowed from collections in every part of the realm, and the result was a compendium of all existing Chinese information from legendary times through A.D. 1400. Originally kept at the capital, Nanking, the set was transferred to Peking when Yung-lo moved his court there in 1421. In 1567, two complete copies were made, and the original and one of the copies went back to Nanking, where they were destroyed in the uprising that ended the Ming Dynasty in 1644. The surviving copy remained at Peking, and went up in flames in 1900 during the Boxer rebellion. Just 368 volumes were saved, and these are scattered in museums and libraries all over the world.

In the same year as the completion of the encyclopedia, Yung-lo began to wage war against the Mongols. Although they had been driven beyond the Great Wall, they still remained a threat to China's internal security. During the Hung-wu reign, Chinese armies had gone deep into the steppe, twice seizing Karakorum and marching as far north as the borders of Siberia as they put the discouraged Mongols to flight. There were dynastic struggles in Mongolia that further weakened the outcast nomads, but early in the fifteenth century they were once more unified by a chieftain named A-lu-t'ai. In 1405, A-lu-t'ai overthrew the reigning Mongol khan and replaced him with a puppet descended from Kublai. Yung-lo promptly sent an emissary asking that this khan, Ben-ya-shi-li, acknowledge the Ming Emperor's supremacy. At A-lu-t'ai's direction, the khan refused, and Mongol forces began to harass the Great Wall frontier. (A threat from a different direction had failed to materialize. In the western Chagadai Khanate, with its capital at Samarkand, there had arisen a conqueror named Timur, known as "Tamerlane" in Europe, who had much of Genghis' fighting spirit. Tamerlane swiftly and violently overran Persia, Mesopotamia, southern Russia, and northern India, and was planning to invade China and convert it forcibly to Islam. His death in 1405 ended the threat.)

In 1408, Yung-lo sent an army into the steppe to deal with Ben-ya-shi-li and A-lu-t'ai. The army was driven back in defeat. The following year, Yung-lo himself led the troops that marched through the Great Wall. More than 100,000 soldiers and 30,000 cartloads of supplies took part in the campaign. Awed by the size of the force, Ben-ya-shi-li and his minister were unable to agree on a defensive strategy; the khan fled westward, where he was slain by a rival Mongol chief, and A-lu-t'ai escaped eastward with a Mongol army that was surrounded and defeated by Yung-lo. A-lu-t'ai survived, and acknowledged the supremacy of the Ming Emperor, who rewarded him with a title.

The Mongols of the steppe had now divided into two factions. In the east, beyond the Kerulen River, they called themselves Tatars; the nomads of the mountainous west were known as Oirats. There was constant strife between these two groups, while Yung-lo enthusiastically encouraged the division by favoring now one, now the other faction. In September of 1410, the Emperor led an army eastward to the Onon River and dealt the Tatars a crushing defeat. A few years later, the Oirats went on the warpath again, and between April and August, 1414, Yung-lo campaigned against them, subduing them with the aid of cannon, and suffering heavy Chinese losses.

The struggle was a never-ending one. A-lu-t'ai, who had made himself the leader of the Tatar faction about 1413, threatened an invasion of China in 1421, but before it could materialize he was himself raided by the Oirats, and had to flee into Manchuria. The following year, he recouped his strength and troubled China's borders again; Yung-lo led forth an army of 235,000 men, requisitioning 117,000 carts and 340,000 donkeys from the peasants of northern China to carry his supplies. A-lu-t'ai escaped, but the Chinese seized a great deal of booty. Again in 1423 and 1424 Yung-lo pursued the Tatar chieftain, without ever quite catching him, and it was on the latter campaign, his fifth in the steppe, that the Emperor suddenly died after a vigorous and active reign.

III

In 1421, a few years before his death, Yung-lo had taken an important step that signalized a return to earlier Chinese attitudes. He transferred the capital from Nanking to Peking. For five hundred years, since the downfall of the T'ang, the political center of *Chinese* China had been the south; Peking, under its various names, had served as the capital of such barbarian masters as the Khitan, the Chin, and the Mongols. In one stroke Yung-lo repudiated the Sung tradition of a capital in the south and his own father's preference for the same region. For the first time, a Chinese Emperor ruled from Peking, only a few dozen miles from the Great Wall.

It was a momentous decision. The court left the rich and culturally developed center of Nanking to take up residence in the heart of a region that had been devastated in civil war and nomad raids. Peking had to be completely rebuilt once more, and the Grand Canal restored. The motive for the move was largely a strategic one; A-lu-t'ai was persistently troublesome beyond the Great Wall, and the best way to prevent a new Mongol invasion of China was to establish the imperial authority along the northern frontier. The official dynastic annalist explained it in this way:

"The descendants of the Yüan Dynasty, after being driven out of China, constantly endeavored to regain their lost dominion. When the capital was removed to the north by Yung-lo, the Great Wall was near to it on three sides, and from that time the enemy became day by day more troublesome. Therefore, to the end of the Ming Dynasty, the defense of the Great Wall became a leading object. Beginning on the east at the Yalu River and extending westward to the Kiayukuan, in length 3,500 miles, this long line was subdivided between numerous garrisons. The first was on the borders of Korea at Liao-tung. . . . Four others were successively established, extending to Ninghsia

in Kansu. This Emperor, Yung-lo, was especially attentive to the defenses from Süenhuafu and westward to Shansi; this reach extends over high hills and deep defiles, where he established watchtowers and guardhouses connected together.

"At each transit pass capable of admitting carts and horsemen, guard posts of one hundred men each were established. At the smaller passes for carriers of fuel and herdsmen with their flocks, ten men. The instructions given to the generals ran thus: 'At each signal station let the towers be built higher and stronger; within must be laid up food, fuel, medicine, and weapons for four moons. Beside the tower let a wall be opened, enclosed by a wall as high as the tower itself, presenting the appearance of a double gateway, inner and outer. Be on your guard at all times with anxious care.' Such were the commands of the Emperor."[110]

Since the Yüan Dynasty had had no reason to maintain the Great Wall, it had fallen into disrepair during the two centuries since the defeat of the Jurchen. Under Yung-lo and later Ming Emperors, the most extensive campaign of Great Wall reconstruction since Ch'in Shih Huang Ti's time was carried out. The heaviest concentration of effort was in the east, naturally, to protect Peking from the raids of A-lu-t'ai's Tatars. The Oirats of the west were also troublesome, though, and the Kia-yü-kuan end of the Wall was not neglected.

One travel account of the time tells us something about the state of the Kia-yü-kuan end of the frontier in Yung-lo's reign. In 1419, Shah Rukh, the Timurid Khan of Persia, tried to reopen the lines of communication with China that had been broken at the collapse of the Yüan Dynasty. The youngest son of the bloody conqueror Tamerlane, Shah Rukh began his rule at a time when the old Mongol empire was in ruins, and presided over something of a renaissance in western Asia.

His embassy to China included three Persian nobles and a painter, Khoja Ghayath-ud-din. Ghayath-ud-din compiled a narrative of his journey which was incorporated into a Persian history of Shah Rukh's reign, and so we know that the envoys followed a traditional eastward path. They left Herat in December, 1419, and passed through Balkh, Samarkand, and Tashkent, and thence through the other oases of the Old Silk Road, at length making a twenty-five day journey across the desert to the border of China proper.

On August 24, 1420, they were met by Chinese officers, and, a day later, still in the desert, they were conducted to a place where awnings had been erected and an elegant feast spread. A Chinese official counted all the members of the party—there were five hundred and ten, including the merchants and servants accompanying the envoys—and careful affidavits were drawn. On the 26th, at another desert outpost, the commanding general of a frontier fort was their host at a second feast, placing the envoys at his left, that being the position of honor in China "because the heart is on the left side." Dishes of meat and poultry, excellent bread, walnuts and pickles, and wine in silver and porcelain goblets were put before the Persians, while dances were performed by "handsome youths adorned like women with their faces painted red and white."[111]

All this took place somewhere east of Tun-huang, evidently, but no mention is made of any kind of fortification. So the Han extension of the Wall must have passed from use at that time. We learn from Ghayath-ud-din's account that on August 27 the party proceeded on their way through the desert and arrived at a strong castle in a mountain defile, through the middle of which the road passed. This was Kia-yü-kuan, the outer limit of Ming China. Here, the entire party was counted and their names registered, and they continued eastward to the walled city of Suchow, within the Great Wall. Not until December did they reach Yung-lo. The Emperor was at Peking, which he was preparing to designate as his capital, and the buildings were still under construction. "He was a man of the middle height," Khoja reported, "his face neither very large nor very small, and not without some beard; indeed two or three hundred hairs of his beard were long enough to form three or four curls upon his chest." The Persians spent five months in Peking, set out for home in May, 1421, and reached Herat in September of the following year. The report of their embassy provides the first non-Chinese mention of Kia-yü-kuan's revived status as the western terminus of the Great Wall.

The fortifications at Tun-huang had served to watch over the travelers passing along the Old Silk Road; Tun-huang was an outward-looking frontier. Kia-yü-kuan, when it served as the last outpost both in pre-Han days and again in the Ming time, faced inward. Those who journeyed thither were received hospitably, but they were numbered and registered, and regarded with a certain degree of suspicion by the xenophobic Ming Chinese, who had no yearning for commerce with foreigners. Such sparse traffic as came over the Pamirs in the fifteenth and sixteenth centuries met treatment similar to that accorded Shah Rukh's envoys. Thus, about 1560, Gislen de Busbeck, ambassador of the Holy Roman Emperor Charles V to the Turkish Sultan at Constantinople, took down a Turkish account of the route to Kia-yü-kuan that sounds much like that of the Shah Rukh party. The Turk told Gislen that beyond Samarkand and Bokhara lie extensive deserts, "some occupied by savage and inhospitable tribes, others by people of more civilized character, but everywhere scantily supplied with food and forage, so that everyone has to take his victuals and other necessaries along with him, and this involves a large number of camels to carry the loads.

"Such large companies of men and beasts," Gislen was informed, "they call caravans. After a fatiguing journey of many months they come to a defile which forms, as it were, the barrier gate of Cathay. For a great part of that empire consists of inland country, and here there was an inclosing chain of rugged and precipitous mountains, affording no passage except through a narrow strait in which a garrison was stationed on the king's part. There the question is put to the merchants, 'What they bring, whence they come, and how many of them are there?' The answer being given, the king's guards pass it by signal—by smoke if in daylight, by fire if by night—to the next watchtower; then to the next, and so on, till in a few hours the message reaches the king at Cathay: a thing which would by any other communication require many days. The king sends back his orders in the same manner and with equal rapidity, saying whether all shall be admitted, or only a part, or the whole put off. . . . For the people of Cathay do not approve of the prolonged stay of foreigners among them, lest their indigenous manners should be corrupted by some foreign infection."[112]

Though few merchants came from the west, many foreigners entered the Great Wall further to the east at Ta-t'ung in Shansi. These were tribute-bearers from the Oirats, who from 1408 on sent annual missions to Peking except in times of war. Sometimes the Oirat embassies numbered several thousand individuals, including Central Asian merchants who, unable to get into China in any other way, labeled themselves "ambassadors," entered under diplomatic auspices, and proceeded to do business. It was the rule that the Oirat delegation had to be quartered and feasted at the expense of the frontier authorities, and if for any reason there was a delay at the Great Wall, it could prove expensive for the guardians of the gates; one Oirat mission, while waiting for clearance, devoured in a single month 3,000 cattle and sheep, 3,000 jars of wine, and 100 large bushels of rice, along with other provender, all at government cost.

The Oirat tribute consisted of horses and furs. In return the barbarians received imperial "gifts" of silk, satins, musical instruments, and articles of clothing. The gifts were measured out on a strict scale—so much silk for so many first-grade horses, etc.—and the elaborate tributary system was nothing other than a disguised means of carrying on trade with the nomads. To signify their vassalage, the ambassadors performed certain ritual acts of obeisance before the Emperor, the so-called "three kneelings and nine prostrations," but this was no hardship for the sake of trade. The system ultimately became a mockery; Ming annals vainly boasted of tribute from dozens of potentates, many of them mythical, while actually the "ambassadors" were merchants. Benedict de Goes, a Jesuit traveler who reached China in 1604 via the overland route, spoke acidly of "sham embassies" of merchants who "forge public letters in the names of the kings whom they profess to represent" and "under pretense of being ambassadors go and offer tribute to the Emperor." But the Mongols were being turned into middlemen for a strange but fruitful sort of foreign trade, and the sham was a cunning way of keeping the frontier pacified.

<h2 style="text-align:center">IV</h2>

Yung-lo died in 1424 while commanding troops beyond the Great Wall. His corpse lay in state for a full year while the astrologers of the court waited for an auspicious day for the royal funeral. Eventually he was laid to rest some thirteen miles south of the Great Wall, in a ring of hills that formed a horseshoe around the burial place. Yung-lo had chosen the site himself, and his successors were buried there in turn, their monuments comprising the famous Ming Tombs. An impressive avenue leads to the tombs, lined with giant statues of men and beasts, two by two, in blue limestone: a pair of unicorns, a pair of camels, two lions, two elephants, and many more. The awesome creatures make a grand array, so noble that a later Ming Emperor thought of collecting them all from the road and placing them around his own grave. A chamberlain, it is said, hurriedly chipped a small piece from each, rendering them unsuited for tomb decorations, and so they

The famous animal statues on the road to the Ming tombs.   *University Museum, University of Pennsylvania*

still remain on their splendid highway today, with the Great Wall rising in the distance to shield the tombs from malevolent spirits out of the north.

Yung-lo's eldest son succeeded him and ruled for a single year, in which he released all political prisoners and attempted to alleviate some of the heavy burdens his father's public works and military programs had placed on the people. He was followed by his eldest son, Chu Chan-chi, whose reign-period, 1426–1436, is called Hsüan-te. Hsüan-te's reign was marred by an uprising led by his father's brother, who, after the manner of Yung-lo, tried to take the throne from his nephew, but failed and perished. The Emperor was childless; the son of an imperial concubine was named as heir apparent, though his fatherhood was highly uncertain, and this prince came to rule in 1436 at the age of nine, as Ying Tsung.

His reign was ill-starred. Within three years a new Oirat chieftain had arisen in the steppe, Esen, who gathered tribe after tribe behind him until he had assembled a confederation that hailed him as chief from Liao-tung to Kansu. The boy Emperor was completely under the sway of the court eunuchs, and one of them, Wang Chên, promised an imperial princess to Esen. When the Oirat envoys arrived at Peking to collect their chieftain's bride, they were bluntly informed by Emperor Ying Tsung that he knew nothing of the promise and would yield no princesses to Esen.

It was virtually a declaration of war. In 1449, Oirat troops massed along the borders and broke through the Great Wall at Ta-t'ung. Ying Tsung, twenty-two years old and asserting his prerogatives for the first time, raised a badly prepared army of half a million men and hastened to meet the Oirat invaders. At a town on the road between Peking and Kalgan, the armies met and the Chinese were routed. The hapless Emperor was captured by Esen's men. The imperial armies fell back in disorder, but managed to defend Peking, whose colossal walls were impregnable in any case. With Chinese cannon jutting from the city's fortresses, Esen turned to negotiation. He demanded a stiff ransom for the Emperor.

To his surprise, the Chinese showed no interest in redeeming Ying Tsung. The Chinese Minister of War, Yü Ch'ien, had already placed the Emperor's brother on the throne as Ching Ti, and Esen was welcome to keep Ying Tsung. Puzzled at this turn of events, the Oirat leader returned to Mongolia, taking Ying Tsung with him. After a year, he released the useless prisoner, who returned shamefacedly to Peking.

Esen's ransom scheme had backfired, but he had won a notable victory all the same, and he proudly proclaimed himself khan of the Mongols in 1454. Almost at once, two of his commanders turned against him; he was driven into flight, and was assassinated in 1455. The Mongols were divided again; the Chinese annals report, "The Mongolian tribes dispersed in the search for water and good pastures, and their armies no longer formed a fighting unit."

Esen's brief supremacy had created an odd situation in Peking. Yü Ch'ien, having put Ching Ti on the throne, kept him there, and Ying Tsung was forced to go into seclusion. The court split into two factions. During the illness of Ching Ti in 1457, a general named Shih Hêng engineered the restoration of Ying Tsung. Shortly afterward, Ching Ti died, and at Shih Hêng's urging the restored Emperor put to death many of his brother's partisans,

including Yü Ch'ien. At this moment, a comet appeared in the sky, portending heavenly disapproval. Ying Tsung blamed the cosmic disturbance on Shih Hêng, and jailed him. Immediately storms and floods broke out all over the empire, and the perplexed Emperor, still seeking the favor of the deities, had Shih Hêng freed. Next came word from an astrologer that Shih Hêng was destined to found a new dynasty. This was too much. Shih Hêng and his son were apprehended at Ta-t'ung and were compelled to take poison. The crisscrossing court intrigues continued, however, until Ying Tsung's death in 1464.

The work of repairing the Great Wall went on, Esen's invasion serving as a grim reminder of what might happen if the Mongols became unified again. The eighth Ming Emperor, eldest son of Ying Tsung, adhered to the dynastic tradition of work on the Great Wall, even though his reign was a weak one, marred by disturbances and drought at home, difficulties beyond the frontiers, and excessive reliance on eunuchs, who practically ruled the country after 1471.

This Emperor's reign-title was Ch'êng-hua. In the third year of his reign the Oirats began to attack along the western zone of the Great Wall, and by 1472 they descended through the Ordos to take possession of the loop of the Huang Ho. Ch'êng-hua raised an army, drove the nomads out, and built new sections of the Wall where needed. In the next reign, that of Chu Yu-t'ang, forts were built outside the Wall, and cannon were cast in great numbers to arm them. These weapons were known at first as *Ta Chiang Chün,* "Great

Generals," but later, when Europeans were in China once again and teaching new techniques of destruction, they were called *Fa Lang Ch'i,* "Foreign Weapons."

The Great Wall was now taking the shape by which we know it today: the solid brick rampart topped by elegant battlements and parapets. Along the mountains north of Peking there ran the finest section of all, twenty-five feet thick at the base, fifteen to thirty feet high, fifteen feet across at the top. The Ming rulers kept that section of wall in constant repair, and it is still the joy of such tourists as manage to get to Peking. To the west, though, no such wonders were attempted; the Wall there was still fashioned of clay and rammed earth, sometimes faced with brick and stone, as it had been in the days of Ch'in Shih Huang Ti.

V

In 1514, with the tenth Ming Emperor on the throne and amusing himself with concubines, wine, and the study of the Tibetan and Mongol languages, the foreign devils arrived. They were Portuguese adventurers who arrived by sea, not too many years after Vasco da Gama and his comrades had sailed around Africa to give Portugal a sea route to the Indies.

The Chinese were startled by the appearance of the strangers, who, swarthy though they may have been, seemed sickly hued and most un-Asiatic. The visitors, too, were aware of the racial difference. A letter exists under date of January 6, 1515, to Duke Lorenzo de' Medici of Florence, written by one Andrew Corsalis, who had heard of the Portuguese feat, and who said of the Chinese:

"They are people of great skill, and on a par with ourselves, but of uglier aspect, with little bits of eyes. They dress very much after our fashion, and wear shoes and stockings like ourselves. I believe them to be pagans, though many allege that they hold our faith or some part of it. During this last year some of our Portuguese made a voyage to China. They were not permitted to land; for they say 'tis against their custom to let foreigners enter their dwellings. But they sold their goods at a great gain, and they say there is as great profit in taking spices to China as in taking them to Portugal; for 'tis a cold country and they make great use of them. It will be five hundred leagues from Malacca [a Portuguese base in Malaya] to China, sailing north."[113]

So dense was the darkness that had fallen since Marco Polo's day that the Portuguese did not realize, nor did any other Europeans for quite a while, that their China was the Cathay of an earlier era. The Portuguese had little enough opportunity to discover it, at first, since they were compelled to do business from their vessels, anchored in the Chinese harbor.

In the early days of Ming rule, China had looked ambitiously outward to the sea. Yung-lo had sent out a Moslem eunuch named Chêng Ho in 1405 with 62 vessels and 28,000 men; he reached India. A second and a third expedition went the same route, bringing back such notable plunder as ostriches, zebras, giraffes, and the kings of Palembang and Ceylon. Voyages in 1413–15 and 1417–19 attained Aden, at Arabia's southwest tip. By 1433, Chinese vessels had touched the east coast of Africa, and seven Chinese made the pilgrimage to Mecca. After 1433, the series of formidable expeditions abruptly halted. The Chinese huddled away from the sea as though a Great Wall hemmed them in to the east as well as to the north. The commerce of such coastal centers as Canton, Amoy, and Ning-po dried up; the waterways were relinquished to the Arabs, and to the Japanese pirates who preyed upon them. When the Portuguese made their unexpected appearance in 1514, they struck a China wrapped in fear of anything alien, anything strange.

Early contacts between Chinese and Europeans were unsuccessful. The Portuguese returned to Canton in 1517, carrying an ambassador named Pires. But everything went wrong; the behavior of the Portuguese so outraged the Chinese that the Europeans were expelled, and the unfortunate Pires was arrested in 1521 and died in chains somewhere in China. Strongly entrenched in Malaya, though, the Portuguese continued to work toward opening of regular trade relations with China.

In 1537, a new Portuguese expedition ventured toward the Orient. On board was a certain Fernão Mendes Pinto, twenty-eight years old, who succeeded not only in reaching China but in entering and (involuntarily) exploring it. He may have been one of the first Europeans ever to see the Great Wall—if we can believe the robust, flamboyant book he left as his monument. That book has been roughly handled in its day; some wit dubbed its author *Mendax* Pinto, using the Latin word meaning "liar," and in the seventeenth century Congreve had a character in one of his plays remark, "Ferdinand Mendes Pinto was but a type of thee, thou liar of the first magnitude." Marco Polo was given the lie too, and time has vindicated him; much of Pinto's book has been recognized, by now, as factual, and, even if he never reached the Wall, he knew how to tell a grand story.

Pinto sailed east in the fleet of Pedro da Gama, one of old Vasco's many sons. After putting in at Goa, the Portuguese haven on the Indian coast, Pinto embarked on wanderings that took him to Ethiopia, Arabia, Malaya, and Indonesia, now as a soldier, now as a doctor, now as a merchant. During a sojourn in Sumatra he met a trader named Antonio de Faria, who was working the trade routes of Southeast Asia. Set upon again and again by pirates off the Malay Peninsula, Faria eventually became a privateer himself.

Pinto cruised with him. They went to Pulo Condore, an island off the mouths of the Mekong River in Indochina; they landed on the coast of Cambodia; they visited ports all the way north to Ning-po in China, looting and plundering as they went. Ning-po was one of the few Chinese ports where foreigners were allowed to trade, though they could not go inland. While they were there, Pinto and Faria heard of an island called Calempluy, on which seventeen Chinese Emperors had supposedly been buried amid great wealth. They set out to carry off the treasures of these tombs.

No such funereal island is recorded in Chinese annals. Pinto tells us that Calempluy lay not far from Nanking, and so at no great distance from Ning-po. But his narrative claims that the voyage to Calempluy took eighty-three days, and that nearly a thousand miles were covered. His description of the island is a detailed one, speaking of gilded pagodas, gardens and fruit trees, and statues of the Buddha. Since Buddhist statues would have no place in an imperial burying ground, Pinto and Faria probably had found and looted a Buddhist monastery on some offshore island.

Coming back from this voyage, the Portuguese were shipwrecked in what Pinto calls the "Gulf of Nanking," probably Hangchow Bay. They were cast up on the Chinese mainland, emerging on a bleak, rocky promontory. The survivors made for Nanking on foot, hoping there to find a ship that would take them to Siam, and, as they legged it through the Chinese villages, they identified themselves to the Chinese as citizens of Siam. The ruse worked for nearly two months. They supported themselves by begging and made their way by a roundabout route to Nanking, but while they were still fifty miles from that city they made the mistake of entering the important town of Taiping. An imperial commissioner from Peking happened to be there on a tour of inspection, and he questioned the "Siamese." A clerk in his entourage pointed out that the strangers were undoubtedly vagabonds, who were subject to arrest under Chinese law. Pinto, Faria, and their companions were promptly jailed, flogged, and left in irons for twenty-six days. "Six and twenty thousand years it might have been in regard to the great misery we suffered," Pinto wrote, observing that the jail crawled with lice and that one of his comrades perished from the bites of the creatures: "It was almost a miracle that the rest of us escaped alive from those filthy vermin."

On the twenty-seventh morning, the prisoners were hauled from the dungeon and sent onward to Nanking, where a high court was to consider their case. Pinto was struck by the grandeur of this city, with its "fourscore thousand mandarins' houses, threescore and two great market-places, a hundred and thirty butchers' shambles, each of them containing fourscore shops, and eight thousand streets, whereof six hundred that are fairer than the rest are compassed about with balusters of copper."[114] In Nanking they were thrust into a huge jail, said to hold four thousand criminals. "One could hardly sit down in any place without being robbed and filled full of lice," Pinto declared. They were beaten again, two of the Portuguese dying of their injuries; at length they came before the court, and a member of the party explained in halting Chinese that they were neither beggars nor thieves, but honest merchants of Siam who had suffered shipwreck. The court was sympathetic, but could not order their release; they were remanded instead to a higher court in Peking.

Under guard, the Portuguese were sent by boat up the Grand Canal to the capital. They were kept in chains, but a Prisoners' Welfare Society supplied them with food, money, and clothes. Pinto gives the date of his arrival in Peking as October 9, 1541. After lengthy legal disputes, the Portuguese were released by the court—but, before they could leave the country, they were required by the judges to serve a one-year tour of labor on the Great Wall in lieu of other punishment.

The Portuguese found themselves being taken after sentencing to a place whose name Pinto renders as Xinanguibaleu—"that is to say," he explains, "the enclosure of the exiles." This was a prison "two leagues square, or little less, both in length and breadth: it is enclosed with a very high wall with-

An early German engraving of the Great Wall, obviously based on hearsay. *Picture collection, New York Public Library*

out any battlements; the wall on the outside is environed with a great deep ditch full of water, over the which are a many of drawbridges, that are drawn up in the night with certain iron chains, and so hang suspended on huge cast pillars; in this prison is an arch of strong hewed stone abutting in two towers, in the tops whereof are six great sentinel bells, which are never rung but all the rest within the said enclosure do answer them, which the Chinese affirm to be above a hundred, and indeed they make a most horrible din."[115]

In this place, Pinto informs us, were kept three hundred thousand men between seventeen and fifty years of age, all condemned to hard labor on the Great Wall. As for the Wall, Pinto offers this bit of historical information:

"In the fifth book of the chief places of that empire, is written, that King Crisnagol (which reigned as we may accord our computation with theirs about the year our Lord 528) builded the wall, the people contributing ten thousand pikes of silver (which are fifteen millions of cruzados) and two hundred fifty thousand men (thirty thousand officers and the rest laborers), which was continued seven and twenty years."[116]

The Wall, Pinto says, had a length of three hundred fifteen leagues—more than two thousand miles, which is accurate enough, though he was probably just guessing at random. "This wall," he writes, "I have seen and measured, being generally six fathoms high, and forty spans thick: and four fathoms runneth a kind of rampart, twice as thick as the wall, strengthened with a bituminous substance on the outside like potters' work; and instead of bulwarks it hath houses of two lofts with beams of black wood, called Caubesy, that is, Iron-wood, seeming stronger than if they were of stonework. This wall or Chanfacau (so they call it, that is, strong resistance) runneth with an equal course till it encounters with hills, which are all . . . made so that it is stronger than the wall itself, the wall being only in the spaces twixt hill and hill, the hills themselves making up the rest."[117]

Pinto reports, incorrectly, that in the entire length of the Wall there are "but five entrances, caused by the Tartarian rivers." Evidently he had learned (for he certainly never traveled the length of the Wall) of the five major gates, at Shanhaikuan, Kupeikou, Kalgan, Yenmên, and Kia-yü-kuan. But these were cut not by rivers but by roads, leading, respectively, to Manchuria and Korea, to Jehol, to Urga in Outer Mongolia, to the cities of Inner Mongolia, and to Turkestan and the west. And there were many subsidiary gates aside from these five.

"At every one of those five entrances," Pinto adds, "the King of China hath one fort and the Tartar another: in every of the China forts there are seven thousand men, six thousand foot and one thousand horse, in continual pay; most of them strangers, Mogors, Champaas, Pancrus, Coracones, and Gizares of Persia, the Chinese being but mean soldiers. In all the space of this wall are three hundred and twenty regiments, each of five hundred men (in all one hundred and sixty thousand), besides ministers, commanders, and their retinue. . . ."[118]

Pinto provides few details of his year of labor on the Wall, and it is conceivable that the entire episode was an invented one, allowing him to insert this information about the Great Wall into his book. The story grows more fanciful: he tells of an invasion by Tartars that freed the prisoners working on the Wall, and describes a visit to the nomad encampment, but his tale of life in Tartary is vague and unconvincing, as if he had made the whole thing up out of third-hand reports. In time, Pinto says, he parted from the Tartars and marched through western China from north to south, reaching Tongking and finding his way from there to Macao, the coastal city near Canton that was becoming Portugal's chief Chinese foothold (and is still part of the Portuguese empire). Unable to find countrymen in Macao, Pinto and two companions took passage on a Chinese junk heading north toward Ning-po. The junk was driven far off course by strong gales, landing them eventually on an island off the coast of Kyushu, the southernmost major island of Japan.

Thus Pinto, by his own account, became the first European to reach Japan, and demonstrated firearms to the curious Japanese, accidentally wounding a Japanese nobleman in the process. This part of Pinto's narrative has been most scornfully denounced by his detractors, but his description of Japan rings true, and there is no reason why he could not have made the journey as he claims. From Japan he returned to Ning-po, where he met Portuguese friends and told them of the wonderful new Japanese market that he had discovered so unexpectedly. The Portuguese merchants thereupon resolved to make a trading voyage to Japan, buying Chinese silk to sell to the Japanese. Again Pinto suffered shipwreck, this time on the island now called Okinawa in the Ryukyus. Remarkable adventures followed; he was enslaved in Burma, a shipwreck victim once more off Cambodia, and involved in a military adventure n Siam. In 1547 he was in Malacca, where he met the missionary priest and future saint, Francis Xavier, and resolved to become a Jesuit. (The resolution did not last.) He was sent to Japan in 1554 as part of an official Portuguese mission, journeyed on to Goa in 1557, and the following year returned to Portugal. There he occupied himself with writing a voluminous memoir of his travels, but made no effort to publish it before his death, at the age of seventy-four, in 1583. The book finally saw print in a Portuguese edition in 1614 and became an international favorite, enjoying nineteen editions in six languages by 1700. The book was regarded generally as an entertaining fable, but gradually it became possible to correlate many of Pinto's statements with the evidence brought back by later explorers, and it appeared that Pinto was not the *mendax* he was said to be. No doubt he invented a good deal of what he set down, but it is quite possible that he and his Portuguese companions did indeed toil to strengthen the Great Wall about the year 1540.

VI

Pinto's account of having been freed from his servitude by Tartar raiders would have been more convincing had he set it a few years later. For, in 1550, nomad warriors did break through the Great Wall in the vicinity of Peking, creating the kind of terror that China had not known since Esen's raids a full century before.

The new menace was the work of Altan Khan, known to the Chinese as Anda. About 1530 he cobbled together a federation of nomads in the Ordos region, and set about the customary process of building a frontier empire. The weakness of the eleventh Ming Emperor, Chu Hou-tsung, made the task easier; while the Emperor spent his days in the search for the elixir of life, Anda harried the provinces of Shensi and Shansi, as well as forcing the submission of the nomad tribes to the west. By 1550, Anda was supreme in the steppe from the borders of Tibet to the sea, and he gathered a striking force for an attack on Peking. The nomads broke through the Great Wall fortifications north of the city without much difficulty and sacked the area around Peking, though the defenses of the capital proved impregnable once again. Anda's raids continued at intervals for the next quarter of a century. Not until the 1570's did the thirteenth Ming Emperor succeed in pacifying him. By then, Anda had abandoned the nomad life and had built a capital city at Kuei-hua outside the Wall, northwest of Ta-t'ung. The Chinese offered him favorable trade concessions and bestowed upon him the title of Shun-i Wang, "Obedient and Righteous Prince."

The transformation of Anda from a wild raider into a settled, obedient, and righteous prince is an indication of a change coming over the entire Mongol culture. The Chinese had never abandoned the old idea of creating a border fringe of "friendly" nomads who would aid in the defense of the northern frontier. With the pacification of Anda, this idea was again carried into reality. Anda adopted Lamaism, the Buddhist creed that had been favored in Kublai Khan's day, and this helped to undermine Mongol strength. This religion required an enormous contribution of manpower; every family contributed one or more sons to the church. Since the lamas were celibate, the spread of the religion caused a sharp population drop, and the Mongol had never really been numerous to begin with. During the sixteenth and seventeenth centuries, the Mongolian region just north of the Great Wall began evolving from a nomad territory to a land of cities and monasteries. The old pastoral economy gave way to a mixed economy based on trade. The wild men of the steppe turned into merchants and lamas—a development that naturally was heartily encouraged by the Chinese. Ultimately, staggering under the burden of their nonproductive lamas, the Mongols of the frontier ceased to be a military threat to China, and began their long slide into helpless poverty.

Anda's raids, incidentally, did not go unnoticed in Europe. Since Pinto' exploits in the late 1530's and early 1540's, Europeans in ever larger number had been entering China. The Portuguese had made permanent settlement in Macao and Amoy from 1544 on; other settlements at Canton, Ning-po, and Fukien were uprooted between 1545 and 1549, but the Portuguese influence spread none the less. The Spaniards had tried to enter China in 1543, without success, but from 1565 on they began to occupy the Philippines and used those islands as a base for frequent trading missions to China. The first Jesuit missionaries reached China in the middle of the sixteenth century with uncertain results at first; their reports filtered back to Europe and were widely published.

In the late 1550's, an anonymous Portuguese who had been imprisoned for six years in China escaped and reached Malacca, where he dictated to the Jesuits an account of his captivity. This account was dispatched to Europe and found its way into print in 1561, as an appendix to Francisco Alvarez' *Historia de Ethiopia*. It included this description of Anda's raid on Peking:

"At the boundary of the kingdom of China, where it borders on the Tartars, there is a wall of wondrous strength, of a month's journey in extent, where the king keeps a great military force in the bulwarks. Where this wall comes upon mountains, they cut them in such a manner that they remain and serve as a wall; for the Tartars are very brave and skilful in war. At the time we were prisoners, they broke through a part of the wall and entered into the territory for a month and a half's journey; but as the king prepared great armies of men provided with artful contrivances (in which the Chinese are very crafty), he kept back the Tartars, who fight on horseback. As their horses had become weak and were dying of hunger, one of the Chinese officers commanded a large quantity of peas to be placed in the fields, and thus it was that the horses (being so hungry as they were) set themselves to eat against the will of their masters; and in this manner the army of the king of China put them in disorder and turned to drive them out. And now a strict watch is kept on the wall."[119]

VII

The late Ming Emperor most closely associated with the Great Wall is Chu I-chün, known under the regnal-period title of Wan-li. The Wan-li Emperor, thirteenth of the Ming line, came to the throne in 1572 and ruled for thirty-eight years, during which time the ruin of the dynasty was accomplished.

For the first decade of his reign, Wan-li was under the influence of his strong and able chief minister, Chang Chü-chêng, who recognized a new enemy arising in the north: not the increasingly impotent Mongols, but a wilder tribe whom we know as the Manchus. Prodded by this minister, Wan-li had so much work done on the Great Wall that many Chinese in later centuries thought that he was its original builder. The Chinese name of the Wall, *Wan Li Ch'ang Ch'eng,* or "Wall of Ten Thousand Miles," was often taken to mean "Wan-li's Long Wall."

Much of the present-day Great Wall is Wan-li's work. A new section was built west of the Yellow River; in the eastern section, the crumbling barrier was restored. Inscriptions up and down the length of the Wall testify to the building of so many feet of "First Class Wall" here, so many of "Third Class Wall" there. One tablet records the building of "two pieces of First Class Wall," each piece 148 tens of feet long plus eight feet, "in the Lucky Days of the Winter Season in the Third Year of Wan-li." Another lists the bureaucrats and contractors, 130 in all, who "cooperated in building this extension of 591 feet 6 inches of Third Class Wall, beginning on the north at the end of the Military Graduate Lung Kuang-hsien's portion of Tower Number 55 of the Black Letter 'Wu' series. The completion of the construction was reported by the Autumn Guard on the 16th day of the 9th moon of the Fourth Year of Wan-li."[120]

Wan-li's engineers did a notable job of construction. The excellently preserved section of the Wall at the Nankou Pass, long a tourist favorite, dates mainly from this reign, though there has been some restoration since Wan-li's time. Here, the Wall is built of granite blocks accurately cut and dressed; some of the blocks are fourteen feet long and three or four feet thick. The

A section of the Great Wall built by Wan-li.   *Geil,* The Great Wall of China

upper part of the Wall is brick, and the brick is of high quality. At fifty-foot intervals along the 14-foot-wide roadway the Ming builders installed stone drains to carry rain water out of the roadbed, letting it pour onto the Mongol side of the Wall. This architectural refinement has had a considerable effect in preserving the Wall at that point.

Not only was there hasty and extensive repair done all along the Great Wall, but the Grand Canal was restored as well, and many other projects of a useful kind were undertaken at the outset of the new regime, when ambition still gripped the Emperor. In Wan-li's third year, a solar eclipse took place, an event solemn enough to stir the Emperor to write down twelve resolutions of virtue and mount them on the right hand of his throne: "Heed the warnings of Heaven. Employ the worthy and the able. Keep virtuous officers near your person. Put the vicious far away. Let rewards and punishments be well defined. Be careful as to those who go in and out of the palace. Rise early. Be temperate. Recall your wandering thoughts. Be reverent toward Heaven. Listen to faithful admonition. Beware of lavish expenditure."[121] Noble sentiments, but Wan-li kept faith with but few of them.

For the first ten years of his reign, China prospered. The population expanded, but the yield of agriculture matched the growth rate, and few went hungry. There were occasional nomad raids, but these were repulsed, as in 1574, when a general named Li Ch'êng-liang used cannon of European design to drive the barbarians back in Liao-tung. These imposing weapons, twenty feet long, were contributions of the Portuguese.

The death of the minister Chang Chü-chêng about 1582 left Wan-li without a controlling force at his side. He abandoned himself to extravagance and debauchery, not the first Chinese Emperor to follow that course. Superstitions possessed him; not only eclipses, but comets, phases of the moon, sudden floods or droughts, or any other unexpected natural manifestation, all struck terror in Wan-li's soul and caused repercussions in the manner of his administration. By 1599, the country was almost bankrupt, and a few years later one imperial minister complained, "The treasuries of the provinces are empty. All enterprises are at a standstill. The Emperor withdraws himself from his people; for more than twenty years he has never called a council of his great ministers. The empire is in danger of revolution." Vast sums of silver had been squandered on private imperial expenditures—90,000 ounces to celebrate Wan-li's marriage, 12,000,000 ounces for the marriage of various princes, 9,000,000 ounces for the building of palaces. While palaces were constructed, dikes and canals were allowed to decay; floods swept northern China, drought the south. The Great Wall, which had been so energetically rebuilt in the early years of Wan-li's reign, now began to deteriorate again as the Emperor's life dragged on into the seventeenth century. The garrisons along the Wall were left without pay or supplies, and many soldiers deserted. By the time Wan-li died in 1620, the empire was in a state of collapse, and within a further twenty-five years China would once again fall under "barbarian" rule—this time for nearly three centuries.

Fifteen. The Collapse of Ming

The annals of Wan-li's interminable and disastrous reign include one significant entry late in the sixteenth century: "This year a man from the Western Ocean, by name Matteo Ricci, begged permission to offer the products of his own country. His request was refused." That is, the aforesaid Ricci asked for permission to come to Peking, and was turned away.

Ricci was a Jesuit missionary, and probably one of the most extraordinary human beings ever to carry the gospels of his creed into a far land. The Jesuits who entered China at this time were more than advocates of religion; they were scholars and scientists, skilled in astronomy, geography, mathematics, and physics, and their effect on Chinese thinking was profound. They came in the wake of the Portuguese and Spanish merchants. Like those pioneers, the missionaries were compelled at first to remain in the coastal cities of southern China, and were given only tantalizing glimpses of the vast hinterland. Europe was awake to the existence of China by now, and every scrap of information that the Jesuits and the merchants sent back was eagerly published, translated, and disseminated. There was a powerful demand at home for news of this wondrous empire, and the Jesuits, men of learning and highly developed curiosity themselves, sought out all the information they could obtain.

The Great Wall, as the most spectacular single aspect of China, was a topic of considerable interest. Since the European travelers generally were unable to view the Wall themselves, the accounts of it that they transmitted were often distorted ones; thus a map of China produced by the great cartographer Ortelius in 1584 shows the Wall running *south* of Peking. A Portuguese treatise on China, printed in Latin at Macao in 1590 and translated into English by the geographer Richard Hakluyt a few years later, repeated another common misunderstanding by declaring that in many places the Wall was a natural one of mountains, rather than a continuous man-made rampart: "It runneth along the borders of three northerly provinces, Xiensi, Xansi, and Paquin, and is said to contain almost three hundred leagues in length, and in such sort to be built, that it hindereth not the courses and

A view of the Great Wall, near Peking. *Chinese collection, East Asian Library, Columbia University*

streams of any rivers, their channels being overthwarted and fortified with wonderful bridges and other defenses. Yet it is not unlikely, that the said wall is built in such sort, that only low and easy passages be therewith stopped and environed; but the mountains running between those low passages are, by their own natural strength, and inaccessible height, a sufficient fortification against the enemy."[122]

The sixteenth-century Dominican friar Gaspar da Cruz had the same idea: "The Chinese have an hundred leagues (others saying there are more) of a Wall between them and the [Tartars], where are continually garrisons of men for the defense of the entries of the Tartarians. It may be believed that this Wall is not continued, but that some mountains or hills are intermixed between; for a lord of Persia affirmed to me, that the like works were in some parts of Persia, with intermixing some hills and mountains."[123]

A more detailed report on the Great Wall was provided by Juan Gonzalez de Mendoza, an Augustine friar born in Toledo, who was a member of an unsuccessful Spanish embassy to China in 1584. Mendoza assembled his book from the reports of various other friars, as well as his own experiences in the Orient. It was published in Rome in 1585, and an English translation appeared three years later as *The Historie of the great and mightie kingdome of China and the situation thereof: Togither with the great riches, huge citties, politike government and rare inuentions in the same.* Mendoza's account of the Great Wall is this:

: 180 :

"There is in this kingdom a defense or wall that is five hundred leagues long, and beginning at the city Ochyou [Ho-chow in Shensi], which is upon the high mountains, and runneth from west unto east. The king of that country which made it was called Tzintzon, and it was for his defense against the Tartaries, with whom he had wars; so that the wall doth shut up the frontier of Tartaria. But you must understand that four hundred leagues of the said wall is natural of itself, for that they be high and mighty rocks, very nigh together: but in the other hundred leagues is comprehended the spaces or distance betwixt the rocks, the which he caused to be made by men's hands of very strong work of stone, and is of seven fathom broad at the foot of it, and seven fathom high. It beginneth at the parts of the sea . . . and doth finish in the province of Susuan [Szechuan].* This king, for to finish this wonderful work, did take of every three men one through his kingdom, and of five, two. . . . They almost all did perish that followed that work.

"The making of this superbious and mighty work was the occasion that his whole kingdom did rise up against the king and did kill him, after that he had reigned forty years, and also a son of his that was called Agnitzi. The report of this wall is held to be of a very truth, for that. It is affirmed by all the Chinese that do traffic to the Islands Philippinas and to Canton, and Macao, and be all confirmable in their declaration as witnesses, because they have seen it: and it is in the farthest parts of all the kingdom, whereas none of us unto this day hath been."[124]

II

Within two decades after Mendoza's book appeared, northern China—and the Great Wall—no longer held many mysteries for the Europeans. This was largely because of the work of the redoubtable Matteo Ricci, the first European since the early fourteenth century to take up permanent residence in Peking.

Ricci was born in Italy in 1552. When he was seventeen, his father sent him to Rome to study law, but after three years he felt the call of a religious impulse, and joined the Society of Jesus. From 1571 to 1577, Ricci studied philosophy and theology at the Jesuit College in Rome. Gradually his scientific curiosity developed, and he took instruction in mathematics, astronomy, and the physical sciences. In 1578, his order sent him to India, where he both taught and studied at Goa. After four years he was transferred to the China Mission. The year 1582 found Ricci in Macao, and he spent the rest of his life in China.

Ricci displayed an unusual linguistic gift. He mastered the Chinese language as well as any European ever has. This ability to speak fluently and hold scholarly discourse in Chinese opened the gates of China to him; he made contact with Chinese scholars and mathematicians, who recognized the keenness of his intellect and made it possible to extend the reach of

---

* Actually the Great Wall goes nowhere near Szechuan.

the Jesuit mission into China's hitherto-forbidden northern regions. After an initial rebuff, Ricci was allowed to establish a mission center at Nanking, and in 1600 he set out for Peking, where he remained until his death ten years later. In 1614, the manuscript of Ricci's diary was brought from China to Rome by Father Nicola Trigault, who translated it into Latin and published it the following year, appending an account of Ricci's death and burial. There were many editions of Trigault's book, at least eleven in the next thirty years, although it was not fully translated into English until 1953.

Before Ricci reached Peking, Europe was still unsure of the relation between the China of the sea trade and the Cathay that Marco Polo had entered via the overland route. It was Matteo Ricci who first clarified the situation. "All authors agree that the great kingdom of Cathay is found in these regions," he reported to the Jesuit Superiors in India, "lying east of Persia and south of Tartary. It seems impossible that if it existed they should not have any relations with it, whether in peace or war. At least they would know of its existence." Hence Ricci concluded that Cathay must be an old name for China, and not a separate land. This was confirmed when he encountered some Central Asian merchants who had journeyed overland to China. They still used the old names: Cathay for the nation, Cambaluc for the capital. But they made it clear to Ricci that Cathay was the land he knew as China, and Cambaluc was the city of Peking. Even then, the myth of Cathay refused to die, and it remained for another man to lay it finally to rest.

While the geographers of Europe debated the nature of Cathay and China, Ricci was winning unusual acclaim at the court of Wan-li. The Chinese knew him as Li Ma-tou, and were delighted by his knowledge of their language, by his sympathetic tolerance of their customs, and above all by his scientific abilities. Early in his Chinese stay, Ricci was asked to draw a map of the world with Chinese characters, after the European maps that the Chinese saw in the Jesuit headquarters. Trigault tells us, "Of all the great nations, the Chinese have had the least commerce, indeed, one might say that they have had practically no contact whatever, with outside nations, and consequently they are grossly ignorant of what the world in general is like." Chinese maps of the world were virtually useless; "their universe was limited to their own fifteen provinces, and in the sea painted around it they had placed a few little islands to which they gave the names of different kingdoms they had heard of."[125]

Ricci prepared a large map of the world, with lengthy annotations in Chinese. With tact that was characteristic of the man, Ricci adjusted the meridians of his map so that China was shown to be in the center of the world. "To them," Trigault said in his edition of Ricci's diary, "the heavens are round but the earth is flat and square, and they firmly believe that their empire is right in the middle of it. They do not like the idea of our geographies pushing their China into one corner of the Orient. They could not comprehend the demonstration proving that the earth is a globe, made up of land and water, and that a globe of its very nature has neither beginning nor end."[126]

The map, though it puzzled the Chinese scholars at first, was a huge success, eventually finding its way to the palace of the Emperor. Ricci next was prevailed upon to make "astronomical spheres and globes, out of copper and iron, illustrating the heavens and demonstrating the proper shape of the earth. At home he also painted sundials or engraved them on copper sheets, which he presented to friendly Magistrates, including the Viceroy. When these various devices were exhibited and their purpose explained, showing the position of the sun, the courses of the stars and the central position of the earth,* their designer and artisan was looked upon as the world's great astronomer. This nation measures all others according to its own standards, and they are thoroughly convinced that what is unknown to them is unknown to the rest of the world."[127]

Ricci also impressed the Chinese by contriving a clock that "not only told the time of day to those passing by but to people at a distance, by sounding the hour on a large bell, and they could never quite make out how it could ring of itself, without anyone touching it."[128] A more striking accomplishment, because Ricci was the only man in the world capable of achieving it, was his translation of the *Elements* of Euclid into Chinese. He carried this out while living at Peking, with the assistance of a Chinese named Hsü Kuangch'i (or Ciu, as the Jesuits called him) who had been received into Christianity under the name of Paul. "Within the space of a year," according to Trigault, "they published a very presentable edition of the first six books of the Elements in clear and elegant Chinese style."[129] With the aid of other learned converts Ricci translated books on astronomy and engineering, and encouraged the compilation of scientific treatises by others. Ricci's library at Peking has been preserved, and still contains the European scientific texts with which he opened a new world of ideas for his Chinese hosts. Ricci's high intellect and noble attainments made it easier for him to propagate his faith; several members of the Chinese court were converted to Christianity, and the Emperor himself, though not a convert, looked favorably upon the Jesuits at his capital. Though the official policy of China toward foreigners had been a chilly one all through the Ming regime, the Jesuits were entrusted with many important responsibilities, such as the reform of the calendar in 1613, and they continued to remain influential at the imperial court even under the barbarian dynasty that soon came to power. (It should be noted that the Jesuits did more than build clocks and draw maps for the Chinese; some of them, though not Ricci, aided in the construction of cannon and cannon balls, and perhaps these men of God would not have been so warmly welcomed at Peking if they had not had access to the most recent developments in European military technology.)

While at Peking, Ricci no doubt rode out to inspect the Great Wall, a short journey to the north. It did not seem to strike him as an engineering

---

* It may seem odd to see the enlightened Ricci teaching the geocentric theory sixty years after Copernicus' death. But bear in mind that the Church's astronomy was still officially geocentric. The persecution of Galileo did not begin until Ricci had been dead for six years, and Galileo's vindication came a good deal later than that.

achievement worthy of much comment, and he disposes of it in a few lines: "To the north the country is defended against hostile Tartar raids by precipitious hills, which are joined into an unbroken line of defense with a tremendous wall four hundred and five miles long. To the northwest it is flanked by a great desert of many days' march, which either deters an advancing army from attacking the Chinese border or becomes the burial place of those who attempt the attack."[130]

III

Matteo Ricci had shown, to his own satisfaction at least, that China and Cathay were one and the same. Yet doubt still remained in the minds of others. The Jesuits living at the court of the Mogul King Akbar in India were particularly concerned with Cathay. They had heard tales of a land by that name a little to the east and a little to the north of the Mogul kingdom, and what excited them was the frequently repeated report that the inhabitants of Cathay were Christians, descendants of the converts made by such missionaries as Archbishop John of Montecorvino three hundred years before.

There was no way for these Jesuits in India to know that Christianity had long since perished in Cathay. Both the Roman Catholic and the much older Nestorian Christian communities had become extinct not long after the xenophobic Ming Dynasty had replaced the tolerant Mongols. Fired by the myth of a Christian Cathay, the Jesuit Father Nicolo Pimenta "became greatly taken up with the desire of holding the people of Cathay in the true faith, all the more because it might well be supposed that Christians separated from their head by such vast distances must have fallen into sundry errors." Letters passed from the Jesuits of India to the King of Spain and to the Pope, and by 1601 an expedition was being prepared to seek the Christians of Cathay, despite Ricci's report that Cathay was China and that no Christians were to be found in the land. Chosen to lead the expedition was Benedict de Goes, a Jesuit lay brother serving at Akbar's court.

Goes, born in the Azores about 1561, had gone to India at the age of twenty-six. Originally a soldier, high-spirited and adventurous, he had undergone a religious experience in a small church in the Indian port of Kolechi, and in 1594 entered the Jesuit order, though he steadfastly refused to become a priest, and remained a lay brother to the end of his days. He accompanied a group of Jesuit missionaries to the court of the great ruler Akbar in 1595, and evidently won the esteem of that tolerant and unusual Indian monarch. When the expedition to Cathay was organized, Goes was selected because he was "an eminently pious and sensible man, who from his long residence in the Mogul's territories had an accurate knowledge of the Persian tongue, and a thorough acquaintance with Mohammedan customs, two qualifications which appeared to be indispensable for anyone attempting this journey."[131]

The expedition was financed by Philip III of Spain. When Goes arrived in the Indian city of Agra in 1602 to assemble his party, Akbar contributed four hundred pieces of gold toward his expenses, along with letters of introduction to the princes of the states lying along his intended route. On the sixth of January, 1603, Goes set out for Cathay. To make his way more easily, he adopted the dress of an Armenian merchant, allowing his hair and beard to grow, and called himself Banda Abdulla, "Servant of the Lord," adding the surname Isai, "the Christian." To make his merchant guise seem more convincing he carried a variety of wares with him. Goes was accompanied by two Greeks, a priest named Leo Grimanus, and a merchant called Demetrius. At Lahore, the secondary capital of the Mogul empire, Goes acquired a genuine Armenian named Isaac as a servant.

The eastward route took Goes first across the Himalayan passes to Kashgar. For reasons of safety, he traveled with a Kashgar-bound caravan of about five hundred persons. The progress was slow, the caravan often halting upon hearing rumors of bandits on the road ahead. One stretch of the road was so badly infested with brigands that the caravan hired an escort of four hundred soldiers. Even so, the travelers were attacked by robbers who swooped down from the hills. "Many of the company were wounded, and life and property were saved with difficulty," a seventeenth-century Jesuit account of Goes' travels declares. "Our Benedict fled with the rest into the jungle, but coming back at night they succeeded in getting away from the robbers."[132] A further journey of twenty days brought the party to Kabul, in Afghanistan, where many of the merchants left the caravan.

The number of those continuing on to Kashgar was so small that it was unsafe to proceed. Goes remained in Kabul for eight months while new traders joined the group. Among the new members of the caravan was the sister of the King of Kashgar, who "was now on her return from that immense journey to Mecca, which she had performed for the sake of her blasphemous creed." She had run short of cash, and Goes aided her in her temporary embarrassment by advancing her six hundred pieces of gold, to be repaid without interest at Kashgar. The noble lady "would not, however, let herself be outdone in liberality, for she afterwards paid him in pieces of that kind of marble which is so highly esteemed among the Chinese, and which is the most profitable of all investments that one can take to Cathay."[133] The "marble" was jade, which the Chinese have for centuries imported from the western countries, and Goes made good use of his supply later.

Before the caravan proceeded on its way, Leo Grimanus and the trader Demetrius decided they had gone far enough, and parted from Goes. He continued on accompanied only by the loyal Isaac. Following in Marco Polo's track, the caravan wound upward into the Pamirs, troubled repeatedly by bandits. At one point, Goes fell behind the party and was attacked by four brigands, but he fooled them by throwing his Persian cap at them; they fell to quarreling over the cap, with its glittering jewel, "and while they were kicking it around like a football," Goes "put spurs to his horse, got the safe distance of an arrow's flight away from them, and safely joined the caravan."

Heavy rains halted them several weeks later, and then more bandits descended. In the ascent of the Pamirs, many of the company froze to death, Goes himself barely escaping, when for six days they were snowed in. A little later, Isaac the Armenian fell into a river and was nearly drowned, and then, as Yarkand drew near, the "roads were so bad that six of our brother's horses died of fatigue." Goes went ahead of the caravan, reaching Yarkand in November, 1603, and sent back fresh horses and provisions for his companions.

The caravan dispersed here, and Goes had to wait a full year before a new Cathay-bound party was assembled. Shrewdly, Goes used this time to acquire a good supply of jade, as an investment which could be redeemed in Cathay. While waiting in Yarkand, the Jesuit visited the king, bestowing upon him a pocket watch, looking glasses, "and other European curiosities." The king, in gratitude, gave Goes a passport permitting him to continue eastward.

When six months had gone by at Yarkand, the Greek merchant Demetrius reappeared. "Benedict and Isaac the Armenian were greatly delighted at his arrival; but their joy was of short continuance, for very soon after this Demetrius caused our friend a great deal of trouble. At that time, with the king's leave, one of the merchants was elected mock emperor, whilst all the rest, according to a custom of theirs, paid homage to him and offered him presents. Demetrius, to save his pocket, held back; and as the emperor had the power of putting rebels against his authority in irons, or even of flogging them, Demetrius had great difficulty in escaping both penalties."[134] Goes helped him out of this predicament, and in November of 1604 the caravan left Yarkand.

After various adventures, not all of them pleasant, Goes arrived at a town called Cialis in the Jesuit narrative—probably Karashahr, on the Old Silk Road. While the caravan halted there, the caravan of the previous year, now westbound out of Cathay, also arrived. "They had made their way to the capital of Cathay as usual by pretending to be an embassy," the account relates, "and as they had been quartered in Peking at the same hostelry with the members of our Society [the Jesuits], they were able to give our brother most authentic information about Father Matthew [Ricci] and his companions, and in this way he learned to his astonishment that China was the Cathay that he was in search of."[135]

The westbound merchants, who were Moslems, told Goes how the Jesuits at Peking had presented the Emperor with clocks, a clavichord, and other European novelties. For proof, they produced a scrap of paper on which a few words of Portuguese had been written, which they had found in their Peking hotel and were taking home as a curio. They described the physical appearance of Ricci and the other Jesuits at Peking, but could not supply Goes with the fathers' names, since they knew only the Chinese names by which the Jesuits were called.

Fortified by the news that members of his own faith lay at the end of his long journey, Goes left the caravan and, accompanied only by Isaac the Armenian, pressed on through the oasis towns of Turfan and Hami into the desert that awaited all travelers to Cathay. It was a dangerous trip; the territory west of the Great Wall was bandit country, with "an evil fame on account of its liability to Tartar raids," and "our travelers found on the way the bodies of sundry Mohammedans who had been miserably murdered." Nine days out of Hami, the wasteland gave way to signs of civilization, as they came to "the celebrated northern wall of China, reaching it at the place called Chiaicuon."[136]

This was Kia-yü-kuan, the Jade Gate, and Goes was perhaps the first Christian to reach it in three centuries. Having reached the Great Wall, Goes had to camp for twenty-five days while awaiting permission to enter. At length the permission came, probably hastened by a bribe to the local governor. It was not very satisfactory, though: Goes could enter China, but could not continue on to join his brethren at Peking. He was ordered to remain at the walled city of Suchow, just within the Wall.

Brother Benedict arrived at Suchow late in 1605, nearly three years after his departure from Agra. Both he and Isaac had come through the grueling trip in good health, and moreover Goes had prospered, having with him thirteen horses, five servants, two boys whom he had bought in slave markets, and a goodly supply of precious jade. At Suchow he met a second westbound caravan of Islamic merchants returning from Peking. They confirmed all that he had earlier been told about the Jesuits at the capital city, adding an improbable detail that must have aroused some suspicions in Goes—"that they had from the Emperor a daily allowance of silver, not counted to them, but measured out in bulk!" From Suchow Goes wrote to Ricci at Peking, informing him of his arrival. The letter was given to Chinese messengers, but it was addressed in European characters, which the Chinese did not understand, and it was addressed to Ricci under his European name, since Goes did not know what the Chinese called him. As a result, the letter was never delivered.

At Easter of 1606, Goes was still detained at Suchow, and he wrote to Peking a second time. He begged the fathers to find some way of rescuing him from Suchow. He had not seen a fellow Christian in all too many years, and he longed to end his travels, particularly since his health was giving way. This second letter did somehow manage to reach its destination.

The Jesuits at Peking had already been informed of Goes' expedition, and had been awaiting his arrival for several years. They had been unable to obtain news of him from travelers reaching Peking from inland, and they assumed that he had perished on the journey. When his second letter reached them, in November of 1606, they delightedly made plans to bring him somehow to Peking. It was considered unwise for any of the Jesuits to attempt to cross China, and so a Chinese convert who had adopted the Christian name of John Ferdinand was entrusted with the task. Though it was a four-month trip from Peking to Suchow, and northern China was then in the grip of a fierce winter, Father Ricci insisted that the rescuer set out at once.

Goes, meanwhile, not knowing that his letter had arrived, was morosely eking out his days in Suchow, troubled by the high price of food, by his failing health, and by the constant need to offer hospitality to local officials. He began selling off his pieces of jade, and was compelled to accept less than half their true value. To keep the remainder of his dwindling supply from being stolen, he buried a hundred pounds of it in the ground.

John Ferdinand left Peking on December 11. A long and fatiguing journey, complicated by the defection of a thieving servant midway across Shensi, brought him to Suchow at the end of March, 1607. He sought out Benedict de Goes and found him in bed with a mortal disease. The night before, Goes had been told in a vision that a messenger from Peking was about to arrive, and he had sent the faithful Isaac to the bazaar to buy goods for distribution to the poor, as a thanks offering. John Ferdinand encountered Isaac in the bazaar, and was led to Goes' bedside. As he entered, carrying letters from the Jesuits at Peking, John Ferdinand "saluted our brother Benedict in the Portuguese tongue. From this he at once understood what the arrival was, and taking the letters he raised them aloft with tears of joy in his eyes, and burst into the hymn of *Nunc dimittis servum tuum, Domine*. For now it seemed to him that indeed his commission was accomplished, and his pilgrimage at an end."[137]

There was no question of going to Peking. John Ferdinand nursed the ebbing Goes; the Chinese convert even cooked some European dishes in the hope of restoring the dying man's strength. Nothing could save him; eleven days after John Ferdinand's arrival, Benedict de Goes breathed his last.

The Moslem merchants at Suchow hastened to seize as much of the dead man's property as they could get. Among the things that disappeared was Goes' detailed diary of his trip, which the merchants thought might contain records of their debts to Goes; its loss was a great one, for we now must rely on a sketchy third-person account for our knowledge of his important expedition. The merchants attempted to have Goes buried after the Moslem fashion, but John Ferdinand and Isaac managed to thwart this, and gave him the best sort of Christian burial they could manage, lacking all prayer books. The Moslems also attempted a legal seizure of Goes' property, according to a custom whereby in the caravans the goods of any merchant who happened to die on the road were divided among the others. This went to court, and the merchants accused Ferdinand and Isaac of being Moslems themselves. Ferdinand dealt with that accusation straightforwardly, declaring that "if he really did belong to that faith he would never touch pork; and taking a piece of pork out of his sleeve he offered it to Isaac, and both of them began to eat it, to the intense disgust of the Mohammedans and to the amusement of the other spectators."[138] The court ordered whatever of Goes' property could be found to be restored to Isaac and Ferdinand, and at last the pair reached Peking with an account of the late pilgrim's epic journey and lamentable passing.

Though he had not reached Peking, Brother Benedict de Goes had settled the question of Cathay forever. He had passed through the Great Wall—indeed, had died almost in its shadow—and he had put an end to the quest for Cathay. One of his Jesuit brethren supplied his epitaph: "Brother Benedict, seeking Cathay, found Heaven."

IV

While Jesuits of Spain, Italy, and Portugal were penetrating China from east and west, men of a harsher clime were coming down out of the Russian northlands to make contact as well. The Russians had been overwhelmed by Mongols in the twelfth and thirteenth centuries, and had not begun to assert their independence until the middle of the sixteenth. Now, with the Tartar yoke gone, the Russians sought new fields for trade, and looked southward across the steppe to China.

The first Russians recorded in China arrived about 1540, if we can trust a hazy passage in the narrative of Mendes Pinto. But as late at 1611, one

Russian account of China included this startling statement: "As to China . . . it is completely surrounded by a brick wall, from which it is evident that it is no large place."[139] Evidently the state of Russian intelligence was still primitive in the early seventeenth century.

Soon afterward, adventurous Cossacks began making their way down through Siberia, and into the Mongolian steppe. By 1620, one of them reached China. He was a certain Ivan Petlin of Tomsk, who was sent by Czar Michael Feodorovich to obtain information about the great river called the Ob, and about the land of Khitai that lay somewhere to the southeast. Petlin proceeded southward from Siberia into the western part of the Mongolian desert, where he was met civilly by the Mongol khan. Ultimately he came to the Great Wall, perhaps at the Kalgan gate. He called the wall *Krym,* a Russian word for a fortification, and observed that the Mongols were allowed to come to the gate with horses to sell to the Chinese, but were not permitted to come within the walls, except in small numbers. Petlin described the Great Wall in these words:

"The bordering or frontier walls stand under the south toward Bokhara, two months travel, all made of brick of fifteen fathom high, whereupon they told about a hundred towers in sight, on both sides of them, but towards Bokhara, and towards the sea, the towers are not to be numbered, and every tower standeth from another about a flight shot distant. The said wall stretcheth down towards the sea four months travel. The people of Cathay say, that this wall stretcheth alongst from Bokhara to the sea, and the towers upon it stand very thick; it was made, as they say, to be a border between Mugalla [Mongolia] and Cathay. The towers upon it are to the end, that when any enemy appeareth, to kindle fires upon them, to give the people warning to come to their places where they are appointed upon the wall. . . . In the wall to Cathay are five gates, both low, and straight or narrow, a man cannot ride into them upright on horseback, and except these five gates there is no more in all the wall. . . ."[140]

Petlin ended his journey at what he called the White City, which was Peking. Inside this city was another, which he called Magnit; it was the residence of the Czar Taibun of Cathay, by which he meant the Emperor T'ai-ch'ang, successor to Wan-li. Petlin did not visit the Chinese "Czar," because he had not brought the proper presents with him, and after viewing Peking he returned home.

The Cossack had arrived in China at a time when the dynastic cycle was coming full once again. Wan-li, whose reign had begun in brilliance and had ended in disaster, had died in 1620, living thirty years too long for his nation's good. His son and successor, Chu Ch'ang-lo, died, after a reign of two months, under suspicious circumstances, and the throne went to fifteen-year-old Chu Yu-hsiao.

Boy kings have almost always meant catastrophe for China. At this time, with the country a shambles after Wan-li's long reign, a man of iron was needed to restore order; but the new Emperor was helpless, and the sinister eunuch Wei Chung-hsien was the real ruler. Infatuated with power, the eunuch appropriated not only authority but honor, causing temples to be erected to himself in many of the provinces, and demanding veneration almost equal to that accorded an Emperor. During this time of misrule, the province of Liao-tung was invaded by Manchu tribesmen and was abandoned to them without a struggle; similarly, in 1624, when the Yellow River broke through the neglected dikes at Hsü-chow, no attempt at repair was made, but, instead, the city was evacuated. At about the same time, the Dutch made their first appearance in China and seized possession of the island of Taiwan, which the Portuguese had called Formosa. The Chinese offered no defense.

The sudden death of the Emperor in 1627 was Wei Chung-hsien's undoing. The throne passed to the late ruler's brother, Chu Yu-chien, who took the throne as the Ch'ung-cheng Emperor and promptly dismissed the powerful eunuch. When Wei Chung-hsien hanged himself to escape trial, his corpse was disemboweled. But it was too late for the new Emperor to repair the damage of half a century. In Manchuria, barbarians were on the march.

V

The new enemy came from the forested northeast. Tribes descended from the Jurchen who had conquered northern China in the twelfth century had begun to unite. Their first center of operations was along the Liao River, and by the middle of the sixteenth century they were clustered not far from the borders of China.

The Great Wall, meeting the sea at Shanhaikuan, cut Manchuria off from China. From Shanhaikuan there ran in a northeasterly direction a secondary wall known as the Willow Palisade, erected during Ming times to mark the frontier. This Willow Palisade was little else than a ditch and an embankment planted with willows, and its value was more symbolic than strategic.

On the far side of the Willow Palisade a chieftain named Nurhachi (1559–1626) began to play the same role that had been played before by Mao Tun, Genghis Khan, Esen, Anda, and other unifiers of the nomad tribes. He built a confederation out of the remnants of the old Jurchen. Fighting his way to power on the pretext of avenging the treacherous deaths of his father and grandfather, who had been killed in 1582 in a border war, Nurhachi gathered strength slowly—by 1584 he had only fifty followers—but gained authority in a steady fashion. In 1590 Nurhachi was able to lead more than a hundred lesser chieftains to offer tribute at Peking. The Ming court, impressed by his achievement in wiping out the bandits that had plagued the area of Liao-tung, gave him the title of "Dragon-Tiger General" in 1595, a notable honor. No one in Peking seemed to realize the potential threat that Nurhachi represented.

His people were not then known as the Manchus. That term did not come into general use until about the time Nurhachi died, and its derivation is uncertain. According to one theory, the name stems from that of a Jurchen ancestor of Nurhachi, one Manjusri, whom the Chinese called Li Man-chu. Another suggestion is that *Manchu* is an old tribal name for "chief," going back to the fifth or sixth century.

Nurhachi's people called themselves Aisin Gioro, the "Golden Tribe." This

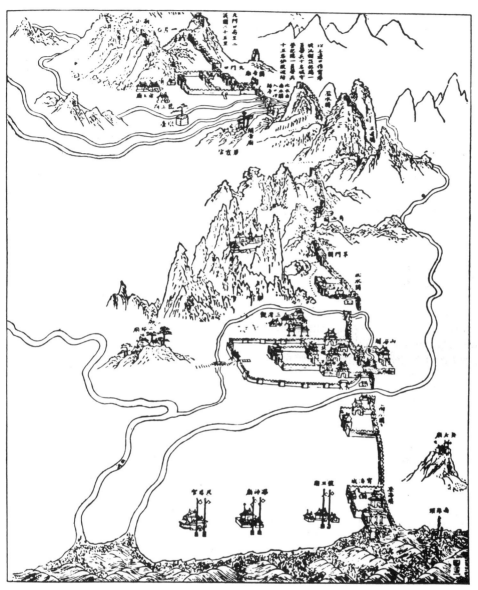

An ancient topographic map of the Wall near Shanhaikuan. From Shanhaikuan in the center of the picture to the sea (foreground) is about five miles. *Harvard Yenching Institute*

echoed the Jurchen dynastic style of Chin, which meant "golden," and soon Nurhachi was calling his own dynasty Hou Chin, meaning "Later Chin."

In 1601 Nurhachi divided his troops into four "banners," or regiments, known by the color of their flags—blue, yellow, red, and white. This system of banners became the fundamental political organization of the Manchus; eventually four more banners were added, and all subjects, including slaves and prisoners, were registered in one of the eight banners, taxed and conscripted through it, controlled and mobilized through it. The banners were led by appointed officers rather than by hereditary tribal chieftains, although Nurhachi's descendants in the imperial clan always reserved the highest posts for themselves.

Shrewdly, Nurhachi amassed strength without giving his neighbors cause for alarm. He was a man of the border, not of the deep steppe, and he understood the factors of conquest in a brilliantly intuitive way. To the south he saw the rotting Ming Dynasty, which he planned ultimately to displace. To the west were the Mongols, disorganized and weakened but still foes to contend with. Nurhachi took care not to stir apprehension in his Mongol neighbors while he consolidated his plan of southward expansion, since he was aware he could not fight on both fronts at once.

The Chinese still regarded the Mongols as more dangerous enemies than the tribesmen of the northeast. Hence their eagerness to decorate Nurhachi and shower favors upon him: to them he represented a force to keep the Mongols in line, not a threat to China herself. Chinese strategy had been summed up by one political commentator in 1541, who wrote, "This is the supreme scheme for holding the reins and controlling them: if the tribes are divided, they are weak and easy to control; if the tribal groups are separated, they become estranged from each other and submit easily. We make every one of them feel like a hero, and make them fight among themselves. This is the theory formulated: internal war among the barbarians is China's opportunity."[141]

The system now failed because the Chinese, leaderless in the days of Wan-li's senility, did not notice what Nurhachi was doing. He was more than a local chieftain. He was an empire builder. One action that should have marked him as a man to reckon with was his building of a fortified castle on the northeast border of Liao-tung to serve as his capital. An innermost fortress was surrounded by several hundred sturdy dwellings for high officers, with the homes of thousands of soldiers ringing the outside. An elaborate system of trade and agriculture supplied this new city. Nurhachi took advantage of the always fluid border situation to detach Chinese of weak loyalties and enroll them in his service, such as Kung Chêng-lu, an intimate adviser of the Manchu chieftain for thirty years.

In 1616, Nurhachi declared himself Emperor of the Later Chin Dynasty. A favorable omen marked his accession: the jade seal of Genghis Khan, which had miraculously appeared at his coronation in 1206, had been lost in the desert during the flight of China's last Mongol Emperor. Now, two hundred and fifty years later, the seal was discovered by a Mongol shepherd, who brought it to Nurhachi. The omen was interpreted to signify Nurhachi's divine right to occupy the Chinese throne.

Two years later, he began open hostilities against Ming China by attacking Liao-tung. Chinese resistance was feeble, and Nurhachi lopped off the northeastern segment of China without difficulty. He gained the services of a number of Chinese officials who enrolled under his banners without hesitation. The death of Wan-li and the succession of his weak sons did not bolster Chinese morale. The forces of Nurhachi raided northern China as they pleased.

Nurhachi died in 1626. After the Chinese custom, he was given a posthumous title: T'ai Tsu, "Grand Progenitor." A struggle for power among his numerous sons followed, and the eighth son, Abahai, emerged as the new leader. Under Abahai the men of the banners broke through the Great Wall in 1629, laying siege to Peking. This thrust ended only when danger developed of their being cut off from the line of retreat; Chinese troops along the Great Wall had been rallied by an able general named Wu San-kuei, and the invaders, fearing that they might be locked into China by the Wall, quickly returned to their home base in the north.

In 1634, Abahai felt strong enough to challenge the Mongols as well as the Chinese, and he sent an expedition of 11,000 men into Inner Mongolia to secure a striking position along China's border to the west. The invasion succeeded. So did an attempt to capture all of Liao-tung in 1635, and Korea in 1637. In 1635 Abahai had decreed the use of the name Manchu for all the Jurchen tribes, and in the following year the dynasty's style was changed from Chin to Ch'ing, meaning "pure" and paralleling the Chinese dynastic name Ming, "Brilliant."

The Manchus now held formidable power. Though there were only some 300,000 of them, their ranks were swelled by the defection of many educated Chinese of the border. This followed Nurhachi's policy statement of 1618: "Our state has always had a generous appreciation of talented men. And if somebody is gifted and quick in administration, we elevate him, appoint him, and bind him in marriage." For example, in 1633 three Ming generals, natives of Liao-tung, went over to the Manchus and later led armies against their homeland. One of them, Shang K'o-hsi, had twenty-three sons, eleven of whom became Manchu generals.

The internal situation of China, meanwhile, was critical. The government's authority was nil; rival warlords were jockeying for position; a Manchu conquest seemed inevitable. The final collapse came in 1644. But when the Ming Dynasty fell, it was because it had been undermined from within.

Sixteen. The Manchu Conquest

The man who shattered the Ming and helped to deliver his native homeland up to barbarian conquerors was Li Tzŭ-ch'êng of Shensi. Tall and thin-lipped, with a beak of a nose and a face marred by smallpox, Li had turned brigand during a famine in 1627, and rampaged through the provinces of Shensi, Shansi, Hupei, and Honan. In time he came to see himself as divinely chosen to found a new dynasty that would rescue China from the chaos brought by the Ming rulers. A constellation of legends and omens adorns Li Tzŭ-ch'êng's biography, such as the story that one hot, parched day he took an arrow from his quiver, thrust it into the ground, and declared, "If I am destined to ascend the Dragon Throne there will be such a snowstorm this night that the shaft of this arrow will be covered." Snow fell all night, and by dawn the arrow was hidden in the drifts.

Malcontents began to flock to Li Tzŭ-ch'êng's side. By 1640, he commanded an army of three hundred thousand men, a third of them cavalry. A superb general and a hypnotic leader of men, he was able to instill fierce loyalty in his followers, and city after city yielded to his irresistible forces. In 1642, he captured the old Sung capital of Kaifeng after a bitter four-month siege. When an imperial army arrived to drive him out, the Ming general chose to cut the two dikes that held back the Huang Ho above the city. Li Tzŭ-ch'êng, warned in advance, managed to get most of his men to higher ground, though ten thousand of them perished. Far worse was the fate of Kaifeng; the unleashed river swept away its northern wall, flooded the city to a depth of twenty feet, and took two hundred thousand lives. When Li entered Kaifeng in triumph soon after, he was rowed down its main street.

Five provinces now acknowledged his sway. At the beginning of 1644, Li somewhat prematurely proclaimed a new dynasty, the Ta Shun or "Great Obedient" Dynasty, and had himself formally crowned at the ancient capital city of Ch'ang-an. His followers hailed him as the Son of Heaven. Peking awaited him now. All that remained to make himself master of China was to push the last Ming, Ch'ung-chêng, from his shaky throne.

Peking's lofty walls had turned back many a hopeful conqueror. Li Tzŭ-ch'êng knew, though, that the great capital was honeycombed with traitors.

Its garrison of a hundred and fifty thousand men was made up mostly of old men and boys; the Emperor was powerless, surrounded by men who planned to defect at the first chance. Li Tzŭ-ch'êng marched north across Shensi and Shansi with an army divided into two columns, passed through the inner loop of the Wall northwest of Peking, and swung around to attack the Nankou Pass, the fortress in the Great Wall that commanded the approach to the capital. In Genghis Khan's day that fortress had been impregnable, but Li Tzŭ-ch'êng took it without a struggle when its commanding officer, after rousing the morale of his troops with a stirring speech, fled to Li's side at nightfall. The defenders of the gate promptly deserted en masse, except for a few loyalists who fled eastward to Shanhaikuan, still a pro-Ming garrison.

Li Tzŭ-ch'êng moved on Peking and sent messengers to demand the Emperor's capitulation. The besieged Ch'ung-chêng sent to Shanhaikuan for help, but it became apparent that no reinforcements could reach Peking in time. On April 8, 1644, the sixteenth and last of the Ming Emperors slew his eldest daughter and sent word to the Empress, to his mother, and to his concubines that they should commit suicide. He sent his three sons, clad in commoner's clothes, toward the gates of the city, telling them to try to escape and go into hiding until the dynasty could be restored. Lastly, he took counsel with his priests, who divined Heaven's will with bamboo sticks. They held a bundle of sticks forward for the Emperor to choose one. The stick he chose was the shortest one. It was a command to take his own life.

Toward dawn, accompanied only by a faithful servant, the Emperor ascended the Wan Sui Hill on the palace grounds, and wrote his last imperial decree on the lapel of his robe: "We, poor in virtue and of contemptible personality, have incurred the wrath of God on high. My ministers have deceived me. I am ashamed to meet my ancestors; and therefore I myself take off my crown, and with my hair covering my face await dismemberment at the hands of the rebels. Do not hurt a single one of my people!"[142] He hanged himself from a beam of the roof of a nearby pavilion. Never again in Chinese history would a native-born Emperor ascend the throne.

II

When morning came, the gates of the city were thrown wide, and Li Tzŭ-ch'êng entered. Since the late monarch's grave at the Ming Tombs site was not yet ready, Li Tzŭ-ch'êng had him interred west of Peking in a tomb originally intended for one of the imperial concubines. The ceremony was a solemn one, with all the dignity an Emperor's funeral merited, for Li Tzŭ-ch'êng had nothing more to fear from the last of the Ming, and wished to begin his reign with the proper tone of respect for the overthrown dynasty.

On that cold April morning Li Tzŭ-ch'êng rode through the nearly empty streets of Peking, enjoying his moment of supremacy. As he approached the marble bridge that led to the inner imperial city, the conqueror halted, looking up at the magnificent series of five archways through which only the Emperor was allowed to pass. A sign over the gate proclaimed its name: *T'ien An Men,* "Gate of Heavenly Peace."

Struck by the need to perform some dramatic gesture, Li Tzǔ-ch'êng drew his bow and fitted an arrow to the string. Pointing to the character *T'ien* in the inscription, he declared, "*T'ien* is Heaven, and it is by Heaven's will that I am here. If I strike the character full center it proves that the empire, All Under Heaven, is truly mine!"

The arrow sped through the chilly air—and missed, striking well below the target. Li Tzǔ-ch'êng's followers vociferously assured him that the omen was meaningless, and hurried him into the palace. But Li Tzǔ-ch'êng was shaken by the answer of Heaven. And the unfavorable omen proved indeed to foretell the cast of events.

The old dynasty was gone, but one of its partisans still survived: the general Wu San-kuei, commander of the garrison at Shanhaikuan. He was a native of the border region, with important family connections in Manchuria. Though loyal to the Chinese Emperor, Wu had watched many of his colleagues desert to the barbarians, and he himself felt a strong pull of sympathy toward the bannermen of the north. A stocky man with small eyes and a hooked nose mottled by a dull purple birthmark, Wu San-kuei had the reputation of being a formidable military man, and he was the only Chinese leader who could offer any kind of challenge to the usurper Li Tzǔ-ch'êng.

The traditional story tells that Wu San-kuei had visited Peking shortly before its fall, and had become enamored of a singing-girl named Ch'ên Yüan-yüan, known as the Roundfaced Beauty. She remained in Peking when Wu returned to Shanhaikuan to defend the Great Wall against a possible Manchu thrust. When Peking was taken by Li Tzǔ-ch'êng, both the lovely Ch'ên Yüan-yüan and the father of Wu San-kuei fell into Li Tzǔ-ch'êng's hands.

At once, Li sent word to Wu at Shanhaikuan, informing him of the change of dynasty and asking for his support. He supported his request with a gift of silver, and enclosed a letter from Wu's father, asking him to submit to the new ruler. Wu San-kuei, realizing that the Ming cause was a hopeless one, agreed to recognize Li Tzǔ-ch'êng as Emperor of the northern and western provinces, maintaining control of the east himself. He reserved the right to transfer his allegiance to the rightful heirs of the Ming Dynasty if they ever regained popular support. And he requested that Li Tzǔ-ch'êng turn over to him his concubine, his father, and the Ming heir apparent, who had been captured by Li while attempting to escape from Peking.

Li agreed to most of Wu San-kuei's proposals. But he refused to surrender the Ming prince, who might become the focal point of rebellion if he ever got free. More puzzlingly, he chose to add Ch'ên Yüan-yüan to his own harem instead of sending her to Wu San-kuei. Perhaps he hoped to use her as a means of keeping Wu in line; perhaps he was simply enjoying the display of power for its own sake. It seems doubtful that he retained her for any reason of passion.

Wu San-kuei was furious when he heard that Ch'ên Yüan-yüan had been enrolled as a concubine of the Ta Shun Emperor. He resolved at once to make no alliances with Li Tzǔ-ch'êng, but rather to hand the country over to the Manchus as a way of gaining revenge. Or, according to a less romantic interpretation, he committed his act of treachery because he was a man of the northern border whose sympathies lay with the Manchus rather than with a Chinese-born usurper.

Abahai, the Manchu Emperor, had died in 1643, and his place had been taken by his younger brother Dorgon, who was serving as regent for Abahai's six-year-old son. Dorgon camped just outside Shanhaikuan at the head of a Manchu army, waiting for an opportunity to invade China. Much to his surprise—for Wu San-kuei had been an obstacle to the Manchu advance for years —Dorgon received a message from the Chinese general, informing him of a willingness to surrender.

Li Tzŭ-ch'êng, having heard of Wu's defiance but knowing nothing of his secret overtures to the Manchus, was at that time marching toward Shanhaikuan with practically his entire large army. He took up a position in a valley south of Shanhaikuan, confident that he could destroy Wu and his garrison. The strategy was to lure Wu from the fortress, draw back in feigned retreat, then close in along the flanks and shut the trap.

With seeming innocence Wu San-kuei led his troops toward the army of the usurper the next morning. Li's men dropped back as planned, then began their encircling movement. Suddenly, to the horror of Li Tzŭ-ch'êng, a mighty force of Manchu calvary burst from the hills just inside the Great Wall and roared down to attack. Li's men panicked and fled at the terrifying sight of the men of the north once again descending like demons onto Chinese soil. Thousands of lives were lost, and Li Tzŭ-ch'êng barely managed to escape, hurrying back to Peking to lick his wounds. In cold fury, he ordered the execution of hundreds of captive Ming officials, and put to death thirty-seven members of Wu San-kuei's family, including his father. The concubine Ch'ên Yüan-yüan was spared to be used as a hostage.

The combined forces of Wu and the Manchus marched toward the capital. Early one morning Li gave orders for evacuation, seeing that it would be impossible to hold the city against the double army. All gold and silver found in the city was melted down into flat disks weighing a thousand ounces apiece, and these, to the number of about ten thousand, went with Li Tzŭ-ch'êng as he fled westward.

The surviving officials of the Ming court admitted Wu and his Manchu allies to Peking. They seemed to be under the impression that the Ming Dynasty was to be restored, but the Manchus quickly and quietly let it be known that they intended to rule China themselves. Dorgon sent Wu San-kuei to the west to pursue and overtake the fleeing Li Tzŭ-ch'êng.

A war of attrition followed. Wu nipped away at the flanks of Li's army in skirmish after skirmish. Li was forced to surrender Wu's captive concubine in order to buy a little delay; he crossed into Shensi, leaving her behind. The massive gold and silver disks of his booty proved too much to carry, and Li dumped them into rivers as he retreated, hoping to salvage them if he ever returned. At last only a few dozen followers remained to him. He wandered from city to city, finding no refuge anywhere, and finally was put to death by villagers in a town of Hupei.

Wu San-kuei returned to Peking. Hopefully, he tried to persuade the Manchus to go home, leaving him as a puppet Emperor, but Dorgon had other ideas. The invaders had come to stay. Wu agreed to pay homage to them as rulers, with four stipulations: that no Chinese women be taken into the harem of the Manchu Emperors; that Chinese women should not be required to adopt Manchu dress or to give up the practice of binding their feet; that the *chin shih,* the highest degree of the Chinese civil service examinations, was never to be awarded to a Manchu; and that Chinese men would be permitted to be buried in the costume of the Ming era. These points were accepted by the Manchus, who insisted on one of their own: that Chinese men would thenceforth shave their heads and wear queues in the Manchu style, and would don Manchu clothing during their lifetimes.

The transfer of power was complete. The young grandson of Nurhachi was raised to the throne as the first Emperor of the Ch'ing, or Manchu, Dynasty. A new caste of barbarian conquerors established themselves as the overlords of China. By 1659, the fifteenth year of Manchu rule, the last prince of the Ming house had been driven from the country. Wu San-kuei pursued him deep into Burma, putting him to death in 1662.

As the man who had given China to the Manchus rather than let it be seized by Li Tzŭ-ch'êng, Wu San-kuei occupied a position of prominence under the invaders. He became enormously wealthy, assembled a private army of his own, and, inevitably, rebelled against the Ch'ing Dynasty in 1673, with the intent of driving the barbarians out and taking the throne himself. His revolt was suppressed eight years later, three years after his own death, and his son, Wu Shih-fan, perished by suicide. In a strange parallel to modern Chinese events, the disgruntled supporters of the Ming Dynasty withdrew to the island of Taiwan after the Manchu conquest, and proclaimed an independent regime with claims to mainland authority. In 1683, the Manchus rooted out the Taiwan diehards with the aid of a Dutch fleet and occupied the island. For a century and a half thereafter, China was at peace.

III

Last of the long line of China's alien conquerors, the Manchus were able to benefit from the errors of those who had come that way before. They made no sweeping changes in the Chinese economy. Holding themselves aloof from their subjects, retaining a separate identity that centered on the structure of the banner system, they employed the Chinese scholar gentry in civil administration, persuading most of the Ming officials to remain at their posts. To preserve their identity as Manchus, the homeland of the Ch'ing was closed to Chinese immigration, and a separate Manchu capital was maintained north of the Great Wall at Mukden. The Willow Palisade was extended several hundred miles, curving northward from Shanhaikuan to Mukden and then south to the mouth of the Yalu, as a barrier to hold back the flow of Chinese culture. Though gradually the rulers at Peking gave up the Manchu language for Chinese, the Ch'ing Dynasty was able to keep a separate identity until its eventual overthrow early in the twentieth century.

The success of the Manchu period grew largely from the wisdom of two unusually gifted Emperors, whose names are familiar to all collectors of Chinese

Portrait of a seated man. Artist unidentified. Ming Dynasty (1368–1644).
The Metropolitan Museum of Art, gift of Hackson E. Reynolds

The Emperor K'ang Hsi of the Ch'ing or Manchu Dynasty (1644–1912).
The Metropolitan Museum of Art, Rogers Fund

porcelain. K'ang-hsi in the seventeenth century and Ch'ien-lung in the eighteenth brought security and stability to the conquered land.

K'ang-hsi* came to the throne in 1661, at the age of seven. He was the third son of Shun Chih, the first Ch'ing Emperor, and the great-grandson of Nurhachi. When he was thirteen he dismissed his regents and began to rule in his own right, proving bold in battle, wise and frugal in administration. Tall and robust, his appearance impressive but for the marks of smallpox, K'ang-hsi enjoyed the pleasures of the hunt and those of the battlefield. Early in his reign, he was required to deal with the rebellions of Wu San-kuei and the surviving Ming partisans—challenges which he met successfully. With China pacified, K'ang-hsi was able to turn to thoughts of conquest north of the Great Wall, at last making that frontier a zone of peace.

The conquest of what has become known as Inner Mongolia had begun as early as 1634. The Manchus followed their successful invasion with a thoughtful program of administration, assigning the tribes to fixed areas, regulating intertribal relations, conferring titles and honors, and carefully averting the rise of any new Mongol unifier in the Genghis Khan tradition. Mongol tribesmen were placed under the banner system and were enrolled in the Ch'ing service, some of them rising to high positions. The Manchus thus gave the Mongols a vested interest in the preservation of the established order. No longer having any reason to invade China, the Mongols of the border "reservoir" grew sedentary and soft, providing a much more effective barrier against invasion than the Great Wall had ever been.

Tougher barbarians still lurked in the remote reaches of Central Asia. In the 1670's Galdan, khan of the Dzungar tribe and a descendant of the Oirat leader Esen, built a following in the Altai Mountains and the valley of the Ili River, and moved southward to occupy the oasis cities of the Old Silk Road as far east as Hami. Galdan's Dzungars began to pillage their settled eastern cousins of Inner Mongolia, and when they had moved as far east as the Kerulen River in 1696, K'ang-hsi personally led an army of 80,000 men to crush them. In a battle south of Urga (the modern Mongolian capital of Ulan Bator) the Manchu artillery routed Galdan's warriors and broke the back of Mongol resistance.

K'ang-hsi followed the customary practice of weakening the Mongols by furthering Lamaism among them. He intervened in the politics of Tibet, the center of Lamaist Buddhism, and in 1705 succeeded in naming a puppet Dalai Lama as the head of the sect. This not only brought Tibet under indirect Chinese rule, but allowed K'ang-hsi to stimulate the expansion of Lamaism in Mongolia. By the end of his reign, between 40 and 60 per cent of the male population of Mongolia were lamas, which produced a vast drop in Mongol numbers and a corresponding reduction of Mongol strength. Indeed, the wreck of the Mongol economy went so far that in certain parts of Inner Mongolia all males of the community had been absorbed into the priesthood,

---

* More accurately referred to as "the K'ang-hsi Emperor," since that was his reign-title; his name was Hsüan-i.

and it was necessary for the descendants of Genghis Khan to hire Chinese as shepherds and as substitutes for compulsory tribal military service.*

In the field of foreign relations, K'ang-hsi dealt extensively with Europeans, particularly the Jesuits and the Russians. Russian ambassadors were frequent visitors to K'ang-hsi's court. In 1670, a Russian named Milovanoff crossed Mongolia and entered China at what he called the Stone Wall, which was the Nankou Pass above Peking. He described the Great Wall as being "of gray stone below, but of brick, laid with mortar, above; and in the wall is a gateway-tower with oaken doors sheathed with iron plates. And from that tower, the wall on either side stretches out endlessly; the Manchus said that it goes from sea to sea, and that it takes about a year to ride alongside it."[143]

Five years later, another Russian embassy under Nikolai Gavrilovitch came to China, and its account leaves no doubt that the Manchus were maintaining the Great Wall: "You can only pass the Wall where gates have been made. Between the high roads, however, there are other, lesser ones by which the subject races of China and the frontier Mongols and Kalmuks enter the kingdom; for there are many gates in the Wall, but it is only over the high roads that the great caravans can pass."[144]

And the Russian traveler Spathary, who saw the Wall near Peking in May 1676, left this description:

"There are frequent towers, 100 *sazhens* [700 feet] one from the other. The Wall is built in this way; at the foundation, cut stone of huge dimensions, undressed granite, and above that, brick. The height is four *sazhens* [twenty-eight feet], the breadth is two *sazhens*. In some places, among the mountains, it has fallen down. The Chinese, speaking of it, boast that when it was built there remained no stone in the mountains, no sand in the desert, in the rivers no water, in the forests no trees."

On his journey Spathary came first to an outer wall fourteen feet high, where he was met by a Chinese escort which took him to the Great Wall's entrance. "There, at the first gate, was a great tower, and at the gate stood the governor of the town, counting all who passed, for such is their custom; and not only the people, but the arms they carry; all which is written down, lest any other man or weapon should pass when these return. And this they do not only at these gates, but at all gates in the Great Wall." He passed through the first gate, which was twenty-eight feet wide and defended by a guard. Twenty-eight yards further on was a second wall with similar gates, and beyond that a third. "And all those gates and towers are very strong," he wrote, "the third (inner) wall thicker than the others, and all three are built across the stony ravine about fifty-six feet wide, with a high and rocky cliff on either side. The doors themselves in the gate towers are sheathed with iron."[145]

These Russian embassies had come to execute commercial treaties. However, the ambassadors declined to perform the obligatory gestures of abase-

---

* When Outer Mongolia became a Communist state in 1921, a vigorous campaign against Lamaism was launched. Forty years later, there were only two monasteries in all Mongolia, and only a few aging lamas.

ment required when approaching the Emperor, and their missions proved fruitless. The encroachment of Russians on the Manchu sphere of influence led to armed conflict along the Amur River in 1684, but a few years later a treaty was negotiated and the Russians withdrew. Gradually, Russian traders filtered into China during the following generation, but in 1722, smarting over some minor offense by the Russians, K'ang-hsi ordered them all expelled, and trade did not resume until a treaty of 1728 gave the Russians the right to use two northern towns as outposts for commerce.

The Jesuits, who had established themselves at Peking in the beginning of the seventeenth century, had remained there through the disorders that accompanied the collapse of the Ming Dynasty. K'ang-hsi recognized the qualities of these unusual men, and made use of them just as his predecessors had. Under the last Ming, a Jesuit named Adam Schall had been an important figure at the court, and at the outset of Ch'ing rule in 1645 he was given the significant post of Director of the Astronomical Board, after he had correctly foretold a solar eclipse not mentioned by the imperial calendar. Schall also set up a foundry for the making of cannon, and this aspect of Jesuit work continued under his successor, Father Verbiest. In 1681, Verbiest demonstrated a new model of cannon for K'ang-hsi, and the Emperor was so delighted by the noisy display that he presented his fur-lined vest and gown to the Jesuit on the spot.

Later in his reign, K'ang-hsi sent his Jesuits on long missions of exploration, in contrast to the Ming rulers, who never let the fathers get out of sight. Some time before 1694, one Father Alexander toured the Great Wall from west to east at K'ang-hsi's command, reporting that parts of it were of such breadth that eight horsemen could comfortably ride upon it abreast. At the beginning of the eighteenth century, Jean François Gerbillon, a Jesuit known to the court as Chang Ch'êng, persuaded the Emperor to undertake a complete survey of all China. The Jesuit chiefly responsible for the assignment was Jean-Baptiste Régis (Lei Hsiao-ssŭ), assisted by Joachim Bouvet (Pai Chin) and Pierre Jartoux (Tu Tê-mei), as well as by several Chinese cartographers. The ten-year project commenced on July 4, 1708, when Fathers Régis, Bouvet, and Jartoux set out from Peking for Shanhaikuan. They followed the outer line of the Wall as far west as Suchow, then went south to map some of the inner spurs. Their map of the Great Wall was fifteen feet long, "which, considering the length of the Wall, cannot be called excessive," one later geographer observed. The Jesuits found the Wall in good repair in the east, but Régis reported, "Along the northern border of Shansi the Wall is made of clay, without battlements, and is only about five feet high. West of Shansi it is a narrow mud rampart, sometimes even only a sand ridge. It is in better repair between Suchow and Kia-yü-kuan, in Kansu. Thence to Hsining, on the Tibetan border, the mountains serve as a rampart, with a moat along their crests." In 1718 the atlas was engraved on copper plates by the Jesuit Matteo Ripa, and it was often reprinted, since it was the most accurate map of any part of the world that had been made up to that time.

The K'ang-hsi Emperor died in 1722, having ruled China for sixty-one of his sixty-eight years. His long reign had seen the power of his dynasty extended far into Asia, and a flourishing of Chinese culture at home. He was succeeded by Yün-chen, the fourth of his thirty-five sons, who ruled as Yung-cheng. Yung-cheng seized the throne in a virtual *coup d'état*, since K'ang-hsi had named no official successor, and consolidated his position by arresting or exiling many of his brothers. Some of the imperial princes had become Christians, which led the new Emperor to turn against that religion. He ordered all the missionaries confined either to Peking or Macao, and, while he did not expel them from his kingdom, he prohibited the entry of new priests. Lacking his father's flair for battle, he began no new military adventures, but conscientiously maintained the empire that he had inherited.

He was followed by a far greater ruler, Ch'ien-lung, the grandson of K'ang-hsi. Ch'ien-lung began his reign in 1735, at the age of twenty-five, and one biographer calls him "an able ruler, with an insatiable thirst for knowledge, and an indefatigable administrator," who "rivals his grandfather's fame as a sovereign and a patron of letters."[146] Shrewd and autocratic, capable of inspiring terror as well as love, Ch'ien-lung held his throne into great old age. In 1793, when he was eighty-three, the Emperor was visited by an embassy of England's George III, and the ambassador, George Viscount Macartney, noted in his journal that Ch'ien-lung's "manner is dignified, but affable and condescending, and his reception of us has been very gracious and satisfactory. He is a very fine old gentleman, still healthy and vigorous, not having the appearance of a man of more than sixty."[147]

He was a warrior in K'ang-hsi's tradition. After ten years devoted to internal reorganization, Ch'ien-lung launched extensive campaigns of conquest on China's western and southern frontiers. Between 1755 and 1757, he devoted himself to the pacification of the Dzungar tribe, which had become troublesome again. The Chinese armies fell on them with such ferocity that nearly a million Mongols were killed, and the survivors fled into Russia. Years later, some of the fugitives began to return to their ancestral territory on the steppe, but the trip across the desert was so grim that only one-fourth of the nomads survived. Since the middle of the eighteenth century, the homeland of the western Mongols has been desolate and almost depopulated, a continuing aftermath of Ch'ien-lung's invasion.

In 1758 and 1759 he attacked Turkestan; he subdued Burma between 1766 and 1770, and Annam in 1788 and 1789. Tibet was invaded and conquered in 1790. Ch'ien-lung had fashioned the greatest empire in Chinese history, far surpassing even the accomplishments of the early T'ang Emperors. A chronicler of the period observed, "The empire was at peace. On the frontiers no more fires were lit in the watchtowers of the Great Wall announcing alarm, the troops and the people enjoyed happiness, and the virtue of humanity was practiced. The people lived until an old age."[148]

In the realm of scholarship, Ch'ien-lung was responsible for the assembly of a great imperial library, known as the *Ssu-k'u ch'üan-shu*, or *The Complete*

Library of the Four Treasuries, the four being the branches of literature: history, philosophy, belles-lettres, and the classics. More than 15,000 copyists worked nearly twenty years to compile this collection, which comprised 36,000 volumes. It thus was more than twice the size of the enormous compilation of Yung-lo; but that was an encyclopedia, while this was simply an aggregation of whole books. Seven complete sets were made. Two were completely destroyed during a nineteenth-century rebellion in southern China, and a third partially so. A fourth set at Peking was burned by a French and British army that put down an uprising in 1860. The remaining copies have survived, two at Peking and one at Mukden.

Ch'ien-lung's motives in this enterprise were not altogether pure. It was intended to be a collection of all the worthy literature of China, but the Emperor decided, for political reasons, what was worthy and what was not. Any book that spoke harshly of the Manchus or insulted previous "barbarian" dynasties was suppressed. By house-to-house canvass the offending works were rooted out and destroyed. Some 2,300 books were proscribed entirely, 350 more partly suppressed. "None may remain to after generations," Ch'ien-lung declared, "in order to cleanse our speech and make straight the hearts of men."

This literary inquisition was broad and sweeping. Typical of the approach was the report of one censor who wrote, "This belongs in the class of fiction. Its words are very confused. It ought to be destroyed."[149] One dictionary-maker dared to criticize a dictionary compiled under K'ang-hsi, and went so far as to print the names of the Ch'ing Emperors in full, rather than using disguised characters as was considered proper. "My hair stood on end," said Ch'ien-lung, "at this revelation of rebellion and lawlessness." The dictionary-maker was executed, his property confiscated, and two sons and three grandsons sent into slavery. (During World War II, when parts of China were occupied by Japan, some of the suppressed books of the Ch'ien-lung era finally were published. They had been hidden in Japanese archives since the eighteenth century, and were made available to Chinese scholars after the invasion.)

V

In old age, Ch'ien-lung grew crusty and opinionated. Though not Chinese himself, he was convinced that the Chinese nation over which he ruled was the most cultured and civilized in the world, and he had little interest in the doings of foreigners. This created problems abroad, for the Europeans were very much interested in China, and sought some way of coming to agreement with Ch'ien-lung on trade concessions.

There had been many embassies to China during Manchu times: the various Russian missions of the seventeenth century, Dutch embassies in 1656 and 1667, an envoy from the Pope in 1720, one from Portugal in 1753. Except for the Russian treaties of 1689 and 1728, the visitors had accomplished little. This was partly their own fault, for the Europeans stiff-neckedly refused to kowtow to the Chinese Emperors in the required manner. Even if they did make the proper obeisance, it did little good; a Dutch ambassador prostrated himself willingly enough before Ch'ien-lung and kowtowed effusively, but only succeeded in making himself look like a clown—particularly when his wig fell off during one extravagant series of prostrations.

In 1792, England sent her first embassy to China under George Macartney. The mission had many purposes. Macartney was directed to negotiate a treaty of commerce and friendship between England and China on an equal footing—not, as other European ambassadors had done, accepting the status of "tributary power" as a sop to Chinese pride. He was to extend British trade in China by opening new ports to foreign ships. He was to obtain cession of an island or tract of land nearer to the silk- and tea-producing areas than Canton, where British jurisdiction could be exercised. He was also requested to obtain every kind of information about China, not merely economical and political, but cultural, social, and military.

George Viscount Macartney, the man entrusted with this mission, had been born in Northern Ireland in 1737. He had spent his early years following the pursuits of an eighteenth-century gentleman: a university education, followed by the study of law, abandoned midway so that he could go on the Grand Tour. When he returned from the Continent, at the age of twenty-seven, he planned to enter Parliament, but the opportunity arose for him to go as envoy extraordinary to the court of Catherine the Great at St. Petersburg. Before leaving England, Macartney was knighted by George III. During prolonged and delicate negotiations, he was able to obtain a commercial treaty with Russia, though not the alliance England had hoped for. After this mission, he served in several government posts, saw action in the West Indies during the American Revolution, and for a while was a French prisoner-of-war after his capture off Grenada. In time he was raised to the peerage, became a member of Dr. Samuel Johnson's circle, and knew such figures of the era as James Boswell and Sir Joshua Reynolds. In 1781, he was sent to India as Governor of Madras; later he resigned and withdrew from public life, but late in 1791, now holding the title of viscount, he accepted the assignment of heading the mission to China.

Macartney took with him an entourage of ninety-five persons aboard two ships. Included were not only diplomats and interpreters but an artist, a watchmaker, a maker of mathematical instruments, five German musicians, a botanist, and various other skilled craftsmen. After a long sea voyage, the party docked at Tientsin in the summer of 1793, and set out for Peking.

The visitors were met by Chinese court officials, who were particularly fearful that Macartney would refuse to perform the ceremonial kowtows. They quickly explained the requirements to the ambassador, who informed them plainly that he would bend one knee before the Emperor, as he might before George III, but would go no further. An anxious interchange of letters among Chinese diplomats followed, the minister Ho-shên suggesting to the minister Cheng-jui that the latter "ought casually in the course of conversation to inform him [Macartney] tactfully that as regards the various vassal states, when they come to the Celestial Empire to bring tribute and have an audience, not only do all their envoys perform the ceremony of the three kneelings and the nine knockings of the head, but even the princes who come in person to court also perform this same ceremony."[150]

Macartney refused to yield, insisting that he had not come as a representative of a vassal state at all, and on September 14, 1793, the Emperor received him without demanding the kowtow. The Chinese officials (who had been so thoughtful as to suggest to Macartney that he would have an easier time genuflecting if he disencumbered himself of his knee buckles and garters before entering the imperial presence) were appalled. Ch'ien-lung did not deign to notice the omission.

The audience with the Emperor took place not at Peking but at the imperial residence in Jehol, north of the Great Wall. Macartney was eager to see the famous structure, and not at all put out that it was necessary to go to the northern capital. The envoys had reached Peking in August, leaving it at the beginning of September, and on September 5 they arrived at the Great Wall at the Kupeikou Pass. Here, rocky mountains rose steeply from the plain, and the road ran through a narrow ravine between the mountain walls.

They found the Great Wall in a state of moderate disrepair. Passing through gate after gate, all of them open and some of them in ruins, they came to the Mongolian side of the Wall and explored it on foot, "there being no other method of approach. In less than half an hour, after traveling over very rough ground, we at last arrived in a breach in the wall, by which we ascended to the top of it."[151]

Macartney made a close examination of the Wall, noting in his journal that it was "built of blueish colored brick, not burnt but dried in the sun, and raised upon a stone foundation, and as measured from the ground on the side next Tartary, it is about twenty-six feet high in the perpendicular. The stone foundation is formed of two courses of granite equal to twenty-four inches or two feet. From thence to the parapet including the cordon which is six inches are nineteen feet four inches, the parapet is four feet eight inches." Some complicated calculations of the number of bricks followed. Macartney observed that "At the bottom the walls are five feet thick, and diminish gradually as they rise. . . . The space or terrepleine between the walls, which is filled with earth and rubbish up to the level of the bottom of the cordon and paved with square bricks is eleven feet in the clear, so that there is room for two coaches or five horsemen abreast. This great wall is strengthened and defended by square towers at one hundred and fifty to two hundred feet distance. They are of different dimensions. I entered one which projected eighteen feet from the ramp on the Tartar side; there is no projection on the Chinese."[152]

A member of Macartney's party took some samples of the brickwork, hoping to discover the reason for the blue color. He reported later that experiments showed that iron in the original clay and also in the ashes and coal used to bake the bricks had imparted the color. This contradicted Macartney's theory that the bricks were sun-dried instead of kiln-baked, and he generously admitted his error in a journal footnote.

Macartney also was interested in the openings in the parapet—holes twelve inches long and ten wide, "which appear much better calculated for musketry than for arrows." Since he had heard—correctly—that the Great Wall dated from a time two centuries before Christ, he concluded—wrongly—that the

A watchtower on the Great Wall.
Collection of the author

Chinese must have had firearms in remotest antiquity. He went astray here because he did not know that the section of the Wall he was examining was Ming work, no more than two hundred years old.

The Wall was every bit as impressive as Macartney had expected it to be. He had been told that it was upward of 1,500 miles in length, and wrote, "If the other parts of it be similar to those which I have seen, it is certainly the most stupendous work of human hands, for I imagine that if the outline of all the masonry of all the forts and fortified places in the whole world besides were to be calculated, it would fall considerably short of that of the Great Wall of China. At the remote period of its building China must have been not only a very powerful empire, but a very wise and virtuous nation, or at least to have had such foresight and such regard for posterity as to establish at once what was then thought a perpetual security for them against future invasion."[153]

He perceived that the Wall had not merely been a defense against enemies, but might have been built "to shut out from the fertile provinces of China the numerous and ferocious beasts of the wilds of Tartary, to ascertain and fix her boundary, and to prevent emigration." And he remarked, "The wall is still in some places which I saw quite perfect and entire, and looks as if recently built or repaired, but in general it is in a ruinous condition, and falling fast to decay, very little care being taken to preserve it. Indeed at present its utility in point of defense seems to be almost at an end. For the Emperor now reigning has extended his territory so far beyond it that I doubt whether his dominions without the wall are inferior to those within it."[154]

Macartney's tour of the Wall was cut short by the impatience of his uneasy guides, who "were astonished at our curiosity, and almost began to suspect us, I believe, of dangerous designs." The party moved on, and when it halted the next day an interpreter regaled Macartney with a Tientsin newspaper's account of the gifts that had supposedly been brought from England for Ch'ien-lung: dwarfs twelve inches high, an elephant the size of a cat, a horse the size of a mouse, and other rarities.

Jehol was reached, and the audience with Ch'ien-lung took place on September 14. The English readied the gifts they actually had brought: telescopes, ornate clocks, Wedgwood vases, and other products of European art and science. When the audience began, there was an exchange of gifts between ambassador and Emperor, Macartney receiving "a whitish, agate-looking stone about a foot and a half long, curiously carved, and highly prized by the Chinese, but to me it does not appear in itself to be of any great value."[155] Ch'ien-lung was gracious but noncommittal, and no serious matters were discussed, though a five-hour entertainment was staged for the amusement of the English. A week went by; the envoys were given a taste of the imperial court's luxury, but no business was transacted, and it began to seem to Macartney that none would be. Ch'ien-lung clearly regarded the English as tribute-bringers, vassals, not as representatives of a sovereign state. The costly gifts sent by George III to the Emperor were accepted casually, and the Chinese presented in return "lanterns, pieces of silk and porcelain, balls of tea, some drawings, etc.," of no great value.

The failure of the mission became evident when Macartney finally got a chance to state his purpose. Ch'ien-lung's ministers had drafted an edict to King George nine days before Macartney's first appearance at the imperial court, which in haughty and condescending tones dismissed the English requests in advance. The edict commended the "sincere humility and obedience" of George III, thanked him for the "tribute articles," and flatly declared, "Strange and costly objects do not interest us. As your ambassador can see for himself, we possess all things. We set no value on objects strange and ingenious and have no use for your country's manufactures."

So, ignominiously, ended England's first embassy to China. Macartney and his party returned to Peking and stayed there through October 7. By January they were at Macao, having toured much of China on the way, and early in 1794 they set out for home. Though George III's envoys had been received with disdain, the mission stirred up great interest in Europe, for Macartney had brought back extensive collections of Chinese articles, and his report caused a sensation in Europe. Nearly every member of the embassy published a book about the journey, including Macartney's valet, a private in the Light Dragoons, and the tutor of a boy whose father had been Macartney's deputy. Curiously, Macartney's own account, by far the best of the literary by-products of the voyage, remained unpublished until it finally was rescued from obscurity in 1962.

Having put the foreign devils in their place, Ch'ien-lung drew his reign to a close. In 1795 he abdicated, explaining that he had ruled for the same length of time as the great K'ang-hsi, and had no wish to exceed the achievement of his distinguished grandsire. He died in 1799, nearly ninety years of age.

China's history after Ch'ien-lung is a wearying business. The succeeding Emperors were weak, and grew weaker as the nineteenth century progressed.

Flood, famine, rebellion, corruption, and bankruptcy harried the Manchu rulers. There were no more invasions from beyond the Great Wall, for all the barbarians had by now been absorbed into the empire, but new invaders came by sea: Germans and French and English and others, who carved up China into spheres of influence and proceeded to transact business atop the still quivering hulk of the Ch'ing Dynasty. The arrogance of Ch'ien-lung gave way to feebleness and to sinister court intrigues, and in 1912 the end came for the Ch'ing Dynasty. It was swept away to join the Ch'in and the Han and the T'ang and the Sung and all the rest in limbo, but this time there was no new dynasty to take its place. After twenty-two imperial centuries China became a republic. The torment and anguish of the giant land in our own time needs no recapitulation here. Today, brisk young archaeologists of the Communist regime conduct explorations along the vast length of the Great Wall, salvaging artifacts as old as Chou Dynasty times, but we learn little of their findings, for China is cut off from our world by a barrier more impenetrable than the Great Wall.

Seventeen.
The Nineteenth Century and After

The crumbling of Chinese imperial authority in the middle of the nineteenth century opened China to European tourists, and they came in droves. All who visited Peking went on to tour the Ming Tombs, and then to the Great Wall, but few were so hardy as to explore the lesser known stretches of the Wall northwest of Peking.

Some were bolder though. In 1892 two English travelers, Mr. and Mrs. St. George R. Littledale, left Russian Turkestan and set out along the Old Silk Road. They passed through Kashgar and the Tarim, through the haunted desert of Marco Polo, and traveled the line of the Great Wall to Peking without guides or interpreters. About the same time, such archaeologist-adventurers as Sven Hedin and Aurel Stein were planning their first expeditions to Central Asia.

Travel in China was halted at the end of the nineteenth century by the bloody uprising known as the Boxer Rebellion, an expression of hatred for foreigners that took hundreds of European lives, saw the Emperor and his scheming aunt, the sinister Dowager Empress, forced to flee, and produced the celebrated siege of foreign diplomats at Peking. Oddly, the Great Wall is said to have figured as a motivating factor in the Boxer Rebellion. According to a possibly apocryphal story, one night in 1899 four bored reporters from Denver's four newspapers, the *Times, Post, Republican,* and *Rocky Mountain News,* found themselves together in a railroad station where they had come to interview a visiting celebrity. The celebrity failed to arrive. Lacking a story, the four cooked one up. They invented a wild tale of American engineers who had stopped over in Denver en route to China, where they were going at the request of the Emperor. The nonexistent engineers had been hired, the stories said, to make plans for demolishing the Great Wall cheaply and efficiently, for the Chinese had decided to tear the Wall down as a gesture of international good will. Razing the Wall was to symbolize China's welcome for foreign trade.

The stories appeared the next day, under such headlines as this from the Denver *Times:*

GREAT CHINESE WALL DOOMED!

PEKING SEES WORLD TRADE!

: 209 :

Denver read the articles, smiled, shrugged, and forgot them. But a New York Sunday supplement picked up the fable and ran it in an expanded and glorified version, complete with illustrations, a political analysis of the Chinese decision, and a "confirming statement" from a Chinese mandarin visiting New York.

The story made its way to China, but got there in upside-down form. The Chinese newspapers shrieked the word that Americans were on their way to demolish by force the Chinese national monument, the Great Wall! Already simmering with revolt after half a century of foreign exploitation, the Chinese rebels were goaded into action by the wild story and by other similar recent events. Rebellion broke out. By June, 1900, the foreign embassies at Peking were under siege, and hundreds of missionaries were butchered all over China. Two months later, an international army of German, Japanese, Russian, American, French, and British troops invaded China, reached Peking, and quelled the uprising, not without burning and looting the imperial palaces in the process and slaughtering an untold number of Chinese. The "Boxer indemnity" of $320,000,000 exacted from China in retribution for the outbreak helped to accelerate the republican revolution that swept the country a decade later.

II

When order was restored after the Boxer Rebellion, the sightseers and archaeologists returned. By 1923, at least three westerners had completed the tour of the Wall from one end to the other. The first was William Edgar Geil, who made the trip about 1908. Geil told his story in a bulky, chatty, atrociously written book distinguished mainly by its scores of excellent photographs. (And by its contempt for Chinese customs and religion, for Geil was robustly and aggressively Christian.) During the First World War a more scientific observer, Frederick G. Clapp, made the journey with several companions, reporting on it in 1920 to the American Geographical Society. And a traveler named Adam Warwick explored the Wall in the early 1920's, telling the readers of the *National Geographic Magazine* about it in a well-illustrated article published in 1923. Of the archaeologists who worked in China during the same period, the one who devoted the most attention to the Great Wall was Aurel Stein, although he concentrated on the Han extension west of Kia-yü-kuan.

Geil began his tour at Shanhaikuan, which he said "boasts a thousand families, on whom the . . . missionaries are making an impression." He noted that there was talk of building a railroad pass through the Wall at that point, but he doubted if it would ever be done, and called it "a cruel sacrilege to pierce the Great Wall with an iron track." It *was* done, though, late in 1909, not at Shanhaikuan but farther west at Nankou. Tunnels, one of them almost four thousand feet long, passed under the Great Wall, and the tracks in one place went through the Wall at the point supposedly destroyed by the weeping Mêng Chiang Nu.

Geil observed a white lighthouse where the Wall met the sea at Shanhaikuan, and commended it as a sign of China's progress. Warwick was also impressed with the lighthouse, remarking on the "contrast between East and West. The eye of the modern searchlight opens and winks with startling effect on the old Pavilion of Literature placed on the very spot where Ch'in's Rampart joins on to the city wall of Shanhaikuan."

The Nankou Pass near Peking, probably the section of the Wall most familiar to western tourists, came in for a good deal of literary attention. Romyn Hitchcock, who visited it about 1891, told the readers of *The Century Illustrated Monthly Magazine* that "formerly the Nankow Pass was the great commercial highway to and from Mongolia. It was then an excellent stone road, laid with great blocks of granite, or cut into the rocky hills, over which carts could travel. It is now a rough and almost dangerous path, where carts do not attempt to pass; the merchandise is still transported on pack-animals —ponies, mules, donkeys, and camels—and of these there is an endless succession of caravans from dawn till sunset." Clapp, thirty years later, described the pass as "wild and gloomy, bounded by towering crags, scarcely leaving room for the stony torrent and the railroad." He commented that the caravan traffic was no longer to be seen, now that the railroad ran through the Great Wall at Nankou.

The decayed state of the Wall farther to the west has brought forth its share of lamentations. Orvar Karlbeck, a Swedish dealer in Chinese art who toured the Wall in the late 1920's, crossed it at Yulin in Shansi, and found that "instead of withstanding the onslaught of sand-storms it had crumbled to insignificance," because "it had been cast from loess but not faced with brick." He reported that "the watchtowers, however, were so faced and were in quite good repair. The lower storey was built of cast loess, and bricked, but the upper one consisted entirely of brick and contained a large chamber with arched openings. The roof had a castellated parapet. A fortress to house the garrison defending that sector was incorporated in the Wall. It was of impressive dimensions and consisted of a square tower with two offsets. It had originally been surmounted by a structure like those crowning the walls of most Chinese towns."[156] The fortress, on high ground, was girdled with a brick wall still in good repair. It had a single entrance, "so low that one had to crouch to pass through it," and a stairway led to the parapet-protected floors above.

On his trip Clapp attempted to follow the Wall through the Ordos Desert, by no means a pleasant chore. Two travelers had come that way in 1912, R. S. Clark and A. de C. Sowerby, and their report hardly made the Ordos sound appealing:

"The country . . . is wild and inexpressibly dreary. Very few trees are to be seen, and the bare brown cliffs and yellow sand are devoid of any vegetation, save an occasional tuft of some sage scrub. In places, especially where, as in the northeast, it rises to any prominence, gloomy chasms, with deadly quicksands lurking in their depths, gape in the sandstone and the half-formed shale. To north and west the prospect is heartbreaking. Sand-dunes and sand-dunes and again sand-dunes shifting with every storm and obliterating every landmark. Only here and there, as tiny islands in a sea of desolation, small clusters of mud huts, where some little oasis marks the site of a spring or well."[157]

Clapp's task was complicated by the fact that many Emperors since Ch'in Shih Huang Ti had built boundary walls across the Ordos at different points, depending on the depth of nomad penetration at the time. Clapp came to the ruins of a desert wall, and commented, "All published maps record this wall as the 'Great Wall.' At Shenmu, however, the natives said: 'This is *not* the Great Wall; this is the 'First Frontier Wall,' built only four hundred years ago; the 'Great Wall' is farther north. And they added that the 'Second Frontier Wall' lies about 30 miles beyond the present frontier, and the 'Great Wall' a long way beyond that. History furthermore appears to corroborate the local tradition that the ruins of the real Great Wall lie buried in the desert sands somewhere in the Ordos. Their exact location makes an interesting archaeological and historical problem. The past greatness and prosperity of the region is attested by numerous walled cities, ancient buried or ruined highways, and the frequent presence, under the sand dunes, of a rich soil which must have constituted a great fertile valley in some distant period. On this region the northern sands have been encroaching, passing one wall after another, and are now far beyond the southernmost one, relentlessly conquering a once prosperous country on which the fiercest Mongol onslaughts were of little avail."[158]

Warwick, visiting the same area, described the Wall as "an earth and gravel mound a few feet high," its "once historic towers . . . now merely rubbish heaps. . . . There is little, if any interest," he went on, "in following this crumbling mound, hastily thrown together, of materials collected on the spot by the builders, who made scarcely any effort to encase it in granite or protect it or embellish it with parapets. The traveler here finds many difficulties without an adequate reward."[159]

The Wall forks at Chunwei, one branch crossing the Yellow River and passing southward to Lanchow, the other running due west toward Kia-yü-kuan. Geil followed both loops. Along the southern one, of which he said "the whole fabric is in ruins, considerable and grass-covered," he came upon the highest altitude reached by the Great Wall—ten thousand feet above sea level, on a pass between Liangchow and Lanchow. At Lanchow the Wall met the Yellow River once again—there are at least five major points of intersection between Wall and river—and Geil pursued the Wall to its southernmost point, beyond the city.

From Lanchow, there are again two lines of Wall. One is the main Kansu loop running to Kia-yü-kuan; the other Geil called the Tibetan loop, because it passed close to the Tibetan borders, though not actually touching them. Hsining, just within this loop of the Wall, is the most important Chinese city in the area. A medical missionary named Henry French Ridley, residing at Hsining in 1895–96, was apparently the first European to explore the Tibetan loop of the Wall. Geil and Clapp both followed his path as far as Kumbum, "the seat of ten thousand images," which has one of the largest lamaseries outside of Lhasa itself. It was at Hsining that the Wall took its curious curve, which gave rise to the story that a dragon had napped against the Wall and pushed it out of shape.

The ruins of the Great Wall bordering Tibet. Geil, *The Great Wall of China*

Only a core remained of the section of Wall that ran along the northern border of Kansu. "Its course is in a wide and lofty valley, over broken hills and upon mountains," Geil wrote. He asked a native why the people did not repair the Great Wall, and received the answer, "We cannot repair our own city, how then the Great Wall?" But farther on, as the Wall neared Kia-yü-kuan, it was in a good state of repair. Geil wrote of Kia-yü-kuan "with its embattled walls and three-storied towers," and said that it "appeared very beautiful to a wearied traveler who for weeks past had wandered over the desert." His account of the very end of the Great Wall, on the precipice overlooking the Tapai Ho, has already been quoted.

The best description of Kia-yü-kuan, I think, is that of Aurel Stein, who approached it from the outside after his explorations in the desert west of the city. In July, 1907, after his work at Tun-huang, Stein rode toward Kia-yü-kuan. "Looking down from a height of close on 8,000 feet I could see distinctly the low gravel ridges closing the valley at its eastern end, and above them a faint white line lit up by the setting sun—the long-expected 'Great Wall.' The distance separating me from it was still over twenty miles. Yet I thought that I could make out towers reflecting the slanting rays and beyond them a great expanse of dark ground, the fertile district of Suchow."[160] The next day, after crossing "four miles of stony waste, slightly but steadily rising," Kia-yü-kuan came into sight again: "The many-storied gate tower built in wood first became visible; then, as we got nearer, the clay wall which stretches away on either side of the square fort guarding the great gate." The gates of the Wall were opened for him, and the distinguished archaeologist entered Cathay.

III

Today China has strange new masters, who fear many enemies but have no dread of the nomads of the north. Manchuria and Inner Mongolia have been made Chinese provinces, and so heavy has been the flow of Chinese settlers into the steppe that the distinctive culture of the north has been submerged. Modern industrialization has destroyed forever the old concepts of an agricultural China and a pastoral northland. Outer Mongolia, now the Mongolian People's Republic, still has a considerable nomad population, but there is small chance of an invasion of China after the style of Mao Tun, Genghis Khan, or Esen.

The Communist government of China does not encourage tourism, but one section of the Great Wall north of Peking has been rebuilt as a showplace for the trade delegations and student groups that still enter the country. A Western news correspondent visited that restored section of the Wall in 1962, in the company of some 100 Chinese, including a party of students from the Marx-Lenin University. New brickwork and refurbished battlements made the Wall seem as majestic as it must have looked during the days when it was an active line of defense. But a sign decreed sternly, "Foreigners not allowed beyond this point without special permission," and the correspondent was able to see that "the ancient stones are crumbling and overgrown as the Wall stretches away." Beer was served and music was played during the visit.

Thus the Wall seems to have come to the end of its long career. No longer is it a barrier against grim warriors of the north. Now it is a tourist attraction—or at least one small segment is. Thousands of scribbled signatures and slogans deface it, for the Chinese authorities do not seem to object. And so an alien hand has scrawled in western characters on the face of the Great Wall of China the incongruous inscription, *"Viva Castro!"*

IV

It was William Edgar Geil who said, "The Wall is not for modern use. It is an ancient fossil—the largest fossil on the planet." There it stands, crumbling and pathetic, a weathered hulk somehow enduring across the centuries. It was designed to turn back invaders, and yet barbarians ruled China for some 850 out of the last 1,500 years. Only during the T'ang and the Ming Dynasties was all China under Chinese control, and even the T'ang was founded by a man of partly Turkish descent. The rest of the time, invaders were triumphant.

Yet were they? Was the Wall really such a monument to futility? Time and again the invaders were absorbed into the civilization they had conquered. "China is a sea which salts all the streams that flow into it," an old proverb has it, and we have seen how the T'o-pa, the Khitan, the Manchus, and many other conquerors found it impossible to resist the lure of Sinification.

: 214 :

It is fair to call the Great Wall, as one writer has, "the greatest example of wasted military effort in the history of the world."[161] But that is not to say that because it failed to stem the nomad tide, it failed to serve any useful purpose at all. Such a verdict would be unkind and untrue. The Wall has always been more than just a mighty rampart; it has been a symbol of China, the concrete and tangible representation of the unity of that vast land. The Great Wall says: *here* is China, and *there* is outer darkness. The story of China is the story of the magnificent Long Rampart that gave her her identity.

THE CHINESE DYNASTIES

PRE-IMPERIAL ERA

Hsia (legendary)	1994–1523 B.C.
Shang (or Yin)	1523–1028 B.C.
Chou	1027–256 B.C.
Ch'in	255–221 B.C.

FIRST UNIFICATION

Ch'in	221–207 B.C.
Earlier (Western) Han	202 B.C.–A.D. 9
Hsin	A.D. 9–A.D. 23
Later (Eastern) Han	25–220

FIRST PARTITION (*Three Kingdoms*)

Wei	220–265
Shu Han	221–264
Wu	222–280

SECOND UNIFICATION

Western Chin	265–317

SECOND PARTITION

Northern Dynasties
(partial list)

T'o-pa Wei	386–534
Eastern Wei	534–550
Western Wei	535–557
Northern Ch'i	550–577
Northern Chou	557–589

Southern Dynasties

Eastern Chin	317–420
Liu Sung	420–479
Southern Ch'i	479–502
Liang	502–557
Ch'en	557–589

| Sui | 589–618 |
| T'ang | 618–906 |

THIRD PARTITION (*Five Dynasties*)

Later Liang	906–923
Later T'ang	923–936
Later Chin	936–947
Later Han	947–951
Later Chou	951–960

FOURTH UNIFICATION (*Sung Dynasty*)

| Northern Sung | 960–1127 |
| Southern Sung | 1127–1279 |

During Five Dynasties and Sung times northern China was ruled by two successive barbarian dynasties:

| Liao (Khitan) | 907–1125 |
| Chin (Jurchen) | 1125–1234 |

FIFTH UNIFICATION

Yüan (Mongol)	1279–1368
Ming	1368–1644
Ch'ing (Manchu)	1644–1912
Republic	1912 to date

NOTES

PREFACE

1. Geil, *Great Wall*, p. 311.
2. *Ibid.*, p. 155.

CHAPTER 1

3. *Book of Odes*, tr. Waley (as *Book of Songs*), p. 248.
4. Petrie, *History of Egypt,* 1st edition.
5. MacKenzie, *Chinese Art*, p. 20.
6. Watson, *China*, p. 103.
7. *Book of Odes, op. cit.,* p. 252.

CHAPTER 2

8. See Lattimore, *Inner Asian Frontiers,* pp. 345–50.
9. *Ibid.*, p. 345.
10. Lattimore, *Studies in Frontier History,* p. 28.
11. Lattimore, *Inner Asian*, p. 363.
12. Tr. Waley, quoted in Lum, *Purple Barrier,* p. 71.
13. *Book of Odes, op. cit.,* pp. 122–3.
14. Lattimore, *Frontier History,* p. 116.
15. Quoted in *ibid.*, p. 108.

CHAPTER 3

16. Quoted in Cottrell, *Tiger of Ch'in,* p. 120.
17. Quoted in *ibid.*, p. 116.
18. Quoted in *ibid.*, p. 117.
19. Grousset, *Rise and Splendor.*
20. Quotations in this section are from the *Shih chi* of Ssŭ-ma Ch'ien, tr. Bodde, *Statesman,* pp. 1–9.
21. Bodde, *ibid.*, p. 22.
22. Bodde, "Basic Concepts," p. 383.

23. Hsün-tzu, quoted in Bodde, *ibid.*, p. 384.
24. Quoted in *ibid.*, p. 385.
25. Confucius, *Analects,* II, 3; quoted in *ibid.*, p. 384.
26. Han Fei Tzŭ, quoted in *ibid.*, p. 385.
27. *Book of Lord Shang,* quoted in *ibid.*, p. 386.
28. Quoted in Fêng Yu-lan, *History of Chinese Philosophy.*
29. *Book of Lord Shang,* quoted in Waley, *Three Ways,* p. 166.
30. *Ibid.*, p. 169.
31. Tr. Bodde in *China's First Unifier.*
32. Quoted by Granet, p. 412.
33. Quoted by Cottrell, p. 181.
34. Quoted by Granet, p. 38.
35. *Ibid.*
36. Quoted in Bodde, *China's First Unifier.*

CHAPTER 4

37. Tr. Bodde, *Statesman,* p. 54.
38. Quoted in *ibid.*, p. 67.
39. Cressey, p. 185.
40. Geil, p. 94.
41. Warwick, p. 123.
42. Geil, pp. 317–18.
43. *Ibid.*, pp. 325–6.
44. *Ibid.*, p. 63.
45. Tr. Joseph Needham and Liao Hung-ying, *Sinologica,* 1, pp. 194–209.

CHAPTER 5

46. Tr. Bodde, *China's First Unifier,* p. 172.
47. *Ibid.*
48. Bodde, *Statesman,* pp. 61–2.
49. Quoted in Granet, pp. 40–1.
50. Bodde, *Unifier.*

CHAPTER 6

51. Pan Ku, quoted in Cottrell, p. 231.
52. Quoted in Granet, pp. 43–4.
53. Quoted in Lum, p. 72.
54. *Ibid.*
55. Lattimore, *Inner Asian*, p. 260.
56. Quoted in Granet, p. 44.
57. Quoted in Goodrich, p. 50.

CHAPTER 7

58. Quoted in Needham, I, p. 234.
59. Tr. Henry Yule.
60. Stein, *Desert Cathay*, I, p. 541.
61. Stein, *Ancient Tracks*, p. 172.
62. *Ibid.*, p. 182.
63. *Ibid.*, pp. 185–6.
64. Quoted in Lum, pp. 23–4.
65. Tr. E. M. Gale, quoted in Goodrich,
    p. 41.

CHAPTER 8

66. Quoted in Lum, p. 80.
67. Tr. Waley, quoted in Lum, p. 87.
68. Quoted in *ibid.*, p. 89.
69. Quoted in *ibid.*, pp. 80–1.
70. Quoted in Needham, I, p. 110.
71. Giles, *Dictionary*, p. 504.
72. *Ibid.*, p. 609.
73. Quoted in Yule-Cordier, *Cathay*, I, p. 50.
74. Quoted in *ibid.*, p. 183.
75. Tr. Hu Shih, quoted in Goodrich, p. 48.

CHAPTER 9

76. Yule-Cordier, *Cathay*, I, p. 16.
77. Giles, *Fa-Hsien*.
78. Giles, *Dictionary*, p. 961.

CHAPTER 10

79. Quoted in Goodrich, p. 118.
80. Quoted in *ibid.*, p. 121.
81. Quoted in Needham, I, p. 219.
82. Quoted in Yule-Cordier, *Cathay*, III, p. 123.

CHAPTER 11

83. *Ibid.*, I, p. 251.
84. Wittfogel, p. 367.
85. Purchas, XI, p. 513.
86. Wittfogel, p. 554.
87. *Ibid.*, p. 422.
88. *Ibid.*, p. 396.
89. Quoted in Goodrich, p. 151.
90. Quoted in Gernet, p. 236.

CHAPTER 12

91. Purchas, XI, p. 173.
92. Giles, *Dictionary*, p. 929.
93. Quoted in Needham, I, p. 140.
94. Lum, p. 122.
95. Tr. Yule, I, p. 382.

CHAPTER 13

96. Olafsson, II, pp. 97–8.
97. Quoted in Baddeley.
98. Jacopo of Acqui, quoted in Power, p. 63.
99. Tr. Yule, quoted in Yutang, pp. 51–2.
100. Tr. Latham, p. 18.
101. *Ibid.*, p. 76.
102. Tr. E. A. Wallis Budge, quoted in Anderson, pp. 22–3.
103. Tr. Pickthall, pp. 218–19.
104. Hakluyt, I, p. 261.
105. Tr. Wilson, p. 591.
106. Quoted in Yule-Cordier, *Cathay*, IV, 117.
107. *Ibid.*, 23.
108. Yule, *Polo*, I, p. 8.
109. Yule-Cordier, *Cathay*, III, pp. 46–7.

CHAPTER 14

110. Quoted by Geil, pp. 82–3.
111. Yule-Cordier, *Cathay*, I, p. 274.
112. *Ibid.*, pp. 296–7.
113. *Ibid.*, p. 180.
114. Ley, pp. 110–11.
115. *Ibid.*, p. 157.
116. Purchas, XI, p. 103.
117. *Ibid.*, pp. 103–4.
118. *Ibid.*, p. 104.
119. Quoted in Hakluyt Society edition of Mendoza.
120. Geil, p. 65.
121. *Ibid.*, p. 74.

CHAPTER 15

122. Hakluyt, VI, pp. 350–1.
123. Purchas, XI, p. 485.
124. Hakluyt Society edition, Vol. I.
125. Gallagher, p. 166.
126. *Ibid.*, pp. 166–7.
127. *Ibid.*, pp. 168–9.
128. *Ibid.*, p. 194.
129. *Ibid.*, p. 477.
130. *Ibid.*, p. 10.
131. Yule-Cordier, *Cathay*, IV, p. 199.
132. *Ibid.*, p. 207.
133. *Ibid.*, p. 208.
134. *Ibid.*, pp. 221–2.

135. *Ibid.*, pp. 235–6.
136. *Ibid.*, p. 239.
137. *Ibid.*, p. 248.
138. *Ibid.*, pp. 251–2.
139. Quoted in Baddeley.
140. Purchas, XI, pp. 279–80.
141. Quoted in Reischauer, p. 348.

CHAPTER 16

142. Giles, *Dictionary*, p. 190.
143. Quoted in Baddeley.
144. *Ibid.*
145. *Ibid.*, p. 321.
146. Giles, *Dictionary*, p. 143.
147. Cranmer-Byng, p. 25.
148. Schramm, III, pp. 103–4.

149. Reischauer, p. 382.
150. Cranmer-Byng, pp. 32–3.
151. *Ibid.*, p. 111.
152. *Ibid.*
153. *Ibid.*, p. 112.
154. *Ibid.*, p. 113.
155. *Ibid.*, p. 122.

CHAPTER 17

156. Karlbeck, p. 82.
157. Clark and Sowerby, *Through Shen-kan*, quoted in Clapp, p. 234.
158. Clapp, p. 234.
159. Warwick, p. 142.
160. Stein, *Desert Cathay*, II, p. 271.
161. Swann, p. 58.

ꓕꓕꓕꓕꓕꓕ

BIBLIOGRAPHY

ANDERSON, ANDREW RUNNI. *Alexander's Gate, Gog and Magog, and the Inclosed Nations.* The Mediaeval Academy of America, Cambridge, Mass., 1932.

ANDERSSON, J. G. *Researches Into the Prehistory of the Chinese.* Bulletin of the Museum of Far Eastern Antiquities, Stockholm, 1943.

BADDELEY, JOHN F. *Russia, Mongolia, China.* Macmillan, London, 1919. 2 vols.

BODDE, DERK. "Basic Concepts of Chinese Law." *Proceedings of the American Philosophical Society,* Vol. 107, No. 5 (October 15, 1963), Philadelphia.

———. *China's First Unifier.* E. J. Brill, Leiden, 1938.

———. *Statesman, Patriot, and General in Ancient China.* American Oriental Society, New Haven, Conn., 1940.

BRETSCHNEIDER, E. *Mediaeval Researches from Eastern Asiatic Sources.* Kegan Paul, Trench, Trübner & Co., London, 1888. 2 vols.

CLAPP, FREDERICK G. "Along and Across the Great Wall of China." *Geographical Review,* Vol. 9, No. 4 (April-May-June, 1920), New York.

COLLIS, MAURICE. *The Grand Peregrination, being the Life and Adventures of Fernão Mendes Pinto.* Faber and Faber, London, 1959.

COTTRELL, LEONARD. *The Tiger of Ch'in.* Holt, Rinehart and Winston, New York, 1962.

CRANMER-BYNG, J. L., ed. *An Embassy to China: Lord Macartney's Journal.* Longmans, London, 1962.

CRESSEY, GEORGE BABCOCK. *China's Geographical Foundations.* McGraw-Hill, New York, 1934.

DABBS, JACK A. *History of the Discovery and Exploration of Chinese Turkestan.* Mouton & Co., The Hague, 1963.

DOUGLAS, WILLIAM O. "Journey to Outer Mongolia." *National Geographic Magazine,* Vol. 121, No. 3 (March 1962), Washington, D. C.

DUYVENDAK, J. V. V., ed. *The Book of Lord Shang.* Probsthain, London, 1928.

EBERHARD, WOLFRAM. *A History of China.* University of California Press, Berkeley and Los Angeles, California, 1950.

FENG YU-LAN. *History of Chinese Philosophy,* trans. by Derk Bodde. Princeton University Press, Princeton, New Jersey, 1953.

GALLAGHER, LOUIS J., S.J. *China in the 16th Century: the Journals of Matthew Ricci,* trans. by Louis J. Gallagher, S.J. Random House, New York, 1953.

GEIL, WILLIAM EDGAR. *The Great Wall of China.* John Murray, London, 1909.

GERNET, JACQUES. *Daily Life in China on the Eve of the Mongol Invasion 1250-1276.* George Allen & Unwin, London, 1962.

GILES, H. A. *A Chinese Biographical Dictionary.* Kelly and Walsh, Shanghai, 1898.

———. *Travels of Fa-Hsien.* Cambridge University Press, Cambridge, England, 1923.

GOODRICH, L. CARRINGTON. *A Short History of the Chinese People,* 3rd ed. Harper Torchbooks. Harper & Row, New York, Evanston, and London, 1963.

✳ GRANET, MARCEL. *Chinese Civilization.* Routledge and Kegan Paul, London, 1930.

GROUSSET, RENÉ. *The Rise and Splendor of the Chinese Empire.* Geoffrey Bles, London, 1952.

HAKLUYT, RICHARD, ed. *The Principal Navigations Voyages Traffiques and Discoveries of the English Nation.* Modern ed. James MacLehose and Sons, Glasgow, 1903–05. 12 vols.

HAYES, L. NEWTON. *The Great Wall of China.* Kelly and Walsh, Shanghai, 1929.

HITCHCOCK, ROMYN. "A Ride to the Great Wall of China." *The Century Magazine,* Vol. 15, No. 3 (January 1893), New York.

HUDSON, G. F. *Europe & China.* Edward Arnold, London, 1931.

KARLBECK, ORVAR. *Treasure Seeker in China.* Cresset Press, London, 1957.

LATTIMORE, OWEN. *Inner Asian Frontiers of China,* 2nd ed. American Geographical Society, New York, 1951.

———. *Studies in Frontier History: Collected Papers, 1929–58.* Oxford University Press, London, 1962.

LEY, C. D., editor. *Portuguese Voyages 1498–1663.* Everyman's Library. J. M. Dent, London, 1960.

LUM, PETER. *The Purple Barrier.* Robert Hale, London, 1960.

MACKENZIE, FINLAY. *Chinese Art.* Marboro Books, New York, 1961.

MENDOZA, JUAN GONZALEZ DE. *History of the Great and Mighty Kingdom of China.* Modern ed. The Hakluyt Society, London, 1854. 2 vols.

MULDAVIN, MARK. "The Fake That Made Violent History." Included in *The Double Dealers: Adventures in Grand Deception,* Alexander Klein, ed. J. B. Lippincott, Philadelphia and New York, 1958.

NEEDHAM, JOSEPH. *Science and Civilization in China.* Cambridge University Press, Cambridge, England. Vol. I, 1954. Vol. II, 1956. Vol. III, 1959. Vol. IV: 1, 1962.

——— and LIAO HUNG-YING, trans. "The Ballad of Mêng Chiang Nu Weeping at the Great Wall." *Sinologica,* Vol. 1, 1948.

NEWTON, A. P., ed. *Travel and Travellers of the Middle Ages.* Routledge and Kegan Paul, London, 1926

OLAFSSON, JON. *The Life of the Icelander Jon Olafsson.* The Hakluyt Society, London, 1923, 1931. 2 vols.

PENROSE, BOIES. *Travel and Discovery in the Renaissance.* Harvard University Press, Cambridge, Mass., 1955.

PICKTHALL, MOHAMMED MARMADUKE. *The Meaning of the Glorious Koran.* New American Library, New York, 1953.

POLO, MARCO. *The Travels of Marco Polo.* Trans. by R. E. Latham. Penguin Books, Harmondsworth, England, 1958.

———. *The Book of Ser Marco Polo the Venetian.* Trans. and ed. by Henry Yule and Henri Cordier. John Murray, London, 1903. 2 vols.

POWER, EILEEN. *Medieval People.* Pelican Books, Harmondsworth, England, 1937.

PRAWDIN, MICHAEL. *The Mongol Empire.* George Allen & Unwin, London, 1940.

PURCHAS, SAMUEL, ed. *Purchas His Pilgrimes.* Modern ed. James MacLehose and Sons, Glasgow, 1906. 20 vols.

REISCHAUER, EDWIN O. and FAIRBANK, JOHN K. *East Asia: The Great Tradition.* Houghton Mifflin, Boston, 1958, 1960.

SCHRAMM, LOUIS M. J. *The Monguors of the Kansu-Tibetan Border.* American Philosophical Society, Philadelphia. Part II, 1957. Part III, 1961.

STEIN, M. AUREL. *On Central-Asian Tracks.* Macmillan, London, 1933.

———. *Ruins of Desert Cathay.* Macmillan, London, 1912. 2 vols.

SWANN, PETER C. *Chinese Monumental Art.* Viking Press, New York, 1963.

SYKES, SIR PERCY. *The Quest for Cathay.* A. & C. Black, London, 1936.

WALEY, ARTHUR. *Three Ways of Thought in Ancient China.* Anchor Books. Doubleday & Company, Inc., Garden City, L. I., 1956.

———, translator. *The Book of Songs (Shih Ching).* Grove Press, New York, 1960.

———. *Translations from the Chinese.* Knopf, New York, 1941.

———. *Travels of an Alchemist,* by Li Chih-ch'ang. Routledge and Kegan Paul, London, 1931.

WARWICK, ADAM. "A Thousand Miles Along the Great Wall of China." *National Geographic Magazine,* Vol. 43, No. 2 (February 1923), Washington, D. C.

WATSON, BURTON. *Records of the Grand Historian of China,* translated from the *Shih Chi* of Ssŭ-ma Ch'ien. Columbia University Press, New York, 1961. 2 vols.

WATSON, WILLIAM. *China.* Frederick A. Praeger, New York, 1961.

WILLETS, WILLIAM. *Chinese Art.* Pelican Books, Harmondsworth, England, 1958. 2 vols.

WILSON, C. E. "The Wall of Alexander Against Gog and Magog; and the Expedition Sent Out to Find It by the Khalif Wathiq in 842 A.D." *Asia Major,* Hirth Anniversary Vol. Probsthain, London, 1922.

WITTFOGEL, KARL A. and FÉNG CHIA-SHÉNG. *History of Chinese Society: Liao.* American Philosophical Society, Philadelphia, 1949.

YULE, HENRY, and CORDIER, HENRI. *Cathay and the Way Thither,* 2nd ed. The Hakluyt Society, London, 1913–16. 4 vols.

YUTANG, LIN. *Imperial Peking.* Crown Publishers, New York, 1961.

INDEX

Abahai (Manchu Emperor), 193, 198
Abulfeda (geographer), 155
Agriculture, Chinese, 20–21, 37, 127
Ai Ti (Han Emperor), 90–91
Akbar (Mogul king), 184
A-ku-ta (Jurchen chieftain), 132
Alexander Book, 151, 153
Alexander the Great, 151–156
Alexander's Wall, 151–156
Altan Khan; *see* Anda
A-lu-t'ai (Mongol chieftain), 162–164
Alvarez, Francisco, 176
Al-Warraq, 120
Amoy, city of, 171, 176
Amur River, 137, 201
An Lu-shan (T'ang general), 121
An Shih-kao, 105
Anda (also known as Altan Khan), 175–176
Andersson, J. G., 1, 3
Anushirvan (Persian king), 153–154, 156
Anyang, 6, 8; *see also* Shang, city of
Argun (Persian khan), 156
Arik-buga (Mongol khan), 144
Art, Chinese, 6–8, 13, 107–108, 119–120, 128, 201
Assurbanipal, 13
Assyria, 12–13
Avars; *see* Juan-juan

Bactria, 76, 80, 94–95, 105
Batu (Mongol general), 142–143, 147
Ben-ya-shi-li (Mongol khan), 162
Bereke (Mongol general), 143, 148
Black Khitai (also known as Kara-Khitai or Western Liao), 133, 141
Bodde, Derk, 29
Bokhara, 121, 124, 137, 142, 148, 166, 190

Book of Lord Shang, 34, 37
Bouvet, Joachim (also known as Pai Chin), 201
Boxer Rebellion, 209–212
Buddhism, 53, 84, 105–109, 112, 116, 118, 120–121, 124, 127, 132, 146, 159, 172, 175, 201
Burma, 77, 95, 145, 149, 174, 199, 202

Cambaluc (also known as Khan-baliq), 144–146, 151, 156, 158, 182
Cambodia, 171
Canton, 119, 145, 147, 156, 171, 174, 176, 181, 204
Catalan Map, 156
Cathay, 147, 149–150, 156–158, 166, 170, 182, 184–186, 189–190, 214
Cathay and the Way Thither, 99
Caucasus, 151–153
Chagadai (Mongol leader), 143, 145
Chagadai Khanate, 145, 162
Chang Ch'êng; *see* Gerbillon, Jean François
Chang Ch'ien (Han explorer), 75–79
Chang Chü-chêng (Ming minister), 177–178
Chang Ti (Later Han Emperor), 94
Ch'ang-an, city of, 67, 72, 92, 99, 104, 106, 108, 110, 112–113, 116, 118, 121–122, 146, 195
Chao (King of Ch'in), 29, 44
Chao Ch'i (Southern Sung Emperor), 144–145
Chao Chün, 88, 90
Chao Dynasty (A.D. 308–333), 99–100
Chao Dynasty, Later (A.D. 334–358), 100
Chao Hsin (Han general), 74
Chao Hsu; *see* Shên Tsung (Sung)
Chao Huan (Sung Emperor), 133
Chao Kao (Ch'in statesman), 58–60, 62–64
Chao K'uang-yin; *see* T'ai Tsu (Sung)

Chao P'o-nu (Han general), 74
Chao, state of, 23–25, 28–30, 42–43
Ch'ao, state of, 23
Chao Ti (Han Emperor, also known as Liu Fu-ling), 86
Chekiang, 19
Ch'ên Dynasty (A.D. 557–589), 109–111
Ch'ên Pa-hsien (Ch'ên Emperor), 109
Ch'en Yüan-yüan, 196–198
Chêng (King of Ch'in); see Shih Huang Ti
Chêng Ho (Ming eunuch), 170
Chêng Kuo (hydraulic engineer), 41
Ch'êng Ti (Han Emperor), 87, 90
Ch'êng Wang (Chou king), 13
Ch'êng-hua (Ming Emperor), 169
Ch'i Dynasty, Northern (A.D. 550–577), 109–111
Ch'i Dynasty, Southern (A.D. 479–502), 104, 109
Ch'i, state of, 13, 17–19, 23, 25, 28, 31, 44, 75, 97
Ch'ien-lung (Ch'ing Emperor), 199, 202–205, 207, 209–210
Ch'ih-ch'eng, city of, 102
Chihli, 102
Chin Dynasty (A.D. 1125–1234), 133, 137–142, 163
Ch'in Dynasty (221–207 B.C.), 39, 41, 45, 56, 68, 92, 210
Ch'in Dynasty (A.D. 351–394), 101
Chin Dynasty, Eastern (A.D. 317–419), 99–100, 103, 106
Chin Dynasty, Later (A.D. 936–947), 123–126
Chin Dynasty, Western (A.D. 265–317), 98–99
Ch'in Dynasty, Western (A.D. 394–431), 101, 103
Ch'in Shih Huang Ti; see Shih Huang Ti
Chin, state of, 18, 21, 23, 26, 28, 30
Ch'in, state of, 16–19, 21, 23–31, 34–36, 42, 46, 65–66
Chin Mi-ti (Hsiung-nu prince), 74, 86
Chinese Biographical Dictionary, 108
Ch'ing Dynasty (A.D. 1644–1912), 7, 159, 192–194, 198–210
Ching River, 41
Ching Ti (Ming Emperor), 168
Ching Ti (Northern Chou Emperor), 111
Chinkiang, city of, 144
Chou Dynasty (1027–256 B.C.), 12–17, 19–23, 25–26, 28, 31, 39–40, 42, 75, 104, 210
Chou Dynasty (A.D. 690–705), 118
Chou Dynasty, Later (A.D. 951–960), 123, 125–127
Chou Dynasty, Northern (A.D. 557–589), 108–111, 116
Chou Hsin (Shang Emperor), 13
Chou Kou Tien, 1

Chou, state of, 28
Christian Legend Concerning Alexander, 152
Christianity, 145, 146–148, 157, 183, 185, 204
Chu Chan-chi; see Hsüan-te
Chu Ch'ang-lo; see T'ai-ch'ang (Ming)
Chu Ch'üan-chung; see Chu Wen (Later Liang)
Chu Hou-tsung (Ming Emperor), 175
Chu I-chün; see Wan-li (Ming)
Ch'u, state of, 19, 23, 25, 31, 35, 44, 56, 63, 65–66, 105
Chu Ti; see Yung-lo (Ming)
Chu Wen (Later Liang Emperor, also known as Chu Ch'üan-chung), 122–123
Chu Yüan-chang; see Hung-wu (Ming)
Chu Yu-chien; see Ch'ung-cheng (Ming)
Chu Yu-hsiao (Ming Emperor), 189
Chu Yu-t'ang (Ming Emperor), 169
Chuang-hsiang (King of Ch'in), 29, 44
Ch'ung-cheng (Ming Emperor, also known as Chu Yu-chien), 190, 194–195
Chüyungkuan, city of, 139–140
Clapp, Frederick G., 49, 210–212
Clark, R. S., 211
Confucianism, 35, 68, 106, 124, 127, 157
Confucius, 12, 31–33, 35, 157
Corsalis, Andrew, 170
Cruz, Gaspar da, 130, 180

Da Gama, Pedro, 171
Da Gama, Vasco, 170–171
De Busbeck, Gislen, 166
De Goeje, M. J., 155
Derbend, 153–154, 156
Dorgon (Manchu regent), 197
Dzungar (tribe), 199, 203

Egypt, 1–3, 6, 8
Elements of Euclid, 183
Erh Shih Huang Ti (Ch'in Emperor), 58–60, 62–65
Esen (Oirat chieftain), 168–169, 175, 191, 199, 214

Fa-hsien (Buddhist pilgrim), 106
Fan San-lang, 53–54
Fang Hsiao-ju (Ming poet), 161
Faria, Antonio de, 171–172
Fêng Tao, 123–124
Ferdinand, John, 187–188
Ferghana, 76–81, 85, 119, 121
Five Dynasties period, 122–123
Five Sovereigns, 5, 31, 39
Flinders Petrie, W. M., 6
Fu Su (Prince of Ch'in), 58–61, 63
Fukien, 56, 176

Galdan (Dzungar khan), 199
Gavrilovitch, Nikolai, 200
Geil, William Edgar, 48, 50–52, 61, 210, 212–214
Genghis Khan (Mongol Great Khan, also known as Yüan T'ai Tsu and as Temujin), 137–143, 150, 157, 159, 162, 192, 195, 199–202, 214
Gerbillon, Jean François (also known as Chang Ch'êng), 201
Ghayath-ud-din, Khoja (Persian painter), 165
Giles, H. A., 108
Gobi Desert, 2, 14, 43, 48, 51, 74, 103, 106, 139, 149–150
Goes, Benedict de, 167, 184–188
Gog and Magog, 151–156
Golden Horde (also known as Kipchak Khanate), 142, 145, 147–148
Grand Canal, 112–115, 146, 163, 178
Great Wall:
  legends of, xiii–xiv, 52–55
  origins as state walls, 23–25
  as projected by Shih Huang Ti, 42–44
  construction by Mêng T'ien, 44–48
  extended by Han Wu Ti, 72, 79–81
  rediscovered by Aurel Stein, 81–84
  rebuilt by Chin Wu Ti, 98–99
  reconstructed by the T'o-pa, 102–103
  extended by Northern Ch'i Dynasty, 109
  repaired by Sui Wên Ti, 112
  rebuilt by Sui Yang Ti, 112–114
  extended by the Khitan, 126
  penetrated by the Mongols, 139–140
  confusion with walls of Alexander and Gog and Magog, 151–156
  reconstructed by Ming Dynasty, 163–164, 169–170
  described by Pinto, 172–175
  restored by Wan-li, 175–178
  described by Mendoza, 180–181
  described by Ricci, 183–185
  described by Petlin, 190
  described by Russian travelers, 202
  described by Macartney, 205–206
  as cause of Boxer Rebellion, 211–212
  described by modern travelers, 213–214
Grimanus, Leo, 185
Grousset, René, 28

Hadrian's Wall, 82
Hakluyt, Richard, 179
Hami, 186, 201
Han Dynasty, Earlier (202 B.C.–A.D. 9), 26, 28, 35, 37, 61, 66–71, 75, 83–92, 95–97, 103, 115, 210
Han Dynasty, Later (A.D. 25–220), 92–93, 95–96, 104–105

Han Dynasty, Later (A.D. 947–951), 123, 125–126
Han Fei Tzŭ (Legalist philosopher), 33, 36
Han, Kingdom of (founded in A.D. 304), 99
Han River, 19, 66, 143–144
Han, state of, 23, 28, 30, 36, 41
Hangchow, 113, 119, 128, 133, 144, 146
Hankow, 109
Hao, city of, 13
Hedin, Sven, 81, 209
Herodotus, 2
Historia de Ethiopia, 176
Hitchcock, Romyn, 211
Ho Ch'ü-p'ing (Han general), 74, 78
Ho Kuang (Han regent), 86
Ho Ti (Later Han Emperor), 94
Honan, 3, 16, 21, 23, 63, 195
Hopei, 23, 58, 101, 124, 126, 140
Horses, 77–78, 80
Hou Chin Dynasty; *see* Ch'ing Dynasty
Hou Ching (Liang Emperor), 109
Hsia Dynasty (1994–1523 B.C.), 5–6, 8, 12, 14
Hsia, Kingdom of (founded c. A.D. 404), 102–103
Hsiang Liang, 66
Hsiang Yü, 66
Hsiang-yang, 144
Hsiao (Duke of Ch'in), 34
Hsiao Tao-ch'eng (Southern Ch'i Emperor), 104
Hsiao Yen (Liang Emperor), 104
Hsien-pi (tribe), 19, 22, 93, 98, 101–102, 109, 125
Hsien-yang (capital of Ch'in Dynasty), 38, 57, 63–64, 66–67
Hsi-Hsia, Kingdom of, 131, 137–138, 141–142
Hsin Dynasty (9 B.C.–A.D. 23), 91
Hsining, 201, 212
Hsiung-nu (tribe), 19, 22, 28, 42–43, 45, 48, 56, 68–72, 74–79, 81, 84–89, 91–94, 98–99, 102, 108, 111, 125, 132, 152
Hsü Chien, 45–46
Hsüan Ti (Han Emperor), 86, 88, 90
Hsüan Ti (Northern Chou Emperor), 111
Hsüan Tsung (T'ang Emperor, also known as Li Lung-chi, 118, 120–121
Hsuan Wang (Chou king), 15, 22
Hsüan-I; *see* K'ang-hsi (Ch'ing)
Hsüan-te (Ming Emperor, also known as Chu Chan-chi), 168
Hsüan-tsang (Buddhist priest), 116–117
Hsün-tzu (Legalist philosopher), 32–33, 35, 40
Hu (tribe); *see* Tung-hu
Hu Hai; *see* Ehr Shih Huang Ti
Huai River, 65, 113, 143
Huang Ch'ao (T'ang rebel), 122

Huang Ho (Yellow River), 2–3, 5–6, 8, 17–18, 21, 23–26, 43, 45, 47–49, 52, 61, 65, 68, 75, 88, 112–115, 131, 133, 138, 140, 142, 169, 177, 191, 194, 212
Huang Ti (Ruler of the Yellow), 5, 105
Hui Ti (Ming Emperor), 161
Hui Tsung (Sung Emperor), 133
Hulagu (Mongol leader), 143, 145, 148
Hung-wu (Ming Emperor, also known as Ming T'ai Tsu and as Chu Yüan-chang), 159–162
Huns, 98, 102, 111, 127, 152–153
Hupei, 195, 198

Ibn Battuta (Arab traveler), 155–156
Ibn Khurdadbih (Arab historian), 154–155
Ibn Muhalhil, Abu Dulaf Mis'ar (Arab traveler), 124–125
I-ch'u (tribe), 74
Index of the Sciences, 120
India, 81, 84, 103, 105–106, 116–117, 119, 135, 142, 149–150, 158, 162, 170, 182, 185, 206
Indochina, 56, 135, 145, 171
Iron Gate, the, 151–155
Islam, *see* Moslems

Jade Gate, 50; *see also* Kia-yü-kuan and Yü-men
Jartoux, Pierre (also known as Tu Tê-mei), 201
Jehol, 121, 174, 205, 207
Jesuits, 150, 179, 181–183, 185, 187–189, 200–203
John of Marignolli, Friar, 158
John of Montecorvino (Archbishop of Cambaluc), 157–158, 185
John of Plano Carpini, Friar, 147, 149, 157
Juan-juan (tribe), 102–103, 110
Jung (tribe), 16, 19, 21–23, 26–27, 42, 45, 75, 98
Jurchen (tribe), 19, 125, 132–133, 135, 137–142, 144, 191, 194

K'ai Ho Chi (Record of the Opening of the Canal), 113
Kaifeng, city of, 123, 125, 128, 133, 140, 142, 194
Kalgan, 25, 55, 103, 168, 174, 190
Kan Ying, 94
Kanchow, 48
K'ang-hsi (Ch'ing Emperor, also known as Hsüan-I), 199–203, 207
Kansu, 3, 12, 14, 25, 42, 45, 48, 74, 78–81, 101, 103–104, 106, 110, 131, 137, 150, 163, 168, 201, 212–213
Kao Hsien-chih (T'ang general), 121
Kao Huan (Eastern Wei Emperor), 108

Kao Huang (Northern Ch'i Emperor), 108
Kao Tsu (Han Emperor, also known as Liu Pang), 64–70, 72, 86, 91–92, 111
Kao Tsung (Southern Sung Emperor), 133
Kao Tsung (T'ang Emperor), 117–118
Kara-Khitai; *see* Black Khitai
Karakorum (Mongol capital), 144, 147, 149, 159, 162
Karlbeck, Orvar, 211
Kashgar, 80–81, 94, 106, 149, 185, 209
Kerulen River, 137, 139, 199
Khan-baliq; *see* Cambaluc
Khitan (tribe), 19, 121, 123–128, 131–133, 138, 140–141, 149, 163, 190, 214
Khorezm, state of, 142
Khotan, 81, 94, 106, 119, 121, 149
Khujanga (Hsiung-nu chieftain), 88, 90
Kiangsu, 19, 65, 105
Kia-yü-kuan, 49–50, 56, 75, 79, 81, 93–94, 149, 155, 163–166, 172, 186–187, 201, 210, 212–213
Kipchak Khanate; *see* Golden Horde
Koran, 153–154
Korea, 75, 102, 113, 115, 117, 119, 121–122, 131, 143, 145, 163, 174, 194
Kou I, 86
Kuang Wu Ti (Later Han Emperor, also known as Liu Hsiu), 92–93
Kublai Khan (Mongol Great Khan and Yüan Emperor, also known as Yüan Shih Tsu), 143–151, 156–157, 162, 175
Kung Chêng-lu (Manchu adviser), 192
Kung-sun Ao (Han general), 74
Kung-sun Ho (Han general), 74
Kuo, state of, 26
Kuo Wei (Later Chou Emperor), 125
Kupeikou Pass, 174, 205
Kuyuk (Mongol Great Khan), 143, 147–148

Lamaism, 146, 175, 199–202
Lanchow, 212
Lao-tzu (founder of Taoism), 105
Lattimore, Owen, 20–21, 23, 43, 71, 145
Legalists, 31–36, 39
Lei Hsiao-ssŭ; *see* Régis, Jean Baptiste
Li Ch'êng-liang (Ming general), 178
Li Chieh (T'ang Emperor), 122
Li Chu (T'ang Emperor), 122
Li Hêng (T'ang Emperor), 122
Li Hsien (T'ang Emperor), 118
Li K'o-yung (Sha-t'o general), 122–124
Li Kuang (Han general), 74
Li Kuang-li (Han general), 78–79, 85
Li Ling (Han general), 85
Li Lung-chi; *see* Hsüan Tsung (T'ang)
Li Ma-tou; *see* Ricci, Matteo

Li Po (T'ang poet), 22, 119
Li Shih-min; *see* T'ai Tsung (T'ang)
Li Shên (T'ang Emperor), 122
Li Ssŭ (Ch'in statesman), 27, 31, 33–36, 38–40, 56, 58–60, 62–65
Li Ting; *see* Su Tsung (T'ang)
Li Tzŭ-ch'êng (Ta Shun Emperor), 194–198
Li Yen (T'ang Emperor), 122
Li Yu (Ch'in administrator), 62–63
Li Yü (T'ang Emperor), 121
Li Yüan (T'ang Emperor), 115
Liang Dynasty (A.D. 502–557), 104, 109
Liang Dynasty, Early (A.D. 313–376), 101
Liang Dynasty, Later (A.D. 386–403), 101
Liang Dynasty, Later (founded c. A.D. 560), 109, 111
Liang Dynasty, Later (A.D. 906–923), 101, 122–123, 126
Liang Dynasty, Northern, 101, 103
Liang Dynasty, Southern (founded in A.D. 397), 101
Liang Dynasty, Western, 101, 103
Liangchow, 48–49, 212
Liao Dynasty (A.D. 907–1125), 125–128, 131–133, 139
Liao Dynasty, Western (founded in A.D. 1124); *see* Black Khitai
Liao River, 25, 121, 126, 190
Liao-tung, 45, 50, 60, 126, 131, 163, 168, 178, 190, 192–193
Lin-t'ao, 45, 60
Littledale, St. George R., 209
Liu Ch'ê; *see* Wu Ti (Han)
Liu Ch'i (Han Emperor), 72, 97
Liu Chih-yüan (Later Han Emperor), 125
Liu Fu-ling; *see* Chao Ti (Han)
Liu Hêng; *see* Wên Ti (Han)
Liu Hsieh (Later Han Emperor), 96
Liu Hsiu; *see* Kuang Wu Ti (Han)
Liu Pang; *see* Kao Tsu (Han)
Liu Pei (Shu Han Emperor), 96–97
Liu Shih; *see* Yüan Ti (Han)
Liu Sung Dynasty (A.D. 420–479), 103–104
Liu Ying (Han Emperor), 70
Lin Yü (Liu Sung Emperor), 103
Liu Yüan-hai (Hun leader), 99
Lo River, 23, 41
Lop Nor, 80–81, 155
Lorenzo de' Medici, Duke, 170
Loulan, 80–81
Loyang, 16–17, 92, 96–97, 99, 104–105, 108, 113, 118, 121–122
Lü (Han Empress), 70–71, 87, 117
Lü Pu-wei, 29, 35
Lu, state of, 13, 19, 31–32
Lung-mên, city of, 108

Macao, city of, 174, 176, 179, 181, 202, 207
Macartney, George Viscount, 150, 202, 204–207
MacKenzie, Finlay, 7
Malaya, 170–171
Manchu Dynasty (A.D. 1644–1912); *see* Ch'ing Dynasty
Manchuria, 14, 18, 20, 25, 42, 49, 75, 101, 121–125, 132, 145, 163, 174, 191, 197, 214
Manchus (tribe), 19, 177, 190, 193–194, 197–198, 201–202, 205, 214
Mangu Khan (Mongol Great Khan), 143, 148
Mao Tun (Hsiung-nu chieftain), 68–71, 76, 99, 102, 191, 214
Marcellinus, Ammianus, 99
Mecca, 171, 186
Mekong River, 171
Mendoza, Juan Gonzalez de, 180–181
Mêng Chiang Nu, 52–55, 210
Mêng I, 44, 57–58, 60–61
Mêng T'ien (builder of Great Wall), 44–49, 56, 58–61, 68, 75, 91
Mercator, 156
Mesopotamia, 1, 3, 8, 12, 143, 162
Ming Dynasty (A.D. 1368–1644), 6, 47, 109, 150, 159–170, 175–178, 183, 191, 192–198, 201, 203, 214
Ming Huang; *see* Hsüan Tsung (T'ang)
Ming Ti (Later Han Emperor), 93–94, 105
Ming Ti (Later T'ang Emperor), 124
Ming Tombs, 167, 195, 209
Mithridates II, 80
Mohammed, 153
Mohammed ben Musa (astronomer), 154
Mohammedans; *see* Moslems
Money, Chinese, 72, 130, 146
Mongolia, 2, 14, 20–21, 41–44, 48, 75, 78–79, 110, 120–121, 125–126, 131–132, 135, 137, 139, 143, 145, 151, 162, 168, 174, 190, 193, 199, 213, 214
Mongols, xiii, 19, 102, 125, 136–148, 151, 156–159, 161–163, 167–170, 175–177, 185, 190, 192–193, 201–202, 204; *see also* Tartars
Moslems, 121, 124, 137, 145–147, 153–154, 156, 162, 185, 187, 189
Mu Wang (Chou king), 75
Mu-jung Huang (Prince of Yen), 101
Mu-jung Hui (Hsien-pi chieftain), 101
Mu-jung Te (Yen Emperor), 101
Mu-jung Tsuan (Yen Emperor), 101
Mukden, 198, 203

Nan-chao, Kingdom of, 143
Nanching; *see* Peking
Nanking, 99, 103, 106, 109, 144, 159, 161–163, 171–172, 182
Nankou Pass, 177, 195, 200, 211–213

Nestorians, 147–148, 158, 185
Ninghsia, 25, 48, 74, 131, 163
Ning-po, city of, 171, 174, 176
Nurhachi (Manchu Emperor), 190, 192–193, 198, 199

Odoric of Pordonone, Friar, 158
Ogödai Khan (Mongol Great Khan), 142–143
Oirats (tribe), 163–164, 166, 168–169, 199
Olafsson, Jon, 150
Ongut (tribe), 139
Onon River, 163
Ordos, 25, 43, 48–49, 68, 74–75, 112, 121, 125, 142, 169, 175, 211–212
Orkhon River, 117
Ortelius, 179

Pai Chin; see Bouvet, Joachim
Palladius, 150
Pamir Mountains, 76, 78, 94, 105, 121, 133, 149, 166, 185
Pan Ch'ao (Han general), 93–95
Pan Ku (Han historian), 67, 93, 95, 127
Pao Ssŭ, 15–16, 44
Paris, Matthew (English chronicler), 136, 138, 142
Parthia, 80, 94
Pegolotti, Francis Balducci, 158
Peiping; see Peking
Peking, 1–2, 25, 47, 55, 103, 109, 113, 124–126, 133, 139–141, 144, 146, 159, 161–165, 168, 170, 172, 175–176, 179, 182–183, 187–190, 193–199, 203–207, 209–212, 216
Periplus of the Erythraean Sea, 95
Persia, 12, 80, 99, 110, 117, 119, 142–143, 145, 149, 154, 156–157, 162, 165, 174, 180, 182
Persian Ilkhanate, 145
Petlin, Ivan (Cossack), 189
Pimenta, Father Nicolo, 184
P'ing Ti (Han Emperor), 90
P'ing Wang (Chou king), 16
Pinto, Fernão Mendes, 171–175, 188
Pithecanthropus pekinensis; see Sinanthropus
Po Chü-i (poet), 88, 119
P'o-hai (tribe), 126
Polo, Maffeo, 148–149, 156–157
Polo, Marco, 81, 133, 139, 144–146, 149–153, 155–158, 170–171, 182, 186, 209
Polo, Niccolo, 148–149, 156–157
Portuguese, 170–172, 174–176, 178–179, 187, 189
Pyŏng-yang, city of, 75, 117
Pyramid of Khufu, xiv, 45

Ramusio, 157
Rashid-ud-din (Arab historian), 120
Régis, Jean Baptiste (also known as Lei Hsiao-ssŭ), 201

Rerum Gestarum, 99
Researches into the Prehistory of the Chinese, 3
Rhazes (Arab physician), 120
Ricci, Matteo (also known as Li Ma-tou), 179, 181–183, 185, 187–188
Ridley, Henry French, 212
Ripa, Matteo, 201
Roosevelt, Franklin D., 131
Russia, 145, 147, 152, 162, 188–189, 200–206
Rustichello, 149, 157

Sallam the Interpreter, 154–155
Samarkand, 80, 121, 142, 150, 162, 165–166
San Ch'uan, 62
Sardanapalus; see Assurbanipal
Sassanid Dynasty (Persian), 119
Scapulimancy, 8, 10
Schall, Adam, 201
Shah Rukh (Persian khan), 165–166
Shan-ching, city of, 126, 132
Shang, city of, 8; see also Anyang
Shang Dynasty (1523–1028 B.C.), 6–8, 10–14, 17, 20, 25, 39
Shang K'o-hsi (Ming general), 193
Shang Yang (Ch'in statesman), 33–34
Shang-tu (Xanadu), 144–145, 149
Shanhaikuan, 48–50, 56, 126, 174, 190, 196–199, 201, 210–213
Shan-shan, state of, 93
Shansi, 6, 18, 21, 37, 69, 99, 101–104, 108–109, 115, 122–124, 126, 139–140, 149, 164, 166, 175, 179, 195, 201, 211
Shantung, 17, 23, 37, 46, 58, 101, 103, 106, 110, 122
Sha-t'o (Turkish tribe), 122–125, 127
Shên Tsung (Sung Emperor, also known as Chao Hsu), 130–131
Shên-nung, 5
Shensi, 12–13, 21, 23, 26, 41, 48, 74, 101–102, 104, 121, 149, 175, 179, 181, 188, 195, 198
Shih chi (Historical Records by Ssŭ-ma Ch'ien), 5, 24, 85
Shih Chiang-t'ang (Later T'ang Emperor), 124
Shih ching (Book of Odes), 4, 12, 22, 39
Shih Hêng (Ming general), 168–169
Shih Huang Ti (Ch'in Emperor), xiii–xv, 4, 26, 28–31, 33–43, 48–49, 51–59, 61–62, 64, 66–67, 69, 75, 79, 81, 86, 91, 102–103, 105, 111–112, 115, 164, 170, 212
Shih Tsu (Yüan Emperor); see Kublai Khan
Shu ching (Book of History), 4–5, 39
Shu Han Dynasty (A.D. 221–264), 97
Shu, Kingdom of (founded in A.D. 221), 97–98
Shun (Hsia Emperor), 5–6
Shun Chih (Ch'ing Emperor), 199
Sian, city of, 13

Silk Road, Old, 78–81, 94, 103, 106, 147, 165, 187, 201, 211
Sinanthropus, 2, 8
Sinkiang, 20
Sogdiana, 76
Sowerby, A. de C., 211
Spathary, 200
Sron-bcan-sgan-po (Tibetan king), 117
Ssŭ of Pao; *see* Pao Ssŭ
Ssŭ River, 37
Ssŭ-ma Ch'ien (historian), 5, 26, 28–29, 35, 37, 39, 45, 56, 58, 60–61, 65, 68–70, 79, 85, 95, 127
Ssŭ-ma Hsiang-ju (Han poet), 74
Ssŭ-ma Tan (historian), 85
Ssŭ-ma Yen; *see* Wu Ti (Chin)
Staunton, Sir George, 150
Stein, Mark Aurel, 81–84, 95, 107, 120, 155, 209–212, 213
Su Tsung (T'ang Emperor, also known as Li Ting), 121
Suchow, 48, 98, 165, 187–188, 201, 213
Sui Dynasty (A.D. 589–618), 111–116
Sun Ts'e (Later Han warlord), 96
Sung Dynasty (A.D. 960–1127), 7, 103, 125–133, 140, 149, 210
Sung Dynasty, Southern (A.D. 1127–1279), 133, 135, 137, 140–145
Sung, state of, 19, 23, 25
Szechuan, 77, 97, 121–122, 142, 149, 181

Ta Shun Dynasty (founded in A.D. 1644), 194, 197
Ta Yüan; *see* Ferghana
Tai Fu-ku (poet), 135
T'ai Tsu (Ming Emperor); *see* Hung-wu
T'ai Tsu (Sung Emperor, also known as Chao K'uang-yin), 125, 127–128
T'ai Tsu (Yüan Emperor); *see* Genghis Khan
T'ai Tsung (Ming Emperor); *see* Yung-lo
T'ai Tsung (Sung Emperor), 127–128
T'ai Tsung (T'ang Emperor, also known as Li Shih-min), 115–118, 147
T'ai-ch'ang (Ming Emperor, also known as Chu Ch'ang-lo), 189
Taiping, city of, 172
T'ai-shan (sacred mountain), 37, 38
Taiwan, 190, 198
Talas River, 121
Tamerlane (also known as Timur), 162, 165
Tan (Duke of Chou), 13–14
T'ang Dynasty (A.D. 618–906), 22, 79, 114–122, 124, 128, 130, 146, 158, 204, 210, 214
T'ang Dynasty, Later (A.D. 923–936), 123–124
Tangut (tribe), 128, 131–132, 137, 141–142, 149
Taoism, 105, 107, 127, 146
Tapai Ho (Big White River), 51, 213

Tardu (Turkish khan), 111–112
Tarim Basin, 78, 106, 117, 209
Tartars or Tatars, xiii, 102, 125, 151, 162–163, 174–176, 180, 187, 189; *see also* Mongols
Tashkent, 121, 165
Ta-t'ung (T'o-pa Wei capital), 102, 104, 108–109, 126, 166, 168–169, 175
Temujin; *see* Genghis Khan
Three August Ones, 5, 31
Three Kingdoms, 97–98
Ti (tribe), 18–20, 22, 27, 42, 45, 98
Tibet, 42, 51, 79–80, 89, 117, 119, 121, 128, 131–132, 143, 145–146, 149–150, 170, 175, 199, 202
Tientsin, 207, 209
T'ien-tsu (Liao Emperor), 132
Timur; *see* Tamerlane
Timur Khan (Mongol Great Khan and Yüan Emperor), 157–158
Tohan Timur Khan (Mongol Great Khan and Yüan Emperor), 158
Tongking, 56, 174
T'o-pa (tribe), 19, 98, 101–103, 109, 111, 125–127, 214
T'o-pa Hung-yen; *see* Wên Ti (T'o-pa Wei)
T'o-pa Kuei (T'o-pa Wei Emperor), 102
T'o-pa Ssŭ (T'o-pa Wei Emperor), 102
T'o-pa Tao (T'o-pa Wei Emperor), 102–103, 107
Tou Ku (Later Han general), 93–94
Toynbee, Arnold, 3
Trigault, Father Nicola, 182–183
Ts'ao P'ei, 98
Ts'ao Ts'ao (Later Han warlord), 96–97
Tu Tê-mei; *see* Jartoux, Pierre
T'u-chüeh (Turkish tribe), 110–112, 115, 117
T'u-man (Hsiung-nu chieftain), 68–69
Tung Cho (Later Han warlord), 96
Tung-hu (tribe, also known as Hu), 24–25, 42, 69, 132
Tungusic languages, 125, 132
Tun-huang, 80–84, 106–108, 120, 124, 155, 165, 213
Turkestan, 42, 48, 93, 101, 103, 110, 121–122, 124, 142, 145, 155, 174, 202, 209
Tzuchingkuan, city of, 140
Tzŭ-ch'u; *see* Chuang-hsiang
Tzŭ-ying (Ch'in Emperor), 60, 63–64, 66

Uighurs (Turkish tribe), 115, 120–122, 125, 127, 132, 137–138, 145
Urga, 174, 199

Verbiest, Father, 201
Vietnam, 56
Volga River, 147

Wang (Han Empress), 87, 90
Wang An-shih (Sung Prime Minister), 130–131, 146
Wang Chên (Ming eunuch), 168
Wang Mang (Hsin Emperor), 90–92, 95–96
Wan-li (Ming Emperor, also known as Chu I-chün), 176–179, 182, 190, 192–193
Wan-yen Hsün (Chin Emperor), 140
Warfare, Chinese, 25–27
Warwick, Adam, 50, 210, 212
Wathiq-bi'llah (Caliph of Baghdad), 154–155
Wei (T'ang Empress), 118
Wei Ch'ing (Han general), 74, 76
Wei Chung-hsien (Ming eunuch), 189–190
Wei Dynasty (A.D. 220–265), 98
Wei Dynasty, Eastern (A.D. 534–550), 104, 108
Wei Dynasty, T'o-pa (A.D. 385–534), 102–109
Wei Dynasty, Western (A.D. 535–557), 105, 108
Wei, first state of, 13
Wei, Kingdom of (founded in A.D. 220), 97–98, 102
Wei River, 16–17, 26, 61
Wei, second state of, 23, 27–28, 30, 34, 41
Wên Ti (Han Emperor, also known as Liu Hêng), 4, 70–72, 86
Wên Ti (Sui Emperor, also known as Yang Chien), 111–113
Wên Ti (T'o-pa Emperor, also known as T'o-pa Hung-yen), 104
William of Rubruck, Friar, 148–149, 153–154, 156, 157
Willow Palisade, 190, 198
Writing, Chinese, 8, 10, 13, 46, 120, 127
Wu (T'ang Empress), 117–118
Wu, Kingdom of (A.D. 222–280), 97
Wu Ling (Chao king), 24, 43
Wu San-kuei (Ming general), 193, 196–199, 201
Wu, state of, 19, 25
Wu Ti (Chin Emperor), 98–99
Wu Ti (Han Emperor), 68, 72, 74–79, 84–87, 91, 93, 97, 112, 130
Wu Ti (Liang Emperor), 109
Wu Wang (Chou king), 13

Yalu River, 198
Yang Chên (Han philosopher), 111
Yang Chien; see Wên Ti (Sui)
Yang Kuei-fei (T'ang concubine), 121

Yang Ti (Sui Emperor), 112–116
Yangchow, city of, 112–113, 115–116, 133, 149
Yangtze River, 14, 19, 36, 61, 65, 97, 105, 110–114, 137, 144, 161
Yao (Hsia Emperor), 5–6, 8, 36
Yarkand, 93, 106, 149, 186
Yeh, city of, 104, 108
Yeh-lü A-pao-chi (Khitan chieftain), 125–126
Yeh-lü Ch'u-ts'ai (Khitan diplomat), 141–142
Yeh-lü Ta-shih (Western Liao Emperor), 133
Yellow River; see Huang Ho
Yellow Sea, 8, 49
Yen Dynasty, Early (A.D. 337–384), 101
Yen Dynasty, Later, 101
Yen Dynasty, Northern, 101
Yen Dynasty, Southern, 101
Yen Dynasty, Western, 101
Yen, state of, 13, 19, 23–25, 28, 31, 42, 75, 97
Yenching; see Peking
Yesukai (Mongol chieftain), 137
Yin Dynasty (1523–1028 B.C.); see Shang Dynasty
Ying Tsung (Ming Emperor), 168–169
Yü (Hsia Emperor), 5, 37
Yü Ch'ien (Ming Minister of War), 168
Yu Wang (Chou king), 15–16, 22, 44
Yüan Dynasty (A.D., 1279–1368), 144–158, 163–165
Yüan K'o (T'o-pa Wei Emperor), 104
Yüan Ti (Han Emperor, also known as Liu Shih), 87–90
Yüeh, state of, 19, 25
Yüeh-chih (tribe), 42, 69, 76, 78, 105
Yule, Sir Henry, 99
Yulin, city of, 211
Yü-men, 50, 80, 124
Yün-chen; see Yung-cheng (Ch'ing)
Yung-cheng (Ch'ing Emperor, also known as Yün-chen), 202
Yung-lo (Ming Emperor, also known as Chu Ti and as Ming T'ai Tsung), 161–165, 167–168, 170, 205
Yung-lo Ta-tien (Ming encyclopedia), 162
Yün-kang, city of, 108
Yunnan, 77, 143, 149
Yü-wen Chüo (Northern Chou Emperor), 108
Yü-wen Hu (Northern Chou regent), 108
Yü-wen Yung (Northern Chou Emperor), 108, 111

Robert Silverberg specializes in the literary exploration of ancient worlds. His prize-winning *Lost Cities and Vanished Civilizations* took thousands of readers to Thebes, Carthage, Pompeii, Troy, Babylon, Machu Picchu, and Knossos. His *Sunken History: The Story of Underwater Archaeology* was a Junior Literary Guild Selection. In *Empires in the Dust,* he brought to life such ancient civilizations as the Phoenicians, the Etruscans, the Incas, and the dwellers of the Indus Valley. In *Akhnaten, The Rebel Pharaoh,* he recreated the life and times of the first temporal ruler ever to lead his people toward the worship of a single God.